D1713974

Es'kia Mphahlele

Professor Es'kia Mphahlele, 1970, at University of Denver.
Photo courtesy of Professor Mphahlele.

Es'kia Mphahlele

Themes of Alienation and African Humanism

RUTH OBEE

Ohio University Press
Athens

Ohio University Press, Athens, Ohio 45701
© 1999 by Ruth Obee
Printed in the United States of America
All rights reserved

Ohio University Press books are printed on acid-free paper ∞ ™
05 04 03 02 01 00 99   5 4 3 2 1

Library of Congress Cataloging-in-Publication Data

Obee, Ruth, 1941–
    Es'kia Mphahlele : themes of alienation and African humanism /
Ruth Obee.
        p.   cm.
    Includes bibliographical references (p.   ) and index.
    ISBN 0-8214-1248-5 (cloth : alk. paper). — ISBN 0-8214-1249-3
    (pbk. : alk. paper)
    1. Mphahlele, Ezekiel—Criticism and interpretation. 2. Literature and
society—South Africa—History—20th century. 3. Alienation (Social psychology) in literature. 4. South Africa—In literature. 5. Humanism in literature. I. Title.
PR9369.3.M67Z83 1998
    823—dc21   98-23472
                                                                    CIP

The author and publisher wish to thank the following publishers and individuals
for permission to use quoted material:

Jonathan Ball Publisher for permission to use the poem "For Don. M.— Banned"
and excerpts from "No Baby Must Weep" appearing in *Selected Poems* (originally published by AD. Donker, 1989) by Mongane Wally Serote.

Mbari Publishers for permission to use quotes from Dennis Brutus's poems "At a
Funeral" and "Waiting (South African Style) 'Non-whites Only,'" from his collection *A
Simple Lust* (originally published by Heinemann in 1973).

Professor Mphahlele for permission to use quotes from his poem "Silences."

Ravan Press for permission to use the poem "Afrika My Music" (1984) from Es'kia
Mphahlele's autobiography by the same title and for use of excerpts from "Fathers and
Sons" from Mphahlele's selected works, *The Unbroken Song* (1987).

The author is grateful to the following individuals for their insights and for permission to quote from their letters: Dr. Linda Brown, Amy Bell Mulaudzi, Professor
Robert Pawlowski, and Dr. H. I. J. van der Spuy.

For Kent

Es'kia Mphahlele—A Dialogue of Two Selves

The dialogue between two selves never ends. The pendulum swings between revulsion and attraction, between the dreams and the reality of a living past and the aspirations, the imperatives of modern living. Ambivalence.

All peoples who have ever been colonized, physically or by 'remote control' have these two selves. The writer, the artist, the musician try to harmonize the two even while they perceive sharp distinctions. They harmonize them through their organic vision of life. The two selves are apt by turns to fight, quarrel, despise each other, hug each other, concede each other's roles.

Contents

Acknowledgments

In the true spirit of African humanism, I wish to express my deep gratitude to kin and the extended family of friends and mentors without whom the writing of this book would not have been possible. First, I am grateful to Professor Es'kia Mphahlele for the *ubuntu* with which he has given of himself and of his time and for the largeness of spirit and the gift of language which renders him in his essential *being* an African humanist. I wish to thank Dr. Peter Thuynsma for his fine lecture on *Down Second Avenue,* for his moving and highly useful anthology *Footprints along the Way* (1989) and for his generosity in sharing out-of-print manuscripts. My gratitude extends to John L. Collier and Professor L. H. Hugo for helping to plant the seed; to Myles Holloway, a wise and patient mentor, and to Dawie Malan, UNISA Research Librarian and keen supporter, for helping the seed to grow slowly like a baobab and, one hopes, into something with the same grand African presence; and to Dr. Linda Brown and Dr. H. I. J. van der Spuy for their knowledge of and profound insight into the human psyche, including that of such unforgettable, fictional characters as Mrs. Plum. Last but not least, my special thanks to my family, Brock, Natalie, and Kiran, for patient endurance and to Kent for putting up with "the other man in my life" for the past seven years.

Chronology

contributes to *Black Orpheus* literary journal. Birth of son, Puso. Later that year is appointed director of the African program of the Congress for Cultural Freedom in Paris. Departs Nigeria for Paris. Is visiting lecturer at the Massachusetts Institute of Technology in the United States. Publication of *The Living and the Dead;* banning order gazetted.

1962   Publication of *The African Image.*

1962–63 Tours and works in such African countries as Uganda, Nigeria, Ghana, Senegal, and Sierra Leone. Also attends professional seminars in Europe and the United States.

1963   Leaves Paris for Nairobi to serve as Director of Chemchemi Creative Centre under auspices of Congress for Cultural Freedom.

1964   Publication of *Modern African Stories.*

1965   Joins the University College in Nairobi as lecturer in English.

1966   Publishes pamphlet *A Guide to Creative Writing.* Receives Farfield Foundation Scholarship to work toward Ph.D. at University of Denver.

1967   Publication of *African Writing Today* and the second collection of short stories, *In Corner B and Other Stories.*

1968   Awarded Ph.D. for novel *The Wanderers.* Leaves Denver for Lusaka to serve as senior lecturer in English at the University of Zambia.

1969   Elected to Phi Beta Kappa and nominated for the Nobel Prize in literature. Awarded first prize by *African Arts/Arts Afrique,* for *The Wanderers.*

1970   Returns to the United States as associate professor of English at the University of Denver. Edits *Thought, Ideology and African Literature.*

1971   Publication of *The Wanderers.*

1972   Publication of *Voices in the Whirlwind and Other Essays.*

1974   Joins University of Pennsylvania as a tenured professor. Publication of the second edition of *The African Image.*

1977   Returns permanently to South Africa.

1978   Fails to secure chair of English at the University of the North. Accepts employment as inspector of schools in Lebowa.

1979   Awarded Ford Foundation grant to record oral poetry in North Sotho, Tsonga, and Venda dialects. Appointed senior research fellow and professor of African Literature, African Studies Institute, University of the Witwatersrand.

1980   Founding member of the African Writers' Association in Johannesburg; Publishes *Chirundu*. Founding member and director of the Council for Black Education and Research in Johannesburg.

1981   Publication of *The Unbroken Song: Selected Writings of Es'kia Mphahlele* and *Let's Write a Novel: A Guide*.

1982   Awarded Honorary Doctorate in Humane Letters, University of Pennsylvania.

1983   Inaugurates Division of African Literature at the University of the Witwatersrand; is appointed its chair. Receives Honorary Doctorate of Literature from the University of Natal.

1984   Publication of *Afrika My Music* and *Father Comes Home*. Visiting professor of African Literature, University of Pennsylvania. Receives the Ordre des Palmes medal from the French government in recognition of contribution to French language and culture.

1985   Receives Honorary Doctorate of Literature from Rhodes University. Publishes *Let's Talk Writing: Prose*.

1988–89 Awarded a Fulbright Professorship at University of South Carolina. Continues as Emeritus Professor in African Literature at the University of the Witwatersrand.

1992   Co-edits *Perspectives on South African English Literature*.

The Present

Es'kia Mphahlele continues to write for numerous periodicals, including a regular column for *Tribute*, and is currently the director of the Council on Black Education and Research and Chairman of the Board of Funda Centre. In May 1994, he received an Honorary Doctorate of Humane Letters from the University of Colorado in Boulder, Colorado, his fourth such honorary degree.

Chapter One

Mphahlele and His Context

Who is Es'kia Mphahlele—the erudite gentleman of warm and unpretentious demeanor frequently seen about town at Johannesburg cultural events in fashionably faded American blue jeans and colorful embroidered West African *dashiki?* Who is this self-professed African humanist and why is it important to study his works? The fact such questions might with any legitimacy be asked today about one of South Africa's foremost black writers is tragic proof (if any were needed) that the Verwoerdian scheme of apartheid succeeded beyond anyone's wildest imaginings.

Banning, listing, censorship, and exile—all have exacted their toll in terms of the published works of Es'kia Mphahlele that are currently out-of-print, which until recently were banned or otherwise are unobtainable either in South Africa or abroad.[1] As a result, several key works, including Mphahlele's autobiography *Down Second Avenue* (1959) as well as his novel *Chirundu* (1980) and the second edition of *The African Image* (1974), are in danger of being condemned to an early and undeserved obscurity.[2] (As of this writing, *Father Comes Home* has been reissued by Ravan Press and *Chirundu,* also reprinted in 1994 by Ravan, is currently available through Ohio University Press, auguring well for the future in the new South Africa.)

The apartheid-induced literary disjuncture between past writers and present, as well as between black writers and their legitimate and intended audiences, is but one of the many forms of alienation—intellectual, cultural, and historical—that has beleaguered black South African writers such as Es'kia Mphahlele for the past several decades, and which in turn, has deprived black youth of mythic heroes and role models of their own. As Mphahlele himself notes, black writers have been cut off from their literary past, particularly from the writers of the 1950s. "They have been cut off from the literature that "captures the agony of the moment. . . . They don't even know it existed. They think that literature begins with them. So there is no resonance echoing the past, foreshadowing the future" (Thuynsma 1989, 140). The malign neglect and active muzzling of black South African writers are among the numerous reasons why studies of the place and importance of such works in the body of South African literature are of value. When the subject of study is Es'kia Mphahlele, an eminent scholar of international repute, a community leader, the elder statesman of African letters, and a philosopher who helped inspire the Black Consciousness movement in South Africa and contributed to a body of aesthetics rooted in Africa, then the need to argue the importance of the study becomes secondary to the need to do the subject full justice.

Mphahlele's life, from 1919 to the present, spans major periods in South African history and parallels the lives and development of other important black South African writers. His extensive oeuvre comprises some fourteen volumes of essays, criticism, short stories, autobiography, and poetry as well as numerous articles. In 1946, Mphahlele published *Man Must Live and Other Stories,* the first collection of short stories ever published by a black South African. His widely acclaimed autobiography *Down Second Avenue* (1959) has been translated into more than a dozen languages. In 1968, he was nominated for the Nobel prize for literature. Three years later, his novel *The Wanderers* was awarded the Best African Novel Prize by *Arts Afrique* at the University of California. With the publication of his landmark critical work *The African Image* in 1974, Mphahlele became one of the first South Africans to have completed a "systematic theoretical and critical overview of writing in South Africa" (De Kock 1987, 36).

Furthermore, as Samuel Omo Assein has observed, Mphahlele, as teacher, writer, scholar, and pater familias, has also been a "moving spirit in the entire process of nurturing the emergent tradition of written English in West and East Africa" (1980, 38).

In 1952, because of his courageous and vocal opposition to the Bantu Education Act, Mphahlele was banned as a teacher. Among the various forms of alienation Mphahlele experienced, one of the most poignant and tragic was surely that of his professional alienation, particularly in view of the immense loss it represented to black South Africa. Mphahlele told students at the University of Denver, where his novel *The Wanderers* (1968) earned him a doctorate, that he believes he does nothing so well on his own terms as teach the discipline he loves (Mphahlele 1973, 33).[3] As Gerald Moore has noted, "it is supremely ironic that Mphahlele's entire life had been an unrelenting struggle to achieve the way of life for which his urban upbringing and liberal education had prepared him. . . . [and] to achieve that life he had finally to become an exile" (1969, 93).

In addition to Mphahlele's banning, related political developments in

South Africa pointed to ominous changes on the horizon that did not bode well for the black majority. In 1948, just four years before Mphahlele's banning, the Nationalist party was voted into power. The election of the Nationalists signaled a triumph for the forces of alienation in South Africa, extinguishing all hope of ending an era of racial discrimination and segregation. Despite growing wealth from mining and industry, South Africa still "rested on the presumptions of slavery." Abundant privileges and luxury enjoyed by whites did not go hand-in-hand with the self-confidence to examine seriously "their actions or ideas. On the contrary, their political retreat into a 'white fortress' continued year by year" (Davidson 1991, 341).

Under the premiership of Dutch-born social engineer, Hendrik Frensch Verwoerd, "apartheid became the most notorious form of racial domination the postwar world has known" (Thompson 1990, 189). The four main pillars that supported the superstructure of state apartheid were: the Population Registration Act (1950), which "provided the machinery to designate the racial category of every person"; the Immorality Act (1950), which made marriage and sexual relations between races illegal; the Separate Amenities Act (1953), which legalized segregation in public places; and Bantu homelands legislation, which provided for the creation of black African reserves and authorized the government to grant homelands independence.

In the meantime, state apartheid evolved its own peculiar form of official "doublespeak"—a self-deluding linguistic whitewash of its draconian laws. A verbal-ideological world unto itself, "its social speech type" was intended to solidify power and "preserve the socially sealed-off quality of a privileged community" (Gardiner 1992, 34). For example, to describe the arid, barren, treeless, unelectrified pieces of land populated by women, children, and old people—those empty wastelands spotted between lush, green, productive tracts owned by whites—as "homelands" is but one example of the ironic disjuncture between appearance and reality. Moreover, it was under the aegis of the Department of Cooperation and Development that blacks were removed from their homes.

Thus, both language and its ideology serve to empty form of content and reduce the world to spectacular symbols and stereotypes. The problem, as Njabulo S. Ndebele suggests in *Rediscovery of the Ordinary,* is for the writer to find a way out of the trap of unreflective rhetoric, since there is always a "'them-us' polarity" and images are reduced to Manichean extremes of "wealth and poverty, of power and powerlessness, of knowledge and ignorance, of form and formlessness" which "may lead to the simplification and trivialisation of moral perception" (1991, 61–63).

Of the many pieces of apartheid legislation, the Bantu Education Act was the most invidious in its devastating effects on future generations.

Based on a blueprint drawn up by the Eiselen Commission and completed in 1951, it resulted in an entire "lost" generation of black youth (Davenport 1989, 372). Under this act and subsequent legislation that amounted to "educational genocide," the government seized control of schools (O'Brien 1992, 73). Although school enrollment increased, expenditure per pupil decreased and teaching standards were lowered. By 1978 black classes were twice the size of white ones, with the government spending ten times more per capita on whites than blacks. Black teachers were poorly trained and compulsory education for blacks was nonexistent (Thompson 1990, 196). In addition, a "tribalized" syllabus was introduced, using African languages as a medium of instruction (Lodge 1993, 116–17). The goal was to ensure that blacks remained hewers of wood and drawers of water, for in Verwoerd's scheme of social engineering, there "is no place for him [the African] in the European community above the level of certain forms of labour" (Thompson 1990, 196). Against the backdrop of this legislation, the fate of the youth Fanyan and his sister Diketso in the "Lesane" stories (1955–57) published in *Drum* magazine are best understood. Furthermore, the Bantu Education Act dealt a mortal blow to English as a medium of instruction and to black writing in general (Barnett 1985, 15), especially when such excellent mission schools as St. Peters, which had educated writers of the stature of Es'kia Mphahlele, Peter Abrahams, Alfred Hutchinson, Todd Matshikiza, and Arthur Maimane, were forced to close their doors (Visser 1976, 2:122–23).

This brief historic sketch lends substance to and provides the context for the dialogue of two selves, between African humanism and themes of alienation in the works of Es'kia Mphahlele. If, as Mikhail Bakhtin suggests, a "word's" meaning is entirely determined by its context, then a thorough examination of context is essential to the understanding of Mphahlele's works. Throughout there is the voice of the disenfranchised, disaffected black exile, who has experienced and written about myriad themes of alienation on three identifiable levels: political, personal, and professional. Racism and apartheid are the backdrop of the first. The abandonment of the Mphahlele family when Mphahlele was still a youngster by his alcoholic father, Moses, provides one subtext of the second. The professional alienation and political exile of both writer and teacher comprise the third. Last but not least, there is the insistent dialogue between "the indigenous consciousness and the consciousness derived from western civilization" (Mphahlele 1974, 281). These dialogues parallel and inform Mphahlele's works providing the contrapuntal themes to his personal odyssey, a self-imposed flight into exile that took him to Nigeria, France, Kenya, Colorado, Zambia, the United States and, finally (in 1977), "back from the wilderness" to South Africa.

Mphahlele's banning, his disillusionment with political developments in South Africa and with the failure of white liberals to provide an effective means of countering them, sent him on a lifelong quest for meaning, self-definition, and a politically forceful mode of national consciousness with which to answer to the self-obliterating negations of state apartheid. For a man with liberal friends and beliefs, "tearing loose from liberalism as a world view" was a painful process (Gerhart 1969, 16). Mphahlele, steeped in a liberal education in the Western humanities when he started, by the end of the search had become a self-declared African humanist. By fusing African values to his fundamental humanism, he achieved a cultural and political synthesis that equates with black nationalism and, indeed, provided a strategic launching pad for the Black Consciousness movement led by Steve Biko and others.

Mphahlele's spiritual and personal odyssey was neither a linear progression nor a process without suffering. There were often shrilly insistent voices struggling aggressively to be heard in the *nduma,* the village council. At first, one or two got the upper hand as Mphahlele set about overhauling his thinking and reinventing himself—a work in progress. There were periods of depression, anxiety, fragmentation—as in the time at a London reception when he saw his own double image. There was alienation, even in black Africa, where he noted that the alienation was not because the "other" rejected you: "In independent Africa and that undefined continent of exile, where mobility on the vertical and horizontal planes is possible, you need to re-educate yourself, to constantly overhaul your values. . . . if you feel alienated it cannot be because your environment rejects you, but the other way around" (Mphahlele 1974, 30). There was, also, the sense that the African quest hero, himself, was always looking restlessly to the future, and that, as he told his biographer N. Chabani Manganyi, the present was an ephemeral place to be. For example, in 1972, Mphahlele stated that the "itch" to move on had started again. Robert Richardson, then head of the English Department at the University of Denver, in a letter to the University of Pennsylvania, to which Mphahlele was being lured, expressed reluctance to lose Mphahlele and describes him as "the leading African literary figure now teaching in America" (Manganyi 1983, 271).

Mphahlele's personal demons also accompanied him into exile. These included such minor insecurities as shyness, but far more importantly, his burning hatred of white racists (that he realized could consume and eventually destroy him if he allowed it), and even his putative rejection of middle-class culture, symbolized by his taking an ax to a piano in the Denver suburbs (ostensibly to clear the space in his work area), despite his undoubted and deep love of Western classical music.

The painful fragmentation, "the consuming fear of annihilation," later brought to life in "Mrs Plum," were helped by the dialogue (Gerhart 1969, 16). Whether externalized on the written page or internalized, the dialogue provided a handle on mood swings, bitterness, and hate. In Mphahlele's works, "discourse lives, as it were, on the boundary between one's own context and another, alien, context" (Bakhtin 1981, 284). At times, there is no distinction between inner and outer speech. The "other" is the ever-changing self.

Mphahlele evolves his own "speech patterns" to describe the fragmenting effects of alienation, including the memorable phrase "tyranny of place," which embraces Mphahlele's sense of being severed from his African roots, cut loose from his moorings. Because he could not feel "the texture and smell" of his native soil, he ceased during part of his exile to write fiction altogether, concentrating instead on criticism. Although active and engaged as teacher, writer, and scholar while living overseas, he never felt a deep, abiding sense of commitment outside his own community in the "painful South" (Mphahlele 1979, 37–44). Political exile ironically had transformed a vibrant, warm, community-loving African humanist into the ultimate outsider and alien.

In a society which routinely dealt in surface realities, in forms, symbols, and rigid polarities, African humanism by contrast is a historically dynamic concept evolving into a nationalist philosophy that transcends and bridges ethnic loyalties. It does not hunker down into monocultural claims based on a self-stereotyping identity. As a lived philosophy, it is not so schematized as to be at risk of becoming dogma. Posited against alienation in the dialectic searching for a synthesis, it contributes balance, warmth of tone, and a humanness that often make the works of Es'kia Mphahlele more rewarding and pleasurable as well as instructive to read than those of his white liberal counterparts whose works, by comparison, frequently strike the reader as being unrelentingly grim, humorless, and beset by guilt.

There is in all of Mphahlele's works an interactive discourse at work not only between Africa and the West, but also between the political exile—be it internal or external—and the African humanist. Urbanization, the breakdown of the family, state oppression and statelessness, racism, father-lessness, and other forms of alienation, conflict and loss, are constantly balanced against the voice of communal culture. This communal voice with its emphasis on the importance of people and on human capabilities—on caring, compassion, humor, and love—imbues Mphahlele's work with a vibrancy and warmth that comes as a welcome relief in the often grim face of stark privation, struggle, and tragedy, as well as in the face of meaninglessness, the ultimate form of alienation to which life is reduced under state apartheid. In Mphahlele's works, humanism more often than not triumphs because people are always people; they are not cardboard victims. Their lives have meaning even when racial oppression and state apartheid work to deny that meaning.

African humanism, to which Mphahlele has devoted the monograph *Poetry and Humanism: Oral Beginnings* and which is a constant underlying theme in his autobiography and critical works, is Mphahlele's answer to Dr. Kwame Nkrumah's African personality, a form of cultural nationalism that emphasized the "spiritual side of 'Africanness'" (Gerhart 1978, 201); Leopold Senghor's negritude, which avers that the "worth of Africans" lies in their being "emotional, experiential and humanistic" as opposed to Europeans who are "mechanistic, rational and calculating" (Khapoya 1994, 207); and Kenneth Kaunda's Zambian humanism, an expression of African nationalism influenced in equal parts by the Christian church, socialist principles of economics, and humanistic thought—all concepts to which Mphahlele was exposed during his twenty years of exile.[4]

When Mphahlele lived in Paris between 1961 and 1963 and was organizing writers' centers and literary conferences in Africa and Europe, he rubbed shoulders with such leading exponents of negritude as Senghor and West Indian poet, Aime Cesaire. Thus, Mphahlele's African humanism as a uniquely black South African expression of cultural nationalism was most certainly shaped by his pan-African and cross-continental wanderings, just as it most certainly evolved as a response to the alienating forces of colonialism, segregation, and apartheid. It was in the interest of state apartheid to depersonalize and to convert individuals into faceless stereotypes since it is easier in good conscience to exploit that which is essentially non-human. Mphahlele fought back by affirming African values and reaffirming his essential humanity. But like another "ardent nationalist," Frantz Fanon, Mphahlele rejects exotica in Africa's cultural revival and believes that there is "no single political context for Africa" (Wauthier 1979, 174–75).

Fanon's book *The Wretched of the Earth* was published a year after Mphahlele's *The African Image* (1963). Fanon, Mphahlele, and Biko are all black humanists shorn of white liberalism. They seek to free blacks from psychological oppression by reaffirming black history, values, and culture and by insisting that blacks must look to their own community for leadership. Black Consciousness in South Africa "borrowed ideas from both Fanon and orthodox African nationalism" (Gerhart 1978, 16). Nevertheless, Biko, at his 1976 "Black Consciousness" trial, continued to profess his belief, until his tragic and violent death at the hands of security police, in the power of persuasion to bring about change. During his trial, he fearlessly declared his belief in an open society. He also stated that his movement, the Black People's Convention, was not interested in armed struggle (Biko 1986, 136).

Fanon, on the other hand, was convinced that a cathartic, apocalyptic, bloody revolution was necessary in order to "cleanse" and "unify," to free blacks not only politically but also psychologically. As becomes increasingly clear in such writings as the revised *The African Image*, on which the censors clamped a ban, Mphahlele had, himself, after the Sharpeville massacre in 1960, begun to doubt the efficacy of the power of persuasion to bring about long-term, meaningful change in South Africa. Nevertheless, he also knew that by virtue of his own temperament and beliefs he could never do more than hurl words as bullets at his enemy.

One criticism of the African National Congress (ANC) in the early days is that it did not have a nation-building component that worked to foster an African sense of pride in the past, in black culture and values, or a sense of self-worth and confidence (Gerhart 1978, 78). In Mphahlele's critical writings, he addresses these very concerns, raising key questions about the course of education, governance, and culture in a new South Africa while, at the same time, reaffirming black culture and values as a means of restoring confidence in the present. Mphahlele's resurrection of ancient indigenous African cultural norms, values, and symbols, to use as a tool, a well-sharpened spear, to criticize the existing order constitutes an ongoing dialogue between text and context. Mphahlele, however, does not reach back that far into the deep African past and certainly not to tribalism, which was used by the apartheid state painfully and destructively to divide Africans. As Fanon observes: "Colonialism does not simply state the existence of tribes; it also reinforces it and separates them" (1963, 94).

Mphahlele is only too well aware of what Bessie Head describes as the "squabbling, petty-minded, vicious little tribalists who . . . repeat the petty little bigotry of tribal wars" (Head 1990, 46) until some colonial power comes along and decides to divide up Africa again. Mphahlele's fellow *Drum* writers like Maimane, Nkosi, Matshikiza, and Themba celebrated urban slum culture with its polyglot colloquial speech, ribald humor, folk-festive, "carnivalesque" atmosphere. In the hands of these writers, township culture throbs with color, life, inventiveness, not to mention a fresh, vibrant subversive potential, in dramatic contrast to the monolithically grim world of officialdom. Only two other major writers of the 1960s, Bessie Head, who put down deep roots in Botswana, and Mphahlele himself, chose to document rural African culture. Of these, only Mphahlele effectively attempts to bridge the gap between rural and urban cultures.

In his evocation of a throbbing and vibrant black urban culture with all its economic deprivations and hardships, Mphahlele did not operate entirely in a vacuum. One important forerunner to Mphahlele, both as autobiographer in *Tell Freedom,* and as one of South Africa's most prolific novelists, is Peter Abrahams. Abrahams's *Tell Freedom* (1954) appeared in print five years before *Down Second Avenue* and a close reading of both autobiographies in terms of thematic parallels, structure, and use of stylistic devices as well as abundant episodic correspondence, suggests a considerable indebtedness on the part of Mphahlele to Abrahams. Abrahams helped establish what later became the conventions of the black township autobiography—mention of the bioscope, gangsterism, fights with Chinese and Indian shopkeepers, depiction of family and township life, and the account of the narrator's gradual political awakening as a result of higher education and through the world of books. In Abrahams's autobiography, the township setting is Vrededorp and the family he portrays strikes the reader as being far more nuclear, far less communal and extended, than that described by Mphahlele in *Down Second Avenue.*

It is all too easy in any analysis of Abrahams's works to be dismissive by conveniently overlooking the fact that Abrahams was an important forerunner. Marxist critics, for example, find Abrahams's work lacking in sufficient ideological commitment or, as in the case of Michael Wade, condemn it for moving away from Marxism toward "bourgeois liberalism" (Chapman et al. 1992, 172). On the other hand, critics such as Ursula Barnett believe Abrahams toes too straight a Marxist line. Black critics fault Abrahams for lacking a black aesthetic. Wole Soyinka, for example, is less than enamored with Abrahams's "multi-racial vision" (1976, 65). Huma Ibrahim in her book *Bessie Head: Subversive Identities in Exile,* refers to his "conciliatory politics" in *Mine Boy* (1996, 33). Other critics, such as Bernth Lindfors, describe Abrahams's direct prose as "wavering between superior reporting and maudlin romanticizing." Lindfors does acknowledge, however, that Abrahams's autobiography is a "superb" work (1987, 186).

Mphahlele very simply states that "Realism burst into full blossom for us [South African black writers] when Peter Abrahams published *Dark Tes-tament* —a volume of stories and sketches" (Chapman et al. 1991, 51). Abra-hams's autobiography *Tell Freedom,* like Mphahlele's *Down Second Avenue,* with its novelistic textures and documentary style, has been universally ac-claimed. It effectively indicts the system of segregation and "parallel devel-opment" of the 1920s and 1930s and, like *Down Second Avenue,* reveals an author/narrator/protagonist whose political consciousness is increasingly awakened both by daily hardships (Abrahams often is starving and jobless) and by educational opportunities. The world opens up to both authors through books and, in particular, their discovery of black American writers and artists ranging from W. E. B. Du Bois, whom Mphahlele had actually met and regarded as "a truly great man," to Cullen Countee, Stirling Brown, Claude Mackay, Paul Robeson, and Langston Hughes. Abrahams affectingly states in *Tell Freedom* that Du Bois's words in *The Souls of Black Folk* had for him "the impact of a revelation" (1954, 193).

Mine Boy (1946), described as the first modern, black South African novel, documents, as Mphahlele's *Chirundu* (1979) also alludes to, an im-portant historic movement in South Africa, which paved the way for the negotiated peace processes in the 1990s by establishing strategies and prece-dents for equal power sharing in the work place and for face-to-face negoti-ations. Through black trade unionism (which Abrahams first became aware of in the early 1930s) with its strikes, organized protests, and boycotts, blacks were able to effectively wield political power and make their voices heard. In addition to its allusions to the trade-union movement, *Mine Boy* powerfully documents the appalling, inhumane, and dangerous working conditions of black gold miners. In *Mine Boy,* unlike in *Down Second Avenue* and much of Mphahlele's fiction, the family "has been completely destroyed, there is no sense of communal consciousness. People band together out of a common need" (Larson 1971, 165). The family structure, of course, could not survive the system of migrant labor that created marginal communities of male la-borers who lived far from their families in military-style barracks. It is not surprising that the all-male hostels located on the outskirts of cities became fertile breeding grounds for tuberculosis, venereal disease, and politically motivated violence.

In Manganyi's psycho-biography of Mphahlele, Mphahlele describes how at St. Peter's Secondary School Mphahlele met a young "coloured stu-dent whose stay . . . was to be a short one." Even then Mphahlele was im-pressed that "Peter was no ordinary individual." He was a poet and an admirer of Marcus Garvey. His verse, says Mphahlele, "was the first version of the black-is-beautiful theme that came my way during my youth" (1983, 56). A seed was planted.

Mphahlele has often expressed his strong dislike of labels, but it may, nonetheless, be useful briefly to attach (for later removal) one last label to the African humanist—that of postmodernist. Postmodernism rejects all labels, categories, and metanarratives. This blanket rejection of categories and even of history itself is ironic, since one cannot discuss any movement or trend without giving it a name. Furthermore, since all things "modern" are contemporary, how can they be "post?"

"Cross the barriers; close the gap" is not an exhortation that may have moved Shaka's Zulu *impis*, but it is the postmodernist battle cry. When Mphahlele discusses African humanism, he likes to make it clear that African humanism is not so much a movement or philosophy as a way of life. People, he states, "do not stand outside it to contemplate it." In such statements Mphahlele has the distinct sound of a postmodernist. He is well aware of the epistemological dangers of absolute truths, ideal social orders, and heroic, universalizing myths—from Nazism to high apartheid. Like Michel Foucault and other postmodernist thinkers, Mphahlele is skeptical of the "enlightenment project" as offering a final answer to mankind's search for meaning or having an ameliorating effect on the "corporate will of a society." Our perception in literature of the "unified sensibility" has not, he states, "been a brake on the march of racism, fascism, the acquisitive drive and its corollary, the rat race, in developed countries" (Mphahlele 1967, 4).

Mphahlele's challenge of received Eurocentric traditions consists of his conviction that "all groups have a right to speak for themselves, in their own voice, and have that voice accepted as authentic and legitimate" (Harvey 1989, 48); of his use of multi-genres, heterogeneous voices; his pastiche of world cultures; of his awareness of multiple "others" (particularly with regard to race, class, and gender); of his insistence on the impenetrability of white liberals; of his allusions to folk and popular cultures; and of his attempts through the healing intervention of narrative, to reintegrate a fragmented self.

The list can be expanded, like praise poem epithets, to include Mphahlele's distaste for an elitist art for art's sake and for technocentric white culture; his belief that there is no single truth—that truth is, at least in part, contextual; his non-linear sense of time; his continual asking of the question also posed by Michel Foucault: "Which world is this? What is to be done in it? Which of myselves is to do it?" There is also Mphahlele's occasional use of what literary critic Terry Eagleton calls a "brutal aesthetics of squalor and shock," and finally his appreciation of a Deweyesque pragmatism. All of this adds up to the fact Mphahlele can stake out a reasonable claim to a postmodernist image.

As a movement, postmodernism emerged "full-blown though still incoherent" between the 1960s and 1970s. One could make a convincing argument that once again there is always something new out of Africa, with Mphahlele its agent. Certainly there is a more than tangential connection between Foucault's "heterotopia," defined as the "coexistence in 'an impossible space' of a 'large number of fragmentary possible worlds'" and Mphahlele's "tyranny of place" (48).

Postmodernism pushes the parameters of how one can both ask and answer the question, "Who is Es'kia Mphahlele?" In autobiography, the narrative through its shaping and selecting is always to some degree fictive, regardless of the validity of the facts being reported. Judith Lütge Coullie argues that the author is in reality several persons—the "(extra-textural) real author . . . the implied author, comprising the norms and values of the text (an 'it' not a 'she' or 'he'), the narrator (a function of the text) and the protagonist" (Nussbaum 1991, 4). All of these voices have a bearing on the text, as do the silences which may have been suppressed within the text or story and that may prove most revealing.

There is no final answer to the question, "Who is Es'kia Mphahlele?" He is, among other things, a survivor, a pragmatist, and a work in progress. In a sense, he survived Foucault's "panopticism" and "the plague"—both fitting images for the malignant paradise South Africa became during state apartheid.

Foucault's description of the plague in his classic study *Discipline and Punish* (1975) is based on a seventeenth-century order in France. The systematic and even sinister way in which a civil machinery was brought to bear in the order's implementation reminds one of the heavy machinery of apartheid, ranging from the bureaucrats who issued passes, to the security police who used surveillance and brutality to enforce the letter of the law:

> First, a strict spatial partitioning: the closing of the town and its outlying districts, a prohibition to leave the town on pain of death . . . the division of the town into district quarters, each governed by an intendant. Each street is placed under the authority of a syndic, who keeps it under surveillance. . . . It is a segmented, immobile, frozen space. Each individual is fixed in his place. And, if he moves, he does so at the risk of his life, contagion or punishment. . . . Inspection functions ceaselessly. The gaze is alert everywhere. (Foucault 1979, 195)

In this case, the disease is racism and those under surveillance, frozen in space, treated like a contagion, are blacks. This lack of mobility and the militant control of space through Group Areas and Pass laws in South Africa are among the reasons why Mphahlele found it difficult to identify with or adopt as his own the cause of African Americans. Both African Americans and black South Africans lived in ghettos, but the difference lies, Mphahlele suggested, in "the fact that the *whole* of the black man's life in South Africa is legislated for—from the cradle to the grave; the fact that we have so many political prisoners . . . the fact that education is not free . . . the fact we do not enjoy the freedom of mobility the black American can boast" (1972, 98–99).

How did Mphahlele manage to survive the incredible strains and rigors of both internal and external exile when so many others did not? As Mbulelo Vizikhungo Mzamane has observed: "No people at any period in their history have produced a higher proportion of exile writers than Africans in South Africa produced during the period of political and cultural repression which followed Sharpeville" (De Vries 1989, 37). Many writers died of drugs, drink, or suicide while in exile. These include Nat Nakasa, who leapt from a building in New York, Can Themba, who died of drink, and Arthur Nortje, who died of a drug overdose at Oxford, to name just a few.

Mphahlele was writing as several personae, past and present, including community. As a black South African, the act of writing was an act of defiance and subversion. Mphahlele's story, in addition, pressed a damning brief against the state on behalf of his community. Writing for him was also, as he tells his autobiographer Chabani Manganyi, a means of survival. In the first case, we are talking about the "implied author." In the second, the real one. Mphahlele's various personae and authorial selves find their way into all his works, fiction and nonfiction. For this reason, some of his narratives might aptly be described as "anatomies," which, according to Northrop Frye in his analysis *Anatomy of Criticism,* present the world in terms of "a single intellectual pattern." There may be "violent dislocations in the customary logic of narrative," which are disruptive only if a reader is careless in reading the text or judges according to "a novel-centered conception of fiction" (1966, 310).

Not only was Mphahlele writing about what he knew, but intuitively he understood that, as physician Jonathan Shay reports in his book *Achilles in Vietnam,* about his treatment of Vietnam veterans for combat post-traumatic stress disorder,

> Severe trauma explodes the cohesion of consciousness. When a survivor creates fully realized narrative that brings together the shattered

> knowledge of what happened, the emotions that were aroused by the
> meaning of the events, and the bodily sensations that the physical
> events created, the survivor pieces back together the fragmentation of
> consciousness that trauma has caused. Such narrative often results in
> the remission of some symptoms. . . . Narrative enables the survivor to
> rebuild the ruins of character. (qtd. Rhodes 1995, 4–5)

In addition to the healing powers of narrative, another secret to Mphahlele's survival and, indeed, to his considerable achievements while in exile, was the presence and support of his wife, the "unsinkable Rebecca." She, a professional social worker, helped provide needed support and stability through all the moves and upheaval over the years.

Lewis Nkosi takes strong issue with Mphahlele's repeated recycling of "self" as exilic wanderer while "still nursing wounds inflicted a long time ago and fighting a private, internal war with himself as a writer." Nkosi states that Mphahlele's novel *The Wanderers* dredges up again "the petty quarrels, the bitter conflicts" of the past. He refers to the novel's lack of objectivity, its turgid prose, and its constant demands "to see the hero as a man of superior qualities." Nkosi concludes that the novel "turns into the deadest tomb of self-love" (1981, 93–94).

All authors are gifted with egos, to help them withstand rejection, but critical rejection is compounded in this case by exile and racism. No doubt the African humanist had learned to overcome deep insecurities, even to love and nurture self. Certainly he was aware of the need to harness his own bitterness, lest it destroy him—a lesson he had reinforced for him by his reading of Richard Wright. Yet despite his many awards and accolades, his international stature as writer, dissident, and educator, he is in person open, friendly, warm, totally without pretense or airs. Like the famous Batswana chief, Tshekedi Khama, Mphahlele "never carrie[s] his fame around with him" (Head 1981, 86). Like Khama he is the product of a humane society, an African humanist who is only too human, and besides being a tough pragmatist, is capable at times of leonine crankiness.

From 1961 to 1963, Mphahlele ran the Paris-based Africa Program for the Congress of Cultural Freedom. The program was intended, in the postcolonial era of the 1950s and 1960s, to support African writers, artists, and intellectuals with grants and travel to conferences on literature, education, and the media in Senegal, Sierra Leone, Mali, Kenya, Uganda, Tanzania, and Cameroon. When it came to light that the Congress of Cultural freedom was underwritten by Central Intelligence Agency (CIA) funding, Mphahlele's response was to wave a hand and say matter-of-factly that for once the CIA had done something worthwhile. After all, the rich had a moral obligation to help the poor. The bottom line was that there were no strings attached. Not everyone shared Mphahlele's views, of course, and there was some sniper fire, some cries of outrage.

For nearly a decade, Mphahlele lived in the United States—a good part of that time spent in the American West. His informality of manner, egalitarian spirit, and earthy sense of humor made him a good match for the setting. Yet, he disdained suburban culture with its pop values and young people who failed to show the respect to elders that Africans consider their due. He disliked the towering Rockies and that "white catastrophe," snow. But the American frontier spirit of cooperative work, from potlucks to barn raisings, and the friendly informality of Westerners in general must surely have held appeal. There was even the analog of the Western campfire around which stories were swapped and songs sung, not unlike the African village campfire where village elders shared their myths, history, folklore, and wisdom.

Mphahlele can also be one of America's harshest critics. His son Tony fell under the sway of a bad peer group and never pulled out of it. Mphahlele had observed on the East Coast, in particular, the urban poverty and powerlessness of American blacks. As he reported in the South African journal *Tribute:* "Racial imbalances in America are savage, as are other inequalities. They are what American capitalism is built upon. . . . All this behind the pious rhetoric about family values and the American God. Meanwhile, crime and greed, part of gross capitalism, continue to corrupt the American characters" (1993, 112). Mphahlele is nonplused by what he regards as American naiveté and an American penchant to "talk, talk, talk," which he attributes to an underlying loneliness of people who are fundamentally isolated and without any strong sense of community. After all it was African traditional life that afforded Mphahlele a support system and sustaining values that saw him through a rocky growing up and into adulthood, that gave him his armor for survival. Mphahlele did not take kindly to what he saw as an American, content-oriented approach to literary study in which "students discuss ideas and the social milieu of a writer even before they have exposed themselves fully to the language in the text" (1973, 35).

Because he is modest and unassuming, Mphahlele—in the loud, indifferent culture of the West—has not always been treated with the consideration that an elder statesman and educator of, for instance, the stature of a John Kenneth Galbraith or an American writer with the name-recognition of a Henry Louis Gates, Jr., would, in similar circumstances, surely have been accorded. When Mphahlele received a Fulbright to a Southern university, after his return to South Africa, and was put up in a noisy dorm, shown little or no home hospitality, and was pretty much ignored, he was understandably disgruntled. The African humanist or "real author," behind the heroic narrative voice of the wandering exile and the "implied" authorial presence who speaks in the African humanist voice, is after all multifaceted, complex, and, above all else, human.

Mphahlele can be ruthlessly blunt. In *Voices in the Whirlwind and Other Essays* (1967) he stirred up controversy in his analysis of the Harlem Renaissance and Black Power poets of the 1920s through the 1960s. Mphahlele's time in America and his reading of black American poets exposed him directly to a political element he found missing in the cultural aesthetics of West African negritude. As Jane Watts states, Mphahlele's "struggle to articulate a black aesthetic for South Africa is immeasurably augmented by his attempts to come to grips with three other areas of literary endeavour: the presentation of black characters in western fiction, the West African negritude movement and the writing of black Americans" (1989, 58). While Mphahlele in his novella, "Mrs Plum," had already written one of his most powerful statements of black consciousness, there is little doubt that his revised, and subsequently banned, edition of *The African Image* (1974) drew some inspiration in its more radical expression from his reading of black Americans. Mphahlele was clearly impressed that in America, "poetry has reached as high a revolutionary pitch as it could ever attain" (1967, 81).

Mphahlele was sympathetic with the black aesthetics of poets such as Larry Neal who linked art with the questions: "Whose vision of the world is finally more meaningful—ours or the white oppressors? What is truth? Whose truth will be valid—that of the oppressor or oppressed?" An unabashed admirer of poet Gwendolyn Brooks, Mphahlele finds LeRoi Jones impenetrable except when he is most concrete, such as in Jones's "Black Art":

> Poems are bullshit unless they are
> teeth or trees or lemons piled
> on a step. Or black ladies dying
> of men leaving nickel hearts
> beating them down. Fuck poems
> and they are useful, would they shoot . . .
> (qtd. Mphahlele 1972, 66)

Mphahlele admires African-American poetry when it reflects what Caudwell calls the "collective conscious and unconscious of a community" and when it works towards Addison Gayle's "proposition that literature is a moral force and an aesthetic creation" (81). Mphahlele disputes the idea that only a black reader "can understand, enter into the emotion of . . . a work of art, and share it." This, he says, would result in "permanent blackout for whites in general in relation to black writing" (77). Because of Mphahlele's critical approach, in which neither ideological content nor literary language is the measure of what he values most in a poem, Mphahlele stirred up something of a hornets' nest, antagonizing both the ideologues and the aesthetes. Professor Peter Thuynsma, a former student of Mphahlele's, called *Voices in the Whirlwind* "the first full-scale critical exploration of the Afro-American dilemma." The book, says Thuynsma, "hit black America in the face" (Manganyi 1983, 272).

Mphahlele's choice of English as a vehicle of expression is purely pragmatic. He notes that Oriental and African cultures are much closer to their own myths than is the West (1967, 5). The Greek and Roman writers exist for the West either in the halls of academe or in the remote past, removed in place and time. African indigenous speech, by contrast, with its proverbs and rich metaphoric elements, continues to inform African thought and expression, particularly in rural areas. Africans remain closer to their own myth and oral poetic traditions than the West is to Shakespeare today (5). That said, Mphahlele insists that language is a tool to be used. In the public domain, its sole ownership can be claimed by no one. As a tool, English serves to expand the reach and range of communication. It lends itself readily to the process of decolonization and domestication. Mphahlele has set out to use it in his search for his own uniquely African voice.

This leads to still another, related question: "Is an African voice in Mphahlele's works a preexistent reality which emerges or is it a perspective that is constructed within the text itself?" One possible answer is that the African voice is both preexistent reality and a perspective that is constructed within the text. It had always been there for Mphahlele, but it was submerged under a Eurocentric education and even the far-reaching effects of such things as American films, jazz, and styles that were the rage in South African townships when Mphahlele was growing up.

Although jazz, unlike some other Eurocentric influences, had purely African roots, it had become a distinctively American idiom. It then returned to South Africa, cross-inseminating with local forms, to give rise to township jazz, an equally distinctive idiom. Indeed, South African township jazz is illustrative of how such a form can borrow from other influences while retaining much of its original character and evolving into something entirely fresh, original, and new.

Through an awakened political consciousness and growing self-awareness, Mphahlele eventually felt the need to go back and reclaim an authentic African voice, which in turn was mediated by history, shifting social conditions, and his own changing perceptions and understanding of it. In his search, Mphahlele synthesizes in much the same way township jazz did, achieving stylistically a similar result.

A more postmodernist reading of this question reflects its true complexity since it postulates a double-coded cultural identity that bears close affinity to Mphahlele's "dialogue of two selves." Postmodernists are, perhaps, not so modern as they suppose in their hypothesizing of

> cultural identities in terms of one, shared culture, a sort of collective "one true self," hiding inside the many other, more superficial or artificially imposed "selves" which people with a shared culture and ancestry hold in common. Within the terms of this definition, our cultural identities reflect the common historical experiences and shared cultural codes which provide us as "one people," with stable, unchanging and continuous frames of reference and meaning, beneath the shifting divisions and vicissitudes of our actual history.
>
> [Cultural identity] is not something which already exists, transcending place, time, history and culture. . . . Far from being eternally fixed in some essentialized past [such identities] are subject to the continual play of history, culture and power. Far from being grounded in a mere "recovery" of the past which is waiting to be found, [they] will secure our sense of ourselves into eternity; identities are the names we give to the different ways we are positioned by, and position ourselves within, the narratives of the past. (Ibrahim 1996, 54)

There is danger in taking too nihilistic an approach to "the narratives of the past" that ends in the rejection of history altogether. The precepts Mphahlele outlines as "implied author" and chooses to call "African humanism" spring from a genuine African antiquity in a concrete, real, identifiable sense. These are core values, overlapping and continuous. Many, if not all, are verifiably pan-African. The peripatetic reader who has lived in African countries will agree with Mphahlele's short list of what these culturally based precepts include. They make up traditions that Bessie Head sees as providing "external discipline—rules of law and conduct created for people by generations of ancestors" (Head 1981, xiv). Bessie Head's sociological study, *Serowe Village of the Rain Wind* (1981), based on extensive interviews and oral history, documents a rural way of life rooted in the same overarching precepts Mphahlele outlines in his monograph.

An attempt to encapsulate the African humanist ethos might be made in the single statement: "I am because you are because we are." In her Serowe study, Head's section on name-giving of the Batswana illustrates the point. A poor man, scorned for his poverty, waited and said not a word until his first child was born. He then named his son, "Kemotho," which means "I am a person." Some grandparents longed for grandchildren, but had none. When, at last, they were blessed with a grandson, they named him "Rebatho" meaning: "Now we are people" (xxi).

What name does Mphahlele give the voice of the African past? How does he seek to position himself within its narrative? The voice he eventually identifies and by which he calls himself is "African humanist." It is an identity not well understood in the West or even by all those who are part of the African diaspora. Because the human mind is more comfortable with definitions and labels in its attempts to come to grips with these shifting selves and concepts, Mphahlele in his monograph *Poetry and Humanism: Oral Beginnings* (1986) spells out the concept of African humanism in some detail, combining careful scholarship with the lyricism of poetry.

African humanism, says Mphahlele, is a way of life that is "deeply embedded in our proverbs . . . oral poetry, and in the way our elders spoke to us, and their children passed on the wisdom." There are no dualities between mind and body, life and death. Humankind, "ancestral presence," and "external nature" are gathered into an organic whole. The Vital Force gives meaning to these interconnecting relationships. Poetry itself "lives in the relationship between beings, alive and alive-in-death, things, time, and space. . . . To make poetry is to be authentically human" (13).

"Social relationships constitute a formidable network . . . people are still family." If you harm another or take a life, you destroy the "God-principle" in yourself. Man is at the center of life, and life is celebrated for its own sake. There is no belief in original sin or man the exile from Eden (9). Since life is sacred, witchcraft, with its stirring up of chaos, "is abhorred; so is suicide. Life and death are not separated by time, only by physical barriers" (9, 15). Ancestors act as a moral force "to help restore harmony." Work, such as farming and house building, is collective. "Respect for elders is one of the traditions that has suffered considerable damage in South Africa as a result" of landlessness, removals, and migrant labor. "The doctor is also a counselor on communal morality . . . as interested in a patient's . . . relations with his folks and neighbours as he is in his ailments" (9).

Because African traditional roots are still traceable to the soil of their origin, these precepts have not yet been entirely lost. Yet, as Mphahlele is the first to acknowledge, "People don't simply regroup in new surroundings and resume the quality of their yesterdays and yesteryears. . . . The uprooting process dislocated the rhythm of their lives" (16). Mphahlele states that:

"The traditional African believes that being is sacred in itself. . . . The relationship with the living dead is the humanistic affirmation of the continuity of life, whose central pillar of support is the bond between people of a family at one level and people of the community at another" (17).

Similarly in African indigenous art there is no duality between the work of art and life experience; no lonely individual artist. There is, instead, a unity and spirituality in African art expressive of Africanness about which Africans feel very strongly. These comments by Mphahlele were made in an inaugural talk at an important exhibition of southern African indigenous art held in Johannesburg in December 1991. Mphahlele, combining a low-key manner with pointed observation, concluded that for too long African indigenous art had been neglected or lost. For too long colonial administrators and Christians and traders have plundered this continent. It is time to recover some of the art and the indigenous culture that informs it, he said.

The past Mphahlele seeks to resurrect is not, however, the exotic tribalized, nostalgic past of a Rider Haggard. Mphahlele, instead, realistically documents rural poverty and, in later works, paints a harsh rural landscape. What he seeks to retrieve, to go back and get, are those overarching precepts of an ancient humanism that can bridge and ameliorate tribalism. For, in what is essentially an African folk, rather than a feudal, culture even class differences, while raising barriers, are not as rigid and insurmountable as those of tribal loyalties.

Rider Haggard serves as a premier example of a writer who deliberately evokes an unrecoverable, nostalgic African past—and revels in that evocation. *King Solomon's Mines,* for instance, is peopled by noble savages, some of whom are even women (with small lips) who "for a native race" are "exceedingly handsome" (Haggard 1962, 126). Unlike the ugly grandmother foregrounded in the opening of *Down Second Avenue,* Umbopo the Zulu in *King Solomon's Mines* is a tall, handsome, magnificent "native" with a proud, handsome face (48). Haggard compensates in places by offering humor and realistic detail in some of his descriptive passages, but the past he evokes is unrecoverable in part because much of it never existed in the first place.

Bessie Head in her writings frequently alludes to an African past that is "a peaceful world of black people simply dreaming in their own skins" (1990, 72), but she invariably balances this lyric picture with references to the extreme poverty and "mud living" that people in their tattered, upright dignity manage somehow to endure on a daily basis. The difference between Head and Mphahlele in their exilic experiences is that while Head wanted to belong, Mphahlele wanted to return.

Even Nelson Mandela portrays his country boyhood in a somewhat lyric fashion, evoking an Eden-like setting less harsh and impoverished than the one portrayed by Mphahlele in *Down Second Avenue*. Mandela's clan, however, with its royal affiliates, was more prosperous than the Mphahleles, even though Mphahlele's father was kin to Chief Mphahlele. In his autobiography *Long Walk to Freedom*, Mandela described his boyhood village of Qunu as "situated in a narrow, grassy valley crisscrossed by clear streams . . . overlooked by green hills," dotted with beehive-shaped huts (1994, 7).

The point for Mphahlele, however, is not so much to valorize the African past as it is to retrieve and preserve from it that which is of value. Mphahlele, idealist and hard-headed realist that he is, eloquently gives voice to the built-in conflict between rural and urban cultures, between educated and illiterate, in a passage tinged with frustration, resignation and sadness:

> Are we talking about personality traits that depend on the distance in time and place between urban and rural life, the distance between literacy and illiteracy? Which are the constants, which are the variants? I do not know. We are still acting out the irony that is the meeting point between acceptance and rejection. Rural communities simply realize that they have to survive. New and time-saving comfort-giving devices arrive and they are used. The intellectual may agonize about the distance between him and the stream of traditional life. He has the ability to select. We shall certainly see some of our traits die out, some revived, some modified. (1974, 31)

Mphahlele here is also addressing the lack of commonality he sometimes finds among fellow Africans, differences based on education, ethnicity, and class as well as rooted in his Westernized, individual person—one of the many dialogizing voices clamoring at the village council.

While following Russian critic Mikhail Bakhtin's injunction to reject a prescribed critical system as potentially damaging to what is unique, nuanced, and fluid in discourse and in art, it is, nonetheless, important to fully examine the context within which the polyphonic voices of alienation speak and to suggest ways in which the counter-voices of African humanism gain increasing definition, ascendancy, and meaning in Mphahlele's works.

There is a close interconnection between text and context which cannot be ignored, particularly in South Africa where, among other issues, "an obsession with the question of race has never ceased to make itself felt." Various critics have noted the close connection between politics and literature in South Africa. This has sometimes meant that the "content of South African literature has usually been examined more carefully than its form" (Klima et al. 1976, 263). Yet it is insufficient in literary works to "raid a work" for its sociological content. A more comprehensive approach (as opposed to system) demands that the critic, as Mphahlele himself suggests, not only "discuss ideas and the social milieu of a writer," but also examine "the language of the text" as a means of communication and a carrier of culture as well as a vehicle for artistic expression and aesthetics (1973, 35).

In my analysis of Mphahlele's work, through close attention to the texts I shall examine elements of structure, style, and content as they tie in with and are promoted by the multi-voiced themes of alienation and African humanism and as they resonate against their historic socioeconomic context.

Through tracking the progress of the African quest hero and political exile I hope to show in Mphahlele's early works, such as *Man Must Live* (1947), how historic context and related thematic content are only dimly in focus, becoming clearer in the *Lesane* stories published in *Drum* magazine (1955–57). These stories, in turn, are bridging points between the romantic escapism of the past and the naturalist realism of *Down Second Avenue;* and, lead the way to Mphahlele's novella "Mrs Plum" (1967)—in which historic context and thematic content informed by Black Consciousness thought combine to achieve searing protest. By examining Mphahlele's later works, such as his ground-breaking novel, *Chirundu* (1980), and his memoir, *Afrika My Music* (1984), as well as his collection of stories and poems, *Unbroken Song* (1981), I will demonstrate how the *nduma* voices grow less clamorous, working toward a resolution, a consensus, affording the reader, in turn, with a thinker, writer, and educator's visionary glimpse of a new South Africa.

Chapter Two

Man Must Live

FROM SOCIAL DARWINISM TO AFRICAN HUMANISM—A DIVIDED VOICE

In apartheid South Africa, the white-controlled capitalist economy dominated and exploited the black labor force. Blacks, no matter how competent, were invariably subordinate to whites, no matter how "feeble," whether in mines, factories, or on the farms. Class and color were thus nearly indistinguishable (Thompson 1990, 155). The human impact of racial domination is clearly articulated in the title story "Man Must Live" from Mphahlele's first published work, his short story collection, *Man Must Live and Other Stories* (1946). In "Man Must Live," the story's black protagonist Zungu, although occupying a supervisory position, cringes before and seeks favor from his "European" employer: "Zungu knew that most of the workers under him disliked him. They murmured complaints among themselves that he was 'driving them like oxen.' Some even went so far as to say that he was only strong in appearance but weak and cowardly within. They said he showed this in the way he cringed before his employer and the European workers to seek favour" (3). Debasement and self-alienation are further compounded when a black worker becomes "a willing tool of the system." Zungu, however, is clearly powerless in the face of controls exercised over black wages, the freedom of labor to organize and bargain, and land ownership by blacks. Such controls formed a deliberate strategy on the part of white politicians during the Botha-Smuts period to safeguard a plentiful, cheap supply of black labor (Davenport 1989, 258). Thus, separate reserves and artificial land shortages forced increasing numbers of Africans into the service of white industry and agriculture. By 1946, white income was ten times that of the average black and most blacks were "preoccupied with day-to-day survival" (Thompson 1990, 156). This theme is incarnated in Mphahlele's *Man Must Live and Other Stories*.

Among the pieces of legislation that served as a cornerstone to segregation was the Natives' Land Act of 1913, which prohibited African land ownership and share-cropping and enforced segregation. In addition, the pernicious Natives (Urban Areas) Act, originally mandated to control endemic diseases, led to the establishment of "locations," and resulted in slum clearances on a massive scale with removal of "black spots" designed to keep "urban areas in white hands" (Davenport 1987, 260).

Efforts to control the influx of blacks into urban areas, in turn, led to a series of increasingly restrictive and humiliating Pass laws, the first of which was the 1937 amendment to the Urban Areas Act. The Pass laws created enormous hardship and, over time, effectively criminalized thousands of otherwise law abiding citizens, rendering blacks stateless in their own country. Under the Pass laws, blacks were restricted to the impoverished "homelands," where 80 percent of the population occupied 13 percent of the land, unless black labor was needed in the cities (Thompson 1990, 166).

As the black labor force continued to expand, in part due to a boom economy stimulated by World War II, the 1940s saw the resurgence of black unionism and—with the rising aspirations of an emergent black middle class, made up of professionals, teachers, landholders, businessmen, and journalists, whose members founded the ANC in 1911—the revitalization of the ANC as a political force (Lodge 1990, 1).

In this important period Mphahlele's *Man Must Live and Other Stories,* a sixty-page volume with pen and ink drawings published by African Bookman's Julian Rolnick, who risked a run of 700 copies at a time when publishing opportunities for blacks were scarce to nonexistent, rolled off the press.[1] The collection of five stories—"Man Must Live," "The Leaves Were Falling," "Out, Brief Candle," "Unwritten Episodes," and "Tomorrow You Shall Reap"—made its debut in the heyday of segregation in the postwar era. Townships were as squalid and violent as ever and tensions were building on the eve of historic elections that ushered the Nationalist government into power. In 1945, Marabastad Township, where Mphahlele spent his childhood, and which he described in *Down Second Avenue,* was leveled "to satisfy the greed of white Pretorians" (Manganyi 1983, 84).

Against a context of increasing white oppression and growing black opposition, the criticism leveled against Mphahlele's early stories, the first such collection published by a black South African writer, is that they fail accurately to mirror prevailing socioeconomic conditions and instead fall under the sway of Victorian prose, the English literary tradition, romantic pulp fiction, and the mission press. One of the most smugly sermonizing blasts directed at the stories was that of Brian Bunting, reviewer for the

Cape Town weekly *Guardian* and a member of the Communist party. Bunting excoriated the work for superimposing European values on "aboriginal raw culture." The reviewer further suggested that the author "has had the gods of his fathers exorcised by missionaries. He has forgotten he is African" (Popken 1978, 313).

The *Guardian*'s critic, however, failed to consider, in addition to questions of content and "pure craft," "values it urges on readers" in terms of a nascent black ethos already in evidence (Chinweizu et al. 1983, 140). Moreover, even when plots are contrived and dialogues marred by artifice, characters frequently undergo the harsh real-life experiences one would expect of impoverished slum dwellers.

Mphahlele cannot be blamed, given his background and education in the Western humanities, for showing signs of a culturally colonized and divided self. In the reception of the text by critics, an extra-textual level of reader-author alienation that Njabulo Ndebele comments on in *Rediscovery of the Ordinary* was at a work. The white liberal audience for whom the text was intended "was schooled under a Eurocentric literary tradition" to reject that same work on grounds of either "the methods of representation" or "the content" (Ndebele 1991, 45). This harsh reception thus may owe something to the application of inappropriate European "theories of style and genre [and] assumptions about the universal features of language" based on the fact Mphahlele's chosen tongue is English (Ashcroft et al. 1991, 11).

Mphahlele later all but rejected his firstborn literary offspring, which he regards with a mixture of embarrassed amusement and outright disdain. One could argue that the collection in itself is, in part, the very embodiment of Mphahlele's self-alienation—cultural, literary, and political. At the same time, Mphahlele finds it galling to be criticized by a white person for failing to describe such things as "pass laws . . . pick-up vans . . . the insolence of the white man . . . or beer raids" when the same white had never experienced the things he was so incensed by and that a black South African could ill afford to forget for a single moment (Manganyi 1989, 93). Perhaps the lesson was not entirely lost on Mphahlele, however, for not only are such things described in his autobiography with consummate skill and artistry, they eventually became conventions in their own right in the genre of the black township autobiography.

By examining themes of alienation and African humanism in *Man Must Live* it becomes possible to identify evidence that refutes one of the *Guardian* critic's more egregious statements, that is, that Mphahlele as a member of "the African intelligentsia has become isolated from [his] people" (Popken 1978, 313). Not only does Mphahlele portray working-class protagonists in an urban setting, such as Zungu in "Man Must Live" and Annah Seripe in "Out, Brief Candle," but several key episodes reflect vividly on the harsh, brutal existence of urbanized slum dwellers. Furthermore, the self-abasement and alienation Zungu in "Man Must Live" undergoes from alcoholism; Annah's loss in "Out, Brief Candle" when Sello, her adopted son, commits suicide; and the dilemma of Sylvia Direko in "Unwritten Episodes" as an unwed mother are not, by any stretch of the imagination, the stuff of escapist literature. In his detailing of such scenes with reference to such historic detail as Annah's ability to support Sello primarily because her property is freehold, Mphahlele shows he is an author who is empathetic and fully in touch with the harsh daily existence of his own people. He has begun to document the lives of a marginalized black world, the first step in the flowering of social commitment and a black aesthetic.

Sello's suicide and Annah's overweening sacrifice and generosity, in "Out, Brief Candle," represent two extreme responses to forces of urban alienation and poverty. Mphahlele shows that there are dire consequences to be paid when life is lived according to a Social Darwinist code instead of an African humanist one. Annah's vulnerability is significantly worsened by her personal isolation from the community and in the end she knows tragedy—a leitmotif in the themes of racial and urban alienation running throughout *Man Must Live*. Neither Sello's nor Annah's response to the struggle for survival in an urban setting is tempered by the humanism of kin and community. The African proverb says: "It takes a village to raise a child." Sello, who exhibits symptoms of Western-style existential alienation, has only Annah. Annah, however, has forsaken community.

Thus, in Mphahlele's early stories the narrator is engaged in a struggle in which the mission-school educated Eurocentric voice is still relatively fresh and is, as yet, linked uneasily to an emergent true African humanist voice. In *Man Must Live* Mphahlele has just begun to document and define the problems of a collectively alienated people. Moreover, he has yet to present a solution in terms of a unifying African humanist vision.

In the story "Unwritten Episodes," the author's divided self further manifests itself in the triangular love story and predictable happy ending with which the story concludes. The suprarational feelings Larry Maphoto entertains toward Sylvia, described as "awful, terrible, mysterious," reflect Victorian ideals of romantic love. African norms would tend rather to define love more in terms of commitment to family and spouse and "much less as an exclusive attraction and affection between two individuals"

(Khapoya 1994, 32). Nevertheless, even the love story has elements of realism and alienation as it deals with a conflict reinforced by social and class distinctions. Thus, prior to meeting and falling in love with Sylvia, Larry was engaged to the better-educated, more socially acceptable Joyce Xaba, who is the preferred choice of Larry's parents. In short, the pendulum swings in the text—between Eurocentric romantic and African realist—as the African humanist narrator searches for his voice, help explain its unevenness despite its evident promise in terms of characterization, realistic themes, and a nascent black aesthetic.

If the gun was the means of Africa's physical subjugation, then language, as a cultural carrier, asserts Ngugi wa Thiong'o, equally might be said to be "the means of spiritual subjugation" (Ngugi 1991, 9). When the language, or what Mikhail Bakhtin calls the social voices and "heteroglossia," in the text are not suitable to the culture, the character, the plot, or the reality of the setting, a glaring discrepancy jars the reader's sensibility and points back to authorial alienation. For example, Annah addresses her suitor with, "You men are such selfish brutes; you speak of love and try to exhibit it by clothing it in gorgeous and dazzling robe of splendour," a speech better suited to a Victorian heroine in a popular romance (Mphahlele 1946, 34). The dialogue does not correspond to the character or with the universe she inhabits. Yet, the "subjugation" here is far from total. In the same passage, Mphahlele shows a more imaginative approach in a line that describes Larry as "chaf[ing] restlessly like a lion caught in a trap" (44). Here the description has vigor and originality and resonates against an African landscape. Thus, the linguistic textual evidence of alienation is ambiguous.

In stories such as "Unwritten Episodes" there are contradictions in style, diction, and the treatment of social and cultural norms that bespeak an alienated and a "divided self." Similar contradictions and polarities are apparent in plots which tend either toward the bleak and the tragic or the sentimental and romantic. For example, "Unwritten Episodes" ends with Larry successfully overcoming his father's objection to his marriage to a woman from a lower economic stratum. Then, the happy lovers ride off romantically into the sunset in a formulaic and contrived ending in which "love conquers all," including class conflict, as the wheels "of the train rolled down their course, carrying them to a new life. . . . Only *they* felt it. No mortal man outside their own world could fathom the depth of their inner hopes, joy, peace. . . . No pen can put it in writing" (47). In the concluding half of "Unwritten Episodes," Mphahlele reflects the alienation of the Westernized, colonized narrator for whom there is a lack of "correspondence" between his "world vision as an experienced reality and the universe" he creates; as well as between "this universe and the specifically literary devices—style, images, syntax, etc. used by the writer to express it" (Goldmann 1964, 315). The story's romantic ending stands in dramatic contrast to such themes as Sylvia's dilemma as a poor unwed mother, Sello's suicide, and Zungu's brutalization and debasement, which are fundamentally not the stuff of escapist romantic pulp fiction. Such episodes convey the harsh realities of township life in sufficiently convincing and realistic detail that they are imprinted with the history of their era.

Whereas Mphahlele's tendency in *Man Must Live* to rely on artificial diction, contrived plots, and stock characters affords evidence of a Eurocentric mission school voice getting the upper hand, the same cannot be said for Mphahlele's overall choice of subject matter. Like Sol Plaatje before him, Mphahlele is a graphic chronicler of the alienating effects on the black majority in South Africa of three centuries of colonialism, segregation, and state apartheid which bracket socioeconomic transitions from "pre-literary to literacy, from pastoralism to industrialisation, from pre-capitalism to capitalism, from a measure of political optimism to increasing pessimism, from hopes of equality to stricter segregation" (Parker 1978, 62). Zungu Khalima is a variant on the theme of "Jim goes to Jo'burg." Indeed, Zungu typifies the flow of black labor from rural to urban areas. At the age of fifteen, Zungu quits school, seeks employment in the city and works his way up the socioeconomic ladder from construction worker to railroad policeman. As a member of the railroad police, Zungu is proud of his "thundering" voice, broad shoulders, and smart uniform. Zungu also enjoys the sense of power it gives him to "herd" the crowds of people as they board the train. The railroad station provides a dramatic backdrop that allows the author to describe the poor masses of relatively unsophisticated urban blacks, who depend on public transport to get them to jobs and who in their ignorance sometimes end up on the wrong train.

In an interior monologue, Zungu continually compares himself with the people he helps direct and to whom he feels himself superior. The commuters remind him of the cattle he once herded in his Zulu village as a boy. Zungu makes repeated use of animal imagery to describe his fellows. For example, earlier on, as a foreman, he drives the laborers like "oxen." As a policeman, he "looks on the commuters as 'cattle' or 'sheep.'" In short, "the animal imagery reinforces both his sense of superiority and [Zungu's] denial or repudiation of humanity" (Hodge 1986, 50). Zungu's class-based denial of the humanity of others is the very antithesis of African humanism—a denial which, in turn, reflects both communal and self-alienation.

Mphahlele's effective use of interior monologue in "Man Must Live" represents an early attempt on the part of the author as African humanist narrator to present a rounded character from the inside out and to probe psychological motivations in behavior. Zungu's smug superiority is undoubtedly rooted in a deep-seated sense of insecurity set against a background of economic exploitation and isolation from his community. Brutal market forces, unequal work opportunities, urbanization, and his adherence to a rigid Social Darwinist ethos have driven a wedge between Zungu and his community. Zungu's isolation stands in dramatic contrast to the throbbing life at the train station. The opening paragraph in the story is evocative and makes imaginative use of local idioms to set the scene: "First Stop Mayfair, Langlaagte, Ikona Westbury, New Clare, Randfontein Train! . . . all stations, Randfontein! *U ya phi? Nkosi yam?* (Where are you going to—My lord!)" (Mphahlele 1946, 1). This passage is a good example of how when Mphahlele's divided self resolves itself into a working synthesis between his mission-educated Eurocentric voice and his Afrocentric humanistic voices, memorable writing results. The author's integration is mirrored by the text. Thus, there is in Mphahlele's use of local idioms the intimation of a rich, polyglot culture in the mix of Zulu, English and Afrikaans names. Yet, at the same time, we are conscious that this is an exclusively black scene as, indeed, it remains throughout, except for the reference to Zungu's cringing before and seeking favor from his "European employer" in a "weak and cowardly" manner while "driving" the workers under him "like oxen." Class analysis of the forms of economic alienation is relevant here, as we observe the rich and powerful (who are invariably white), the aspiring middle stream, and the urban poor—slum dwellers who toil for a mere pittance. Thus, to paraphrase Fanon, "the well-being and progress" of whites "have been built up with the sweat and dead bodies of" blacks (1963, 96).

In Zungu's tendency to cringe before white bosses to gain favor, we gain insight into racial as well as socioeconomic divisions—with the white invariably cast in the superior position of overseer. The overall mood is one of loneliness and isolation—of a man uprooted from his rural background. But unlike Alan Paton's passive "man with the halo" in *Cry, the Beloved Country*, Rev. Stephen Kumalo, in playing out the theme of "Jim comes to Jo'burg," Zungu does not manifest a noble mien of Christian patience, love, and passivity, serving as a living sermon on the theme that "so in my suffering I can believe" (Mphahlele 1962, 131).

The African humanist narrator has stepped forward, while not totally losing sight of his Westernized persona which also affords valuable insights. In his evocation of setting, Mphahlele draws imaginatively on the "heteroglossia" of "open places, of public squares, streets, cities . . . of social groups, generations and epoch" as well as "social dialects, characteristic group behavior," and "language of the authorities" (Bakhtin 1981, 259–63). Mphahlele's use of "diverse social voices" in the narrative enables him to describe and thus to validate a marginalized black world and characters consistent with the universe he inhabits.

As Mphahlele, casting a "sideways" glance at the "other," heeds his true African voice, he moves into a realistic mode of speech patterns and character types that possess the power to condemn and indict even as they document. Although Mphahlele's authorial voice is showing signs of integration, however, his philosophic vision is to some extent still divided. In Zungu's dilemma is seen the conflict between two opposing world views.

Zungu's dehumanization is driven by his Social Darwinism. A process of dehumanization sets in the moment he begins to internalize and enact this essentially Western ethos that is amoral, ruggedly individualistic, and self-serving, rather than cooperative and community centered. In short, Social Darwinism is the very antithesis of *ubuntu* or "participatory communalism" (Sparks 1990, 14). Zungu thus exemplifies the prototypical black male who has become brutalized by the market forces of which he, too, is a victim. Furthermore, he is twice-alienated, since he has no real political consciousness as to the true nature of these forces.

Indeed, "Man Must Live" might be viewed as a satiric parable on the consequences of living according to the dehumanizing precepts derived from Darwin, Adam Smith, and Malthus, which sanction the view that in society as in nature the principle that applies is "survival of the fittest." Taken to its logical conclusion this view is opportunistic, nihilistic, and pessimistic. A more optimistic and affirming African humanist world view sanctions the return to community, not to tribalism or ethnicity in its narrowest sense, but rather to urbanized African community as it is later depicted in *Down Second Avenue*. Mphahlele suggests in the tale of Zungu's rise and fall that the brutal, impoverished life of the black slum dweller does not result in nobility of spirit by virtue of suffering as Paton's hero Stephen Kumalo would suggest. Rather it brutalizes in a truly alienating Hobbesian sense.

Zungu's Social Darwinism dates from the moment when he departs from his Zulu village for the city. First, he severs all connections with family and community. Then the process of urban alienation, as he is cut off from his ancestral roots, sets in and is reinforced by racism. An analysis of the discourse reveals the presence of a divide between the races in the unapologetic use of such terms as "non-European workers" to define workers by what they are *not* in the case of blacks, rather than by what they are. Herein lies evidence of racial labeling that was in practice even before the Population

Registration Act (1950) was on the books. The casual use of such terminology suggests the author has been momentarily co-opted by the alienating forces of colonial imperialism.

Zungu is not an entirely flat character. Through interior monologue and interaction with others, we learn that besides being vain, he entertains social ambitions, and has a capacity for hard work. He is also shy and uncertain of himself with women (an autobiographical note here). As a stubborn survivor, he, unlike Paton's passive victim, Rev. Kumalo, speaks more to black pride. Yet at the same time Zungu's actions and choices are determined by market forces over which he has little control and that further contribute to his dehumanizing downward spiral.

In the end the marriage between Zungu and Sophia Masite begins to falter when Zungu starts to drink (like Mphahlele's father Moses)—at which point Sophia and her children, who never had much use for Zungu in any event, walk out. Zungu then, in a state of despair, decides to burn down the house which deprived of its inhabitants is like an empty shell—a fitting symbol for Zungu's own empty life. In the process of rural to urban migration, Zungu has severed community roots and is an example of how members of the majority culture have been fragmented by a derivative culture from the West that is "spiritually bankrupt" (Thuynsma 1989, 144).

Zungu's abasement and loss of humanity serve as a blistering commentary on Western materialism and its devastating impact on African culture and society. Thus, in his theme and characterization the author shows signs of divesting himself of inappropriate superimposed Eurocentric values, taking a major first step toward arriving at a positive working synthesis in the dialogue of two selves.

Moreover, Mphahlele begins to speak out, tentatively at first, in his true African humanist voice, reflecting a degree of authorial integration with his as yet embryonic world vision, when he reaches back into the deep past and resurrects cultural symbols and myths to criticize the existing order. One example of such a cultural myth being resurrected is Zungu's act of burning down his own house. This example of culturally derived symbolism rests on the fundamental "precept of all Southern Bantu societies that, once established, a house should not be allowed to die out" (Johnson 1984, 6). The burning house serves as a powerful metaphor for the disintegration of the individual, the breakdown of the family, and by extension, the fragmentation of the larger community as a result of alienating forces of urbanization, racism, and economic exploitation.

African humanism, while as yet not fully defined, does find symbolic expression in the story's final episode, suggesting a mode of Africanization or way of being that can help bridge the gaps among undereducated rural Africans and alienated city dwellers. In the concluding scene of "Man Must Live" lies the authentic "value" being urged on the reader by the ideology of the text, and one which is given full reign. Zungu's neighbors in a strong spontaneous expression of community spirit and of *ubuntu* come to his rescue. Pulling Zungu from the burning house, they wrap him in sacking, roll him on the ground, and then take him off to hospital. Later they provide him with food to eat and a place to stay. Even when Zungu has chosen to remain aloof and had isolated himself, African community steps in. Such compassion and community support is what can sustain a man in an otherwise hostile and alien world. Zungu is a victim, but he is also a survivor and unlike Rev. Kumalo he resists stubbornly to the end, as is clear in the following cameo: Zungu's "eyes are expressionless, whether he be happy or not. That twinkle is gone. But there is something in that stolid blankness . . . something of stubbornness. When he looks at you, you cannot help but read the stubborn words: What do you expect me to be—a magician or a superman, or a soft learned genteel animal? My Lord—I *must* live, man!" Although Zungu has been reduced to the amoral ethos of Social Darwinism, even that, the author intimates, is preferable to being a passive victim and grist for the "legal machinery" set up "to control the influx of Africans into the towns and cities." Zungu may be a "wretched picture of frustration" in the city, but unlike Paton's hero, Rev. Kumalo, he cannot be accused of being a "man with a halo," the South African equivalent of the American "Uncle Tom" (Mphahlele 1962, 37). While Kumalo ultimately returns, hat in hand, in a state of passive defeat and resignation to his rural Zululand, Zungu, debased but still endowed with fighting spirit, is stubbornly determined to stay where he is in the city, to resist and to endure.

In "Man Must Live" Mphahlele has crafted a story that corresponds to the universe he inhabits and has begun in a rudimentary fashion to be engaged with the issue of black oppression. The African humanist narrator as black nationalist has begun to speak out here by documenting the history of an era in which, as historian Leonard Thompson states, most blacks were "preoccupied with day-to-day survival." Furthermore, *The Guardian* critic's allegation that the characters in *Man Must Live* are seriously flawed as they all "believe in ideal love, heavenly justice, patience and other delectable virtues" is patently untrue.

Even as "Man Must Live" is closely linked to socioeconomic concerns of the era, "The Leaves Were Falling," the second story in Mphahlele's collection, has a strong historic basis in the politically significant "Africa for the African" movement that became the battle cry of black ministers in the church. Here again is proof that Mphahlele's divided self is not isolated from the black ghetto world with its social ills nor has the author forgotten for a moment that he is "an African in South Africa."

Ironically, it is the rascally Rev. Mushi, and not the reliable Rev. Katsane, who preaches against the raised fees and the "European tyranny in our churches" and who subsequently manages to stir up mass action in the form of peaceful demonstrations (Mphahlele 1946, 20). In a narrative aside, laced with wry humor, the author lets the reader know of his own deep skepticism and growing alienation from the church—whether in the hands of overbearing whites or those of unscrupulous black preachers like Mushi who can stop beer drinkers in their tracks with his fiery oratory, but who cannot put an end to drunkenness: a man, in short, with a strong promotional flare, who cynically uses the "donkey church" to advance his own self-seeking interests.

The comic juxtaposing of these two preachers, one of whom is clearly a bit of a scoundrel, is a measure of Mphahlele's narrative restraint, balance, and objectivity. He pokes fun at the church, draws attention to racism, and, at the same time, does not overcompensate for a negative colonial perception of Africa by "literary re-creation of an alternate, more just picture of indigenous culture" in which all blacks in a world of Manichean aesthetics are "white" (JanMohamed 1988, 8). The story foreshadows Mphahlele's own disillusionment with the church, whose influence is seen in the biblical overtones and moral biases of such stories as "Out, Brief Candle," and in such episodes as Annah's discovery of the orphan Sello in the bushes near the river like a biblical Moses.

An alienation that emerges at times in *Man Must Live* is the inappropriate tenor of the stories. Harking back to days of a Tennyson rural idyll and a gentle pastoral English countryside and utilizing an ornate Victorian English, such stories as "The Leaves Were Falling" describe settings alive with "lowing calves," "golden sunsets," and "eternal abodes," at odds with the vivid humanism of a rural African setting. The description is also not reflective of the harsh conditions in densely populated, overgrazed, impoverished, rural black locations. Perhaps the narrator is more intent on capturing the white man's vision of a Rousseauesque setting peopled with noble savages.

Nevertheless, the African humanist narrator begins to make his presence more boldly felt when he switches from third to first-person narrative voice in "Tomorrow We Shall Reap"—a story that claims strong patrimony to *Down Second Avenue*. In it the African humanist begins to mark his territory. Certain places and sequences, such as the reference to the cruel Lapelle River which divides the Christian village and the "heathen" one where people believed that their lives were regulated by an "All-powerful and All-knowing force," a force that was vested in their ancestors, reappear later in more sophisticated form in *Down Second Avenue* (Mphahlele 1946, 51). Moreover, frequent metaphysical references to a divine force vested in ancestors suggest that, contrary to Brian Bunting's statement, Mphahlele has not entirely "had the gods of his fathers exorcised by the missionaries" (Popken 1978, 313).

"Tomorrow We Shall Reap," in contrast to such stories as "Out, Brief Candle," with its biblical overtones and Shakespearean title reminiscent of Macbeth's soliloquy, moves a step closer toward reifying an African humanist world view. For example, there are references to "a sense of communal unity" which is concretely illustrated in the reaping festival and in the symbolic return of Stephen and Mariah to her village to seek Shikwane Makwe's, Mariah's father's, approval of their marriage. Moreover, there is an African humanist reference to "the sacred ancestral gift" of being able to create (Mphahlele 1946, 50). This pleasing turn of phrase hints at spiritual values rather than at what a mission mentality might mistake for sheer animism or exotica. In such African humanist references, Mphahlele, like all humanists—whether Western or African—operates on the principle of the "golden mean." He thus affords in his disquisitions on ancestors in various texts both balance and a necessary corrective to foreign missionaries in Africa who "became obsessively interested in ancestral spirits and spirits in general—as though that was all there was to African spirituality" (Khapoya 1994, 52).

The reaping festival reveals an increasingly well integrated authorial voice insofar as it largely escapes the trap of the anthropological, tour-guide approach. Instead, the authorial voice encapsulates an African humanist spirit and celebration in which local color comes to life in authentic detail, and we find plausible characters consuming food as real and as African as "roasted mealies" (Mphahlele 1946, 57). The passage is evidence that while book learning may raise a barrier of sorts, it does not mean that Mphahlele, as author and Western-educated intellectual, is in any meaningful sense isolated from or disengaged from people in towns or villages who are only semiliterate. Indeed, he is, in the African sense, very much "there," and the reader is there with him—brought in from the cold, no longer an alien.

In sum, themes of alienation as a counterpoint to nascent African Humanism in the collection *Man Must Live* point to a divided self on primarily the aesthetic literary level. Narrative conflicts are frequently resolved through the escape of romance, rather than the succor of community. Diction and style are too often marked by artifice. Social norms and moral biases reflect a Christian mission upbringing. Authorial alienation is, however, perhaps most poignantly echoed in the semi-autobiographical flight of Rev. Katsane Melato in "The Leaves Were Falling." Melato's is a harrowing mystic journey in which, unlike the African humanist for whom "the all is now," Melato "feared the future" and "hated the morrow" (15). Slightly more than a decade later Mphahlele makes a similar flight himself and has expressed similar sentiments about it with regard to his personal feeling of betrayal toward his own community and his overall disillusionment with mankind—that is: "'You have left them. . . . You distrust mankind . . . [and] your own self—of the same species. You are an exile'" (25). Here Katsane shows some promising characteristics and the beginning of political will and self-awareness as he ponders the seeds of his own alienation from church, congregation, and self, which at root is a factor of the continuing and oppressive racial alienation that informs the dialogue of two selves.

Katsane continues to be torn, moreover, between his agreement with the need to protest the raised fees and his disagreement with the methods used to attain these ends—a dilemma Mphahlele later faces himself when he agonizes over how to protest effectively against the evils of apartheid (especially when peaceful methods seem to have failed) without the use of violent means that are contrary to his own personal beliefs and temperament.

Katsane, failing to take a stand and mirroring the self-restraint of the narrator, then finds himself at odds with the congregation who turn against him and from whom he takes flight, isolating himself from the community which affords him his only hope of salvation. At the end of a long "mystic" flight, in which God appears to have deserted him and he sees a symbolic Virgin Mary, ironically represented by an emaciated black mother with little milk to give, attempting to nurse her child, Katsane collapses and ends up unconscious in hospital. Again, the theme with its telling symbol of the emaciated Virgin Mary is one of alienation from a Christian God and a religion that builds churches and preaches about helping the poor, but which, in reality, has done little to alleviate the suffering of the masses in the face of racism, colonialism, and rampant capitalist exploitation. The conflict is not resolved, however, through political action or a conclusion expressive of a nationalist consciousness. Instead, Lindi, who has all along encouraged Katsane to stand firm on his own principles, manages to track Katsane down in hospital and the two are happily reunited in their love, bringing the story to its somewhat mawkish and predictable romantic ending—in the best tradition of escapist pulp fiction.

On a purely aesthetic level the reader can readily trace Mphahlele's progress, from a culturally colonized and therefore alienated writer to one who arrives at a distinctive idiom fusing two streams of consciousness that speak from the authenticity of his own experience. The author's rapid progress as he divests himself of his colonial baggage is impressive and can be clearly seen by comparing the following three descriptive passages, starting with "The Leaves Were Falling" in which "It was sunset, the big sun was about to rear his head beyond the horizon. His long rays were shooting out fan-like to bid farewell to the world. Hilltops and treetops were flooded with a soft red glow" (13). Here the sun is personified in the manner in which Shelley might personify the moon in his lyric poetry. The tone is romantic. The reader is transported to a bucolic countryside.

In "Tomorrow We Shall Reap," however, there is substantial evidence of the author's beginning to divest himself of colonial influences and to engage instead with the immediate reality of his own universe. The reader, too, gains a commensurate sense of a specific geographic locale as mountains rise up out of the "Low Veld." These are the "high, lofty mountains, fearful in appearance, but which kindly gave me shelter under their huge crags many a night" (51). The mountains are realistically described as "high," "fearful," having "huge crags," but they are also romantically personified as being "kindly" when they "gave me shelter," again reflecting the divided self—with realism on the ascendance and a more believable aesthetic and cultural correspondence between the universe the author inhabits and the world he creates. In *Down Second Avenue,* Mphahlele leaves off such devices as the personification of nature altogether. The tone is consistently one of foreboding and the effect is one of naturalism in what is quite possibly one of Mphahlele's most effective openings, notable because unlike in the Eurocentric descriptive passages in his early works, this is Afrocentric and humanistic. People are a part of the landscape in the village of Maupaneng where "My grandmother sat there under a small lemon tree next to the hut, as big as fate, as forbidding as a mountain, stern as a mimosa tree" (11). In view of the frequent lack of correspondence in *Man Must Live* between the universe he inhabits and the world he creates, it is perhaps understandable why Mphahlele, in his epilogue to *Down Second Avenue,* says of his first published collection of stories: "I can never summon enough courage to read a line from any of the stories that were published in 1947 {sic} under the title, *Man Must Live* again. In ten years my perspective has changed enormously from escapist writing to protest writing, and, I hope, to something of a higher order, which is the ironic meeting between protest and acceptance in their widest terms" (217). Nonetheless, the nascent African humanism evident in the stories along with countervailing forces of alienation belie Brian Bunting's statement that characters only believe in "ideal love, heavenly justice and other delectable virtues." There is a rising vein of realism apparent in which we are made aware of the black man, isolated in separate amenities and group areas, and brutalized by a Social Darwinist code of conduct untempered as yet by the humanizing benefits of kin and community. This polarity in Mphahlele's characters between Western individualism (which contains the seeds of its own alienation) and African communalism recapitulates Mphahlele's own internal discourse and the personal conflict he seeks later to resolve through the synthesis of African humanism.

On the one hand, *Man Must Live* can be, at least in part, regarded as an example of the effects of cultural alienation as shaped by Eurocentric language and learning and by forms of colonialism that controlled not only the people's wealth, but more invidiously "the entire realm of the language of real life. . . . Its most important area of domination was the mental universe of the colonised, the control, through culture, of how people perceived themselves and their relationship to the world" (Ngugi 1992, 160). In all fairness to the author, however, it must also be acknowledged that in these early stories Mphahlele is still an unseasoned young writer learning to master his craft. As Norman Hodge, writing in *English in Africa*, observes, *Man Must Live and Other Stories* belongs to an earlier era before the full flowering of the black South African literary renaissance. It is the work of a writer serving his "apprenticeship . . . yet many of the basic themes and concerns of the later fiction are clearly discernible" (Hodge 1986, 63). For this reason, the collection occupies an important place in the history and development of black South African fiction. Prior to its publication in 1946, only three other fictional works with urban settings had been published by black writers—R. R. R. Dhlomo's *An African Tragedy* and Peter Abrahams's *Song of the City* and *Mine Boy.*

Chapter Three

Formulating a National Consciousness

FROM SLAVES AND NOBLE SAVAGES TO TOWNSHIP *TSOTSIS* AND ANC HEROES

We are born into a world where alienation awaits us.
—R. D. Laing

Mphahlele's first published collection of short stories, *Man Must Live,* reveals the alienation of an author for whom the text and its discourse fail to reflect accurately the universe he inhabits. The author exemplifies the wide-ranging symptoms of colonial alienation as described by Ngugi wa Thiong'o. Such alienation, rooted in mission-school education, manifests itself in a disassociation between the "colonial . . . sensibility" and one's "natural and social environment"—which, in turn, is reinforced by Eurocentric teaching and writing in the humanities (Ngugi 1992, 17). Words frequently do not serve to express an authentic inner voice.

Themes of alienation occur in both the external structure and internal content of the stories in *Man Must Live,* which suffer from a weakening imbalance in which the voice of the African humanist is as yet only dimly heard. Characters in these stories for this reason are not as alive, as fully realized, for example, as they are in the "Lesane" stories. Within the context of *Man Must Live* characters such as Zungu and Sello as well as Rev. Katsane are portrayed as isolated and alienated, if not passive victims of harsh socioeconomic forces beyond their control. It is implicitly understood that such individuals are more vulnerable precisely because of their failure to identify and participate with the group. As becomes increasingly clear in subsequent works by Mphahlele, such as the "Lesane" series and even more in his autobiography *Down Second Avenue,* the remedy for such self-defeating alienation is African humanism—a strong bulwark against the impoverishment, oppression, and violence of an apartheid culture in which "people take a communal interest in one another's joys and sorrows" (Mphahlele 1956, 13). "It is those individuals who are strengthened through dedication to a group . . . who are enabled to act. . . . it is in this way that the impotence, debilitation and alienation of the isolated subject is overcome" (Barboure 1986, 176). This collectivist ethos in which survival is "dependent on people living together . . . sharing tasks, and protecting and comforting each other" (Khapoya 1994, 43) gains increasing definition and clarity in Mphahlele's works as he moves steadily away from a derivative style and subject matter and more confidently into an African mode of expression free of Victorian prose, Christian-mission morals, and plots and characters out of nineteenth-century romances. As Essop Patel asserts, "For an authentic revolution there has to be an aesthetic revolution, only then will there be cultural revolution" (1986, 85).

In his Master of Arts thesis written at the University of South Africa (UNISA) and titled "The Non-European Character in South African English Fiction" (1956), Mphahlele began to lay the groundwork for his own personal aesthetic and cultural revolution and for what later would became a broad-scale black nationalist revolution.[1] The first in a three-part trilogy, this ambitious and imaginative survey is the ancestor and progenitor of Mphahlele's landmark work of criticism *The African Image,* of which the new and revised editions published in 1962 and 1974 respectively are direct descendants.

Mphahlele's early attempts to define an African aesthetic eventually had a far-reaching impact on the later efforts of black consciousness writers and political leaders of the 1970s to shape a national consciousness. According to Jane Watts, "Mphahlele's intellectual explorations of the function of culture ran so closely parallel to the practical aspirations of the black consciousness writers that it is difficult not to assume that a number of them had read his critical writings" (1989, 86). Mphahlele sets as his task in his critical works—including his essays *Voices in the Whirlwind*—the establishing of a "sociological aesthetic" which examines the "relationship between . . . world visions and the universe of characters and things created in a particular work" (Goldmann 1964, 316).

"African humanism" was that sociological aesthetic. One cannot fully appreciate how revolutionary those seemingly innocuous words were at the time, except in terms of their political-historic context. By coming to grips with such a mythic concept in "all its complex mosaic of . . . ever shifting nuances, connotations and meanings," Mphahlele, himself, was actively engaged in nation building through the "discovery and encouragement of universalizing values." At a time when Fanon was writing about the need for black intellectuals to be engaged in this very pursuit, Mphahlele was busily doing just that—making himself into a conduit through which culture becomes an expression of national consciousness. African humanism, it is clear, was already beginning to play an important role in Mphahlele's critical thought—which, in turn, would shape his formulations on questions of negritude and Black Consciousness.

The very focus of Mphahlele's politically topical dissertation "The Non-European Character in South African English Fiction," represents a first step toward breaking away from a Eurocentric, self-alienating world vision. What further establishes Mphahlele's humanist, black nationalist credentials is that his survey centers on the exploration of human character within the framework of an African world rather than with more formal stylistic or structural concerns of setting, plot, or theme. Moreover, the rigorous exercise in poetics of criticizing white and black writers in English—particularly ones who dealt in political clichés and stereotypical characters—may well have acted as a corrective to Mphahlele's own initial tendency to deal in stock characters and situations.

Mphahlele's humanist stance in his dissertation is both more forgiving and more Western-oriented than it is in his later critical works. He does, however, afford a penetrating critical analysis, characterized by balance and realism, of ways in which white writers of English fiction all too frequently portray black characters as stereotypes cast in such molds as that of the "reprobate," "the servant," "the barbarian on the battlefield," or the "noble savage," a concept British settlers may have brought to the frontier (Mphahlele 1956, 21). Mphahlele understood that such historic and literary stereotypes lead to alienation and promote misunderstanding and incipient racism between whites and blacks. Although it is commonplace now to examine works of literature for evidence of racial stereotypes that reinforce bigotry, Mphahlele was well in advance of his time in undertaking to do so in the South Africa of the 1950s. It is ironic that his thesis title, perforce, employs the self-alienating racist label "non-European" then in usage.

As Mphahlele told his autobiographer N. Chabani Manganyi, he required a wide canvas for his dissertation in order to bring into relief the South African literary scene—for, "the problem of a national culture is always also a problem of a national literature" (1983, 146). Racism not only divides and separates, it finds its way into literary works and limits what is written about. South African writers' obsession with the race problem means literature is also subservient to some political message or "preachments as bedevil South African fiction" itself and thus must "remain sectional and sterile as long as such conditions prevail" (Mphahlele 1959, 195–96). Such constraints do not make for either a unifying national consciousness or a great national literature.

Nonetheless, and despite his banning from teaching four years earlier in 1952, Mphahlele remained optimistic about reconciliation—thus showing his true humanistic stripes. He opened his thesis with the unequivocal statement that in the postcolonial era of economic and political exploitation of Africa by Europe, there arises the opportunity to build understanding between "whites" and "non-whites." From the first paragraph, Mphahlele, thus, defined the terms of black-white alienation. At the same time, he expressed a humanistic vision—that is as much Western as African—in the clear assertion that colonial conflicts can be bridged with closer contact and "better mutual understanding" (Mphahlele 1956, 1).

Mphahlele then proceeded to a survey of fiction by such well-known English-language writers as Rudyard Kipling, E. M. Forster, Joseph Conrad, and Pearl Buck in whose works he avers are to be found "non-white" characters effectively and believably portrayed in the round. By contrast black characters in white South African fiction are often, he argued, lacking in any third dimension and their "response-mechanism . . . is not half as complex as human life is in general" (87). They were frequently flat and stereotypical. This, Mphahlele believed, could be attributed to the fact that separation of the races meant whites had only limited contact with (and thus limited understanding of) blacks and what little they did have was based on knowing blacks as enemies, servants, or converts. Furthermore, race issues in South African fiction drove and dominated plot to the exclusion of character development. Characters were of only secondary importance. In effect, they served as message carriers.

Mphahlele's survey of American literature started with Harriet Beecher Stowe's *Uncle Tom's Cabin* and its portrayal of "the type of Negro who adopts the attitude of Christian sufferance to ill-treatment and cringes before the harsh master or mistress" (7). Other stereotypical black literary types include the noble savage, complete with tom-tom drums and all the exotica that entails; and the black as debased, stupid, shiftless, and brutish, such as were depicted in Carl Van Vechten's *Nigger Heaven*. Nevertheless, black writers such as Langston Hughes, Countee Cullen, and Richard Wright, who depart from the "plantation" and "pseudo-paganism" tradition do succeed, stated Mphahlele, in creating multidimensional black characters that help counter widely held racial stereotypes. Clearly, in his analysis

Mphahlele is relying on critical standards and a "poetics" of interrogation of the text which are based on "humanism" and "realism," but increasingly are beginning to be tuned to a more specifically African focus (Manganyi 1983, 147). The fact that Mphahlele also examines the social basis of form and content insures that his "broad canvas" avoids the merely superficial.

Mphahlele, the African humanist, is not himself a racist even in his literary criticism. In the first chapter of his thesis he makes a definitive African humanist statement, reflecting on the "so-called clash of cultures" in which a colonizing technological culture has contact with an African culture which is more humanistic (Mphahlele 1956, 17). He sees the "clash" as offering rich material for the poet and writer as he bemoans the fact that the literary theme of "evangelizing the native" is "a theme that hardly ever suggests what the African can teach the white man" (44). The implication here is that a cultural synthesis could be enriching and beneficial; that Africa does have something to teach whites, and that whites would be welcome participants in the process of educating themselves. Such African humanistic statements concerning racial alienation and potential reconciliation in academe and in the arts provide balance and credibility to Mphahlele's criticism and spare the text from any taint of polemics.

Potential black-white alienation between reader and author is overcome by the generosity and compassion, the inclusiveness, of African humanism. This antidote to alienation is necessary. For just as a black audience may be alienated by the culturally colonized black author, so the white reader may, as Njabulo Ndebele observes, experience the "spectacular 'alienation effect'" of black protest literature "since it shows up the ogre to himself" (Chapman 1991, 442).

If the white critic feels inexcusably ignorant about certain aspects of black arts and culture, now that critic feels empowered in the inclusivist spirit of the "journey" to take a first tentative step forward in the pursuit of new understanding. In the realm of literary criticism as in life itself, it is clear that Mphahlele the African humanist is free from racism. He believes moreover that whites are fully capable of creating rounded black characters and that the southern American writer William Faulkner is a notable example of an author who has done so. In early South African fiction, however, the black character often appears only as an organic part of the setting or is portrayed in works such as those by Thomas Pringle or Rider Haggard as either "a fighter or servant" (Mphahlele 1956, 13).

There is little question that Mphahlele, in his thesis, was the first black critic to draw attention to the brand of liberal, white patronage found in Alan Paton's novel *Cry, the Beloved Country*. Mphahlele, sharpening his spear, takes Paton to task for his portrayal of the clergyman Kumalo as a

South African version of Harriet Beecher Stowe's "Uncle Tom." Kumalo, Mphahlele states, is remarkable chiefly for his eternal fatalism and his passive acceptance of his lot, as well as for his willingness to "uphold the law" even when that law had outrageous built-in inequities—even when it "hurts." Mphahlele suggests that Kumalo's character is deliberately flat because Kumalo serves as a message carrier for the sermon Paton is preaching to his readers with its theme of "comfort in desolation."

Kumalo's story is a variant on the "Jim comes to Jo'burg" theme. Mphahlele had explored that theme himself in his first collection of stories, *Man Must Live,* in which Zungu comes to the city, is brutalized, but endures despite everything. In the "Lesane" series, Fanyan comes to the city and is changed by the experience, not always for the better; but he too shows every indication of being a survivor. As Fanon has also observed, for a "colonized man, in a context of oppression," life does not embody "moral values" or cohesive, "fruitful living. To live means to keep on existing" (1963, 308). Mphahlele, the prototypical hero of his autobiography, *Down Second Avenue* and its fictive sequel *The Wanderers,* is anything but a passive survivor. Both in real life and fiction characters are much less passive and much more complex than Kumalo. Although Kumalo is merely a fictional character, the fact that his passive acceptance of the *status quo* is presented as close to the ideal and as exemplary by an eminent white liberal of the stature of Paton, who in the 1950s was a founder of the Liberal party, may have suggested to Mphahlele that white liberalism itself could not ultimately rescue blacks from oppression. Hence the early signs of Mphahlele's political and literary alienation from liberal white writers and politicians can be seen taking root in his pioneering and (for the 1950s) radical analysis of Paton's well-known work.

Historian Gail Gerhart makes clear that liberalism in South Africa in the late nineteenth and early twentieth centuries was not really liberalism at all, but "in fact really conservative paternalism or trusteeship," and that liberals were responsible for the "anemic state of African political organization during the first 30 years after union." She further states that liberalism recognized only one yardstick—the adoption of "civilized" or "modern western ways" (1979, 7–8).

In his effort to probe the historical reasons behind the South African writer's inability to portray rounded black characters, Mphahlele eloquently summarizes some of the sources of stereotypical thinking that, in turn, help foster tensions, black-white alienation, and a widening gulf in understanding between two streams of consciousness—African and Western; between a colonized people and the colonizer.

For several years in the history of South Africa the white man gets to know the non-white merely as an enemy on the battlefield or as a slave—whether it be as a labourer on the farm or a carrier on an expedition. Often he knows the non-white as a convert or prospective convert at a mission station. In the first two cases, the emotional circumstances of the contact allow for little more than a tendency on the part of the white man to regard the non-white as one of a group rather than an individual. The missionary is perhaps at an advantage because he tries to deal with the individual personality. If he fails to understand the convert, it's because his approach is bedeviled by the same overpowering tendency to regard his "ward" as a member of a group whose culture must be completely destroyed as an antithesis to Christian culture. (1956, 17)

Here Mphahlele shows himself a humanist trying to understand rather than categorically condemn. He ascribes white bigotry to the failure of whites to meet and know blacks as individuals rather than as members of a group. This spatial and geographic separation in place, culture, and time results in stereotypical perceptions, both in real life and literature. Mphahlele then proceeds to the antithesis in the dialectic of alienation and African humanism, making a key statement on several profound philosophical differences between the West and Africa. Such passages as the one just cited reveal Mphahlele as an incisive, original thinker with a felicitous turn of phrase, a true critic in the making. The preceding statement of alienation balanced against early affirmations of African humanism help establish a metronomic rhythm and creative tension that immediately draw the reader in.

Mphahlele differentiates between a world view that focuses on "doing" (and, one might add, that measures self-worth in terms of materialist values such as earning power and personal achievement) and an African world view that emphasizes the importance and value of "being" (with the communal self as important as, if not more important than, the individual self). Mphahlele suggests that the South African writer in the nineteenth century, in particular, lacked the vision to

investigate the contact of a European culture that has had the good luck to produce technical skills with an African culture whose content finds the maximum satisfaction not so much in "doing" (as a Western concept) but in social "being"—in the best human relationship and communal responsibility. The irony of the "clash" should be rich material enough to interest a novelist and a poet; to say nothing of the real clash as it exists in the economic and religious system. (17)

Mphahlele's prose takes a lyrical turn as he elaborates on the richness and value of an ethos deriving from traditional African society, with its communal responsibilities, customs such as harvest festivals, and "beautiful" patterns of family life in which "the whole structure of African traditional life which places the accent on 'being'—could tone down and supplement the white man's highly acquisitive urges" (45). It is interesting from a historic perspective to note that one of Mphahlele's most affecting statements on African humanism and the potential for synthesis between two streams of consciousness is to be found in his earliest critical work, his thesis "The Non-European Character in South African English Fiction."

The irony as well as the reality of the cultural clash between Africa and the West did in fact become rich material for the novelist, short story writer, essayist, and poet Mphahlele. In effect, he threw down the gauntlet, then picked it up again himself. Indeed, the irony of the "clash" became Mphahlele's lifelong study.

> *Do not accept the "mouthings of officials" and never forget.*
> *(Quoted phrase from Ezra Pound's Cantos)*

In 1956, while Mphahlele was still at work on his thesis for Unisa, he began his "brief and unhappy career as a journalist" and literary editor for *Drum* magazine—a popular journal that featured muckraking exposés, romantic fiction, and cheesecake photography, and which gained a reputation for being one of "the most authoritative newspapers on the life of Black South Africans" then in existence (Nkosi 1983, 21). *Drum* was more than just a slick magazine, however. It was almost a state of mind that gave its name to the "fabulous fifties." With the advent of *Drum,* black writers had begun to forge a jazzy new urban idiom (the verbal equivalent of township jazz, such as *mbaqanga*) to match the fast-paced life of the city slums. The style was fresh, upbeat, and innovative—in marked contrast to the stiff Victorian prose of the mission presses (Visser 1976, 12). Although the "Drum decade" was an era of "the truncheon and boot" and of police raids and mass action, it was also an era of optimism and of a great creative outpouring by blacks in the arts and literature.

On one hand, a panoply of repressive legislation had been passed, including the Bantu Education Act and the Suppression of Communism Act (1950), "which defined communism in sweeping terms and gave the minister of justice summary powers" under which Mphahlele was banned

(Thompson 1990, 198). Yet it was an era when blacks and whites still inter-
mingled and when there was still a widespread liberal belief in the possibility of peaceful change through education and persuasion. The white-led
Liberal party, founded in 1953 by a small group of white liberals under the
leadership of Paton, was beginning to cooperate politically with the ANC.
(Mphahlele joined the ANC in the early 1950s when Bantu Education arrived in primary schools and the clearance of Sophiatown began.) Hope of
peaceful change was fueled by the success of such mass actions as the bus
boycotts and the march of 20,000 African women to the Union buildings in
Pretoria in 1955 to protest pass laws. Both of these historic events were cov-
ered for *Drum* magazine by Mphahlele. It was not until 1958 that Nether-
lands-born social engineer Hendrik Frensch Verwoerd—who "plugged"
every hole in the dike of legalized segregation—was elected prime minister
(Thompson 1990, 189).

Mphahlele's journalistic experience at *Drum* meant that he was not culturally isolated while writing his thesis in what amounted to an Eurocentric
ivory tower. Instead, he was in daily contact with the disenfranchized, dispossessed, impoverished black community, both in urban and rural settings, where he gathered some of the raw material for later works such as his
first novel *The Wanderers*. Mphahlele was further stimulated to find his own
African voice through constant exposure to and encouragement of other
talented black writers. It is more than empty speculation to suggest that
in the process Mphahlele became the *de facto* father of the black South
African short story. Indeed, *Drum* magazine, according to Michael Chapman, "marks the substantial beginning, in South Africa, of the modern
black short story" (1983, 183).

Various critics have noted that the exigencies of life in poor, overcrowded, noisy townships where police raids were frequent and privacy and
security nonexistent, made the short story as protest literature (and as a
means of lighting a high velocity charge in a short time) a logical literary
medium for black writers. The choice, reflective of Bakhtin's observation
that there is no dichotomy between form and content, was further reinforced by the constraints placed on the means of production by censorship,
by separate amenities and by a segregated press. The short story was also a
natural choice for black writers with deep roots in a rich African oral tradition of storytelling. Although socioeconomic conditions favored such a
birth, a catalyst and an outlet were also needed. Mphahlele was, arguably,
that catalyst; *Drum* was the sole publishing outlet then available to black
fiction writers. According to Richard Rive, Mphahlele, as fiction editor of
Drum, was "father of it all." Mphahlele "decided to push the short stories for
Drum" and since he encouraged so many talented writers such as Peter

Clarke, Can Themba, and Rive himself, he in effect "made us writers" (De Vries 1989, 47). Thus as an editor and reporter as well as a critic and the first published short story writer, Mphahlele contributed significantly to his own cultural decolonization, as well as that of his fellow South African writers and of African English literature in general. This bears out Jane Watt's observation that Mphahlele is "one writer in whose work it is possible to trace, over a period of 40 years, both the problems of literary production experienced by South African writers and the stages in the development of an appropriate critical approach" (1989, 57).

Between 1956 and 1957, Mphahlele made another important contribution to African literature and to *Drum* in the publication of his "Lesane" series. In this series, not only does Mphahlele show a greater mastery of the short story form, but his stories are now more boldly stamped with the imprint of their historic epoch. Themes of alienation tie in more directly with what is happening to people and, in consequence, "with moral and social questions" (Chapman 1989, 183). The author, in reaching back to oral traditions for inspiration, is commencing to describe with greater accuracy the universe he inhabits, thus overcoming his culturally colonized persona. As the African voice grows stronger, the stories gain in meaning and interest as well as effectiveness. Although concerned with moral and social issues, the "Lesane" stories are not didactic. In their detailed realism, they hold up a mirror to the 1950s with its pass laws, Bantu education, beer raids, and slum clearances (a reference to which provides the ironic conclusion to "The Lesanes of Nadia") that, in turn, disrupted families and obliterated entire communities and their histories. For this reason, as well as for their intrinsic merit, the "Lesane" stories have extraordinary value as "an account of locale and period which cannot be found elsewhere in such detail" (Barnett 1976, 46).

Whenever African idioms and customs enrich the texture of Mphahlele's prose the implied theme is African humanism since these customs and rituals are a part of the total African human experience—the rituals that connect people to one another and to their ancestors. It is these idioms that lend warmth, life, texture, color, and movement to Mphahlele's writings. The narrator is already beginning deftly to weave such idioms into the text in such a manner that the reader does not feel treated to an ethnographic treatise. This approach, focusing on a sociological aesthetic in which the "word" is linked with a particular society, generation and historic period, in Bakhtin's words, and where the word belongs to "no one and to everyone" is very different from what Breyten Breytenbach describes as the "tribal whites" reduction of indigenous South African culture to "folklore" limited to "Ndebele huts, Xhosa pots or Zulu beads" (Brink 1983, 75).

In his story the "Lesanes of Nadia Street," Mphahlele opens with a favorite narrative device—swooping down on the scene with a wide-angle lens, panning it, then focusing in on a particular scene. Nadia Street, like Second Avenue in Mphahlele's autobiography, functions both as stage set and as an African humanist eminence, rather like a character itself. (It is an eminence notably absent in the earlier collection *Man Must Live,* in which, in a more Western vein, individuals rather than community have prominence.) Nadia Street, says the narrator, is the "quietest street in Newclare." Yet there is also a great deal going on there. The street indeed is as full of humanity and movement as it is of gossips. It is typical of Mphahlele's African humanism that he often chooses as his subject real-life experiences that are shared in common with all humanity rather than specific political events. In African townships, weddings are an important communal celebration, as they are everywhere, and it is a wedding that opens the story "The Lesanes of Nadia Street."

> Midday. Nadia Street was bright and gay. Lu-lulu-lu-li-li li-li! the women shouted. Crowds of people converged on Lesane's place. . . . Women shouted and stamped on the street. Spectators nudged and jostled one another. The crown was lovely; the bride's face might have been a little shorter; the bride seemed much younger than her husband; the groom's dress had a rustic flavour about it; the bridesmaids were perfect. Shame, how pathetically beautiful they looked. . . . A tiny man stood like a sentinel at the door, forbidding them to enter. Custom. He had to be there. And it didn't look funny to the spectators that the forbidding majesty of custom should be personified in such a tiny man. (Chapman 1989, 132)

In this passage, it is clear Mphahlele has wrenched himself free from mission-press, Victorian prose. Sound effects include African ululation. Sentences are short and punchy. The scene is urban, yet distinctly African. Customs and people are described with wry humor (the bride's face is too short; a tiny man is the doorkeeper for "the forbidding majesty of custom"). Customs repeatedly in this and other stories are documented in detail and with humor and pride—in an implicit and yet profound statement of Black Consciousness. Mphahlele, the emergent African humanist writer, is able to draw effectively on ironic contrasts between two cultures. His optimism of will allows him to engage in humorous asides while depicting scenes of grim realism. Here as elsewhere humor and hope serve as counterweights to balance pain and desolation, suggesting that there is more to life for blacks than the fate-driven presence of state apartheid and white oppression. Such counterweights permit Mphahlele to avoid the monochromatic effect of tone that occasionally mars works of such eminent white, liberal protest writers as Nadine Gordimer and André Brink.

The communal African humanist scene continues with a dialogue among half a dozen wedding celebrants who speculate on such questions as the receipt by the bride's mother of a new shawl from the Lesanes because, says Ma-Siviya, it is "'custom, didn't you know stupid? . . . It's the Xhosa way. The bride is Xhosa. Where I come from we don't do such things.'" There is also much discussion about what meat will be served, whether goat or oxen will be slaughtered, for "What's a wedding without food?" (Later when the smaller children are eating, we discover just how impoverished life is—for counter to dictates of African humanism and the hospitality that goes with it, they have learned to take turns eating their food in privacy if guests show up at their house so they do not have to share.)

The above vignette reflects back on its context in an implicit commentary on how state-imposed apartheid fragmented and alienated what was becoming a black, urban humanistic culture. Ma-Siviya, for example, is a Mosotho. She is curious about, but accepting of Xhosa customs and the two tribal groups here are living comfortably side by side with other tribal groups. In slum clearances, however, people were grouped according to ethnicity in the divide-and-rule formula of the apartheid system under which Africans were viewed as belonging to "ten distinct nations," making whites the largest "single nation" (Thompson 1990, 190). The effect of such government policies was divisive, alienating, and resulted in ethnic strife.

Mphahlele contrasts the wedding as a joyous celebration with the grim reality of its setting in the impoverished township. The streets are full of flies, dirty water, and "rows of dilapidated houses that stood cheek-by-jowl as if to support one another in the event of disaster" (Mphahlele 1989, 133). A roll call of some of the guests provides a quick indictment of the system. Ma-Ntoi came from a mining town in the Free State "from which she had been expelled because she couldn't own a house as a widow." Shigumbu, the soft-hearted bachelor, "was trying desperately hard not to annoy the authorities lest he be sent back to his homeland."

"Custom" becomes one of the leitmotifs of African humanism. For example, there are comments on marriage and the groom's responsibility that reflect group-held values. "'He's marrying,' people always say in the continuous tense," comments the narrator, "which implies a long, long process" (133). The groom is reminded by his elders of his duty in life in a definitive African humanist statement and admonished not to forget "a man is a man because of other men." At the same time, the new order suggests it is good for the groom to move out of the house: "If you can rear your own cow, why let others do it for you." The African humanism inherent in the litany of communal obligations, in the importance of producing children, and in the lively interaction among extended family and friends at the wedding, as well as the repeated comments on customs, helps set up the tension in the story and establish a dialectic between old ways and new. The expression of an African humanistic ethos also enables Mphahlele to probe the psychology and motivation of individual characters.

The story's conflict arises when Diketso, the groom's younger sister, begins to jive with her lover, openly defying convention. Later in the story, the mood turns ugly when Diketso's father brutally beats her for continuing to see her lover, who lives in a squatters' camp out of town. Mphahlele does not overlook the potential for violence in the African character here nor the socioeconomic reasons behind it. Psychological motivation is provided for these destructive and self-alienating actions. Diketso's father is suffering from ill health brought on by work in the mines. He is also emasculated by his rather too domineering wife and thus beats his daughter in order to feel more like a man. Diketso, in turn, is deeply unhappy and frustrated because she is not in school. Through the African humanist voice of Ma-Lesane, who continues to insist that one day Diketso will be as straight as her little finger (which ironically happens to be quite crooked), the reader learns that the Lesanes cannot afford to keep Diketso in school, although Diketso "loves schooling so, poor girl, and since she left it she's like a door on one hinge." Diketso, rebellious though she is, is self-aware enough to realize that she continues to meet her lover in large part out of deep frustration as well as her personal sense of loneliness and inadequacy. In the end, the hurt and alienation extends to the squatters' camp itself when the story ends with the camp's demolition against a "violent background" over which hangs a "pall of smoke." Diketso, however, still clings to the hope that one day she will return to school and perhaps even train to be a nurse.

By putting community and the African humanist commentaries of Ma-Lebone and "Old Mbata," who sits with his peers "coughing and sneezing out the last years of their lives, reflecting on "the broken purposes of human lives that littered the street," in the foreground, Mphahlele is better able both to dramatize and to highlight themes of alienation and to devise more realistic plots and rounded characters (135). For example, Diketso, who is Rebone's forerunner in *Down Second Avenue,* comes to life through the eyes of several other characters (her father, mother, siblings, and lover) through interactions with them and events in the narrative as well as through interior monologue. Because Diketso is seen as a part of African communal life, but also with a life of her own, she is more than a mere message carrier. She is, in short, a much more rounded, multifaceted character than either Sylvia Direko or Annah in *Man Must Live*. But they, like Diketso, Rebone, Eva, Dora, Karabo, and, indeed, all of Mphahlele's strong women are

> girls in the slums who are moved by an inner strength to try and drag themselves out of their circumstances. Sometimes, tragically, they fail, but they do not despair. [Mphahlele's] older women we can often imagine as the mature version of the younger girls. Ma-Lesane in *Drum* and Aunt Dora in *Down Second Avenue* no longer have ambitions for themselves, but the toughness and refusal to give into circumstances is still there. They rule their families with a hand of iron, but with tremendous affection, and thus give their children a sense of mental stability in an unstable world. (Barnett 1976, 38)

Mphahlele's concern with socioeconomic issues affecting the self-alienating, psychological oppression of blacks stands out as an early indicator of his fundamental black consciousness. Long before Steve Biko articulated Black Consciousness as a political philosophy, these concerns are identifiable in such works as the "Lesane" stories and act as commentaries on the context. They include inferior black education or no education, the powerlessness of the black masses and working class, and the breakdown of traditional African values and the family structure due to apartheid economics and white oppression.

Education, for example, is compulsory for white children. The same is not true of blacks, however, as witness the fact that neither Fanyan nor Diketso has secured a secondary education (Thompson 1990, 196). Furthermore, the government whom Ma-Lesane refers to as "a strange person," does not provide her husband, whose health has been ruined by long years of hard labor in the mines from which he "had been discharged owing to his kidney trouble," with a "sick pension" nor would it grant Fanyan a pass. The "Lesane" stories, in short, bear out the socioeconomic realities of an era in which "the social dislocations resulting from colonialism and the migrant labour system helped to disrupt family life and undermine both women's rights and status in patriarchal rural societies. The insecurities of urban existence would have also contributed to a weakening of traditional patriarchal controls" (Lodge 1990, 140). In her warmth, compassion, and insights Ma-Lesane, along with "Old Mbata," provides the positive African humanist counterweight that keeps the sequel from becoming unremittingly grim. It also enables Mphahlele simultaneously to probe psychological motives such as Fanyan's fears and inferiority, Diketso's frustration and unhappiness, their father's low self-esteem and emasculation, and to link motive to the interplay of themes of alienation.

In the conversational tone of the narrative in the text of the "Lesane" stories and in his use of wise sayings and proverbs Mphahlele draws effectively on the African oral tradition. The metaphoric language is also alive with African imagery. Thus language as "both a means of communication and a carrier of culture" and of values as a part of national identity is beginning to overcome colonial alienation (Ngugi 1992, 77). Mphahlele's language reflects "real life" concerns of "how people interact with each other in the labour process" (15–17). We learn from the stories about colonialism's disruptive effect on society and about economic exploitation as well as of a judicial system that is fundamentally bankrupt and corrupting. Thus Fanyan, age eighteen and fresh from the country where his education in bush schools was inadequate and spotty, much like Mphahlele's own early education, is sent to school in part to circumvent the system and in order to secure a pass. It is also widely acknowledged and accepted that Seleke, the *shebeen* queen, regularly bribes the police—for as wise Old Mbata observes, "In town here your honesty can only carry you to the end of Nadia street."

Because Fanyan is fearful, awkward, and shy, he is intrigued by Seleke who is anything but. With her arms that are "shaped like a constable's baton" and breasts "that parted where they united" she is perceived by Ma-Lesane to be "a hundred Sodoms and Gomorrahs put together." (Here a missionary-school allusion creeps in that is effectively Africanized to achieve a humorous effect in Mphahlele's vividly sketched cameo portrait of Seleke.) Fanyan asks Seleke how she can show such a "strong heart" with the police coming in and out all the time. Seleke in a variation on the man-must-live theme, replies that one must have a "tough heart" to survive. Fanyan then asks, "How did you begin?" Seleke's reply amounts to her township-style resume as *shebeen* queen. It becomes a short telling lesson in apartheid economics and thus serves as an indictment. She tells Fanyan: "Like most of us in the townships. School, no money, school, no money, out, factory, out, no money, out, lie, cheat, bribe, live. Nothing more. Never!" Seleke's reply details a life lived by thousands like her. In order to survive, considerable wit and resourcefulness are needed. There is, for instance, an entire tribe employed in the profession of "hole-diggers"—men who dig holes in people's back yards so as to hide illegally distilled beer (brewed by women to supplement incomes) from police during raids (Mphahlele 1959, 142–43).

Eventually, Fanyan quite innocently falls foul of the law for carrying *dagga*, after being set up by Seleke, and is arrested by the police, whom he fears, much in the manner of Dinku Dikae in *Down Second Avenue*, as a dreaded symbol of the system. Mphahlele shows himself to be firmly in control of the narrative here, using dialogue and character description to advance plot and to foreshadow the trouble Fanyan will find himself in when he makes the *dagga* pick-up from Shigumbu "who went about the room like a cat. . . . The set of false teeth he had gave him an evil, snarling appearance."

Dialogue is lively and humorous. The wily Shigumbu tries to make certain the gossip about *dagga* is squelched by suggesting to neighbors that the packet was, in fact, an herbal remedy for colds. The use of humor, African idioms, and dialect and making the toothless Shigumbu speak are clever rhetorical devices: "I bought the herbs at Mai Mai myself, bludder. For a cough. Well, if people want to think it's dagga let them, my bludder. Look at the moon and say it's a woman's breast, you can fly up and kiss it if you want it bludder. I can't help it if the moon is not a breast, can I? I didn't make the moon what it is. Solly, bludder." It is a part of the narrator's humanism, and his broad perspective, that his characters are not in the Manichean sense either all black or white. There are bad blacks and at least one white policeman who shows signs of compassion when he remarks of Fanyan, "Poor fellow, how green he is still" (Mphahlele 1989, 141). Because of his arrest, Fanyan is now forced to quit school altogether and to look for a job. When he eventually finds a job he soon loses it because of tension with the foreman. These events further exacerbate the father-son alienation that builds throughout, a theme that is taken up again in *Down Second Avenue.* In a sense, Fanyan is the ultimate outsider—taunted by classmates, persecuted by the police, and exploited by the *shebeen* queen Seleke, a hardened survivor, herself, whose tough armor was forged in the cauldron of township life and the need to survive. In short, Fanyan undergoes a process of psychological alienation. In his brief encounters with the white bureaucrat who denies Fanyan a pass because he fails to answer questions accurately about landmarks in the black township and the lift operators who address him as "John" and send him to a separate lift, we witness the corrosive effects of racism and prejudice. Mphahlele documents this self-destructive change in Fanyan as follows: "He was beginning to see city life in clearer perspective. Certain mental habits were forming in him: suspicion, for instance, and a timid alertness" (147). Fanyan in his psychological alienation and loss of innocence is a metaphor for the insidious alienation of township youth.

One of the sadder episodes of alienation that occurs in the "Lesane" series illustrates the class-caste alienation between the Asian and black communities, who for the most part live amicably, but between whom there is friction due, in part, to the fact that the Asians comprise the commercial class and, under the caste system of apartheid, also enjoy better amenities and greater privilege. Again Mphahlele uses the African humanist voice in Ma-Lesane to comment on the scene which begins when Indian fruit hawker Ahmed Moosa arrives and cries out his wares. People are returning home at the end of the week. They spew out of the train "like the . . . vomit of some monster" full of the "conflicts that raged in them during the week" when "tough nerves ached and the flesh longed to hurt itself" (151).

Mphahlele shows a good ear for dialect as he replicates Moosa's accent. Moosa is fond of repartee and likes to crack jokes. The women go into peals of laughter when Moosa says, "See my hoss? My hoss and all its pleas [fleas] and plies [flies] on it love you, love you love you!" (152). The scene, however, turns ugly when a patron discovers a worm in his apple. Suddenly and without warning, an angry crowd gathers and upends Moosa's cart, beats the horse and sends it crashing down the street. The episode hints at ones to come in *Down Second Avenue*, when Aunt Dora takes on Abdool. Again, Mphahlele shows that a cruel existence makes people cruel. In the compassion of Ma-Lesane and her stance of African humanism Mphahlele, however, has a ready-made foil and commentator to enlarge on mob motivation and psychology. People act this way, she explains to her son in the story "Neighbours," because "there is something big on our shoulders, and so we stab and curse and beat one another."

While it is clear that communalism in the slums is not all *ubuntu* and caring, Ma-Lesane in her distinctly African humanist cooperative effort to help Moosa recover his losses saves the episode from becoming too brutish, grim, and meaningless. Sometimes, however, Ma-Lesane is overly generous in her desire to accept and help others. Ma-Lesane is not a one-sided character. Despite her African humanism, she is tough enough to intimidate her husband; and single-minded enough to overlook the obvious. When Rev. Anton Katsane, a man of the cloth, arrives under questionable circumstances and rumors about his irregular use of church funds, Ma-Lesane nonetheless encourages Diketso to clean for him. Town gossips judge this to be inappropriate and unseemly. Nevertheless, as Ma-Ntoi comments: "It wouldn't have happened in the old days . . . because we were human beings. And nothing would have happened because we were clean" (159).

This is a poignant statement on the devastating effect of urbanization, poverty, colonialism, and white oppression on the indigenous culture and its ancient humanism. It is also a commentary on the conflict between old ways and new and between generations with regard to manners, morals, and questions of social conduct. Diketso, upset by the beatings her father administers and frustrated by her lack of education, seeks comfort from the pastor, who is only too happy to oblige with a warm embrace. (In this episode, Mphahlele as satirist holds up a magnifying glass to the church and finds it wanting.) Ma-Mafate, stumbling across the scene, suspects the worst. She issues a warning. In a scene foreshadowing Rebone's actions in *Down Second Avenue*, Diketso, enraged, slaps Ma-Mafate in the face—an action so unthinkable that Old Mbate, like a Greek sibyl, proclaims: "The world is coming to an end, brother!" (161).

So goes the process of dehumanization with its lost opportunities—for education, for personal growth, for purposeful employment; the massive dislocation, the breakdown in relationships between family members and communal groups, leading, in turn, to ethnic strife and youth alienation, to acts of violence and a loss of morality; to a loss of traditional ways and values—to a loss, in the final analysis, of humanity and humanness. In *I Write What I Like* Steve Biko notes the bitter irony of ministers on Sunday preaching "mea culpa" sermons to black congregations about the "thieving, housebreaking, stabbing, murdering, adultery etc." that are rife in black townships and their utter blind failure to connect vice in the townships with socioeconomic conditions marked by "poverty, unemployment, overcrowding, lack of schooling, and migratory labour" (1986, 56–57). In the "Lesane" series Mphahlele, as he realistically documents and describes, succeeds in making the vital, damning link. Yet not all is without hope. Characters in the "Lesane" series are not so hopeless as Zungu is in "Man Must Live," primarily because, despite alienation and conflict, they remain rooted in community. In his evocation of setting, Mphahlele documents a synthesizing process of "elements of old and new," by which "a distinctive African urban subculture" has come into being, "but underneath its often vibrant and gay exterior lingered a continuing crisis of the spirit" (Gerhart 1979, 32).

Unlike Mphahlele, the young black writers with whom he worked on *Drum* did not reach back into the African past or rural culture for inspiration. The idioms they employed were almost exclusively urban. Dialogue was a medley of local vernaculars, American movie slang, and *tsotsi taal* (gangster) talk. Characters in their stories were often, in Bakhtin's words, an "ideological construct." Mphahlele, himself, understood the power of characters as ideological message carriers and used the "African image" as an ideological measuring rod in his own critical analysis of fictional characters, devising what was essentially a more poetic version of Bakhtin's analytic phrase.

Although none of the *Drum* stories is overtly didactic, the depiction of street-wise tough guys in urban settings, who clearly belong where they are and nowhere else, and, particularly, not in a rural setting, constitutes an ideological statement of sorts—a response to the "other's already articulated word." The stories stand collectively as an assertion that flies in the face of state apartheid's intent to retribalize in "homelands" those "surplus" blacks not required as laborers in cities—with resettlement engineered along ethnic lines, in a calculated strategy of divide and conquer.

No matter how thugish or debased the characters in the *Drum* stories—whether they be alcoholics like Marta, in Can Themba's story by the same name, or boxers who stab their lovers, as in Nat Nakasa's "The Life and Death of King Kong"—they, nonetheless, are about urban blacks in urban settings written by and for urban blacks. The *Drum* style is sometimes referred to as "Matshikize." Todd Matshikiza, the composer of the musical score of *King Kong,* which became a hit in South Africa and abroad in the early 1960s, transformed the English language into the verbal equivalent of Kwela folk jazz. He played his typewriter as if it were a combination saxophone and machine gun—a syncopation felt in his writing (Barnett, 1983, 219).

In his autobiographical fragment, *Chocolates for My Wife,* Matshikiza juxtaposes life for a black in Johannesburg with that in London, where his jazz opera was then being staged, creating a mirror image in which black and white are reversed. Wry humor is effectively deployed as a weapon to critique state apartheid. Like an innocent abroad, Matshikiza can never quite get over the oddity of seeing whites employed at blue-collar jobs or of his being repeatedly and courteously addressed as "sir." His wife, Esme, and their two children are brought to life as the narrator, who manages throughout to exude a flip, but engaging charm, interacts with them in the family circle. In his hands, the English language is played like an instrument with the same virtuoso flair that marks the playing of Hugh Masekela on the trumpet. The narrative—episodic and full of flashbacks—reflects both a fragmented existence and the pulse and improvisation of jazz. Of the several *Drum* voices, Matshikiza's is among the most original. The prose narrative often spills over into poetry as in the following passage:

> the chimney pots . . . grouped at the top of the roofs, bent at the elbows or sitting down close together huddled like gossiping old women come out to say, "Isn't it awful, or isn't it great, isn't it shocking, this constant influx of foreigners into our quiet country."
>
> Anthony Sampson was there to meet us. He was all there. Bigger.

Stronger. Blue and bright in the eyes as ever. I had worked with him when he was editor of *Drum*. . . . Here he was, talking and walking as upright as ever. Warm and comfortable as the central heating in London. (1985, 10)

The easy conversational style, the jazz beat, the charm of the narrator, the poetic imagery all are unmistakably vintage Matshikiza. His was, sadly and like so many others, to be a short-lived brilliance, but it burned brightly while it lasted. Yet one does not find in Matshikiza's work the distinctively African imagery, the use of proverbs and aphorisms, the references to a rural African past or to an African cosmology that mark Mphahlele's work.

Using Mphahlele's *The African Image* as a means of examining several stories of the *Drum* era, one is struck by the more humanistic cast of Mphahlele's fictive characters. In such *Drum* stories as Mphahlele's "The Suitcase," we are presented in Timi with a character who (like Mphahlele himself) is a responsible family man, loyal to wife and family and abstemious, having refused offers of drink. He is also struggling desperately to find employment in order to put food on the table. His wife, who is ill, finds courage and offers comfort by quoting the African sages who say: "Even where there is no pot to boil, there should be fire." Timi in a weak moment succumbs to the temptation to keep a suitcase left behind on a bus by a pair of young women, one of whom appears unwell. It is New Year's and the dead child that is later and shockingly discovered inside serves to reverse the traditional symbolism of Christmas—in the same way blacks experience so many other reversals. Timi is ultimately caught by the police and sentenced to 18 months of hard labor for theft, hammered by a legal system that hands out disproportionate and unjust sentences to blacks. Thus, we see a man, fundamentally decent, driven by despair into acting against his own better instincts. In this way, Mphahlele links vice with socioeconomic injustices and exploitation in a story that indicts without being didactic.

By contrast, most characters portrayed in the *Drum* stories, whether fiction or nonfiction, are township toughs and degenerates, who unwittingly serve to confirm certain stereotypes. For example, in "Battle for Honour" by Alex La Guma, we have a pair of hard-drinking, tough-talking characters who womanize and fight it out over a love triangle. Setting is evoked naturalistically and in journalistic detail. Characters and scene serve in their specificity and concreteness to reflect the harsh realities of historic context. We do not, however, witness individual change and so there is no overt link between degradation and socioeconomic conditions as there is in Mphahlele's story where Timi changes before our eyes. We know Arthur as a hard-drinking lorry driver, Fancy as a womanizer and braggart, the shark as brutish and good with his fists, and so on. The fight that ensues would make good reading in any sports section of a newspaper with its bear hugs, yelling, hoots, and "the sudden wrench sideways," when Fancy "staggered away crazily, making mewling sounds with his pain-twisted mouth" (Chapman 1989, 164). The fight is highly realistic, in its blow-by-blow, documentary recreation. La Guma's racy dialect packs an equal punch.

Henry Nxumalo movingly documents the "Birth of a Tsotsi," in the nonfiction story by the same title, in which are utilized such storytelling techniques as dialogue. In it Nxumalo, known as "Mr. Drum" for his fearless reportage, interviews a young inmate at Diepkloof Reformatory, where Alan Paton served as principal for thirteen years. The youth describes his career in crime, starting from age thirteen. Although the youth is resolved to stay straight when he returns to society, the reader realizes that social conditions will make that almost impossible. It is a heartrending account— even though the *tsotsi* never comes fully to life, but rather stands more as a symbol of a collective tragedy.

Arthur Mogale (Maimane) wrote escapist pieces for *Drum*, featuring a tough detective who is cast in the trickster mold. Casi Motsisi, whose style most closely resembles Matshikiza's in its breeziness, whimsy, and jazzy dialogue, wrote a promising and clever series featuring such characters as "the playboy," "kid hangover," and "kid journalist."

This lineup of characters, however, tends to bear out Lewis Nkosi's observation that blacks in the 1950s, unlike in other parts of the world, "had no literary heroes . . . who would serve as moral examples for us" (1983, 6). Mphahlele counters the rogues' gallery by offering *Drum* readers in his story "Guts and Granite" an inspired portrait of the first African woman to be on the Transvaal Provincial Executive of the ANC, Lilian Ngoyi. A gifted and persuasive orator, Ngoyi makes her points "with vivid figures of speech." These include such statements as: "We women are like hens that lay eggs for somebody to take away. That's the effect of Bantu education." She is an inspired and inspiring role model for nation building. Mphahlele's sketch of the remarkable Ngoyi is balanced by absence of any hagiography and by the effective use of African idioms: "Mrs Ngoyi's weakness lies in being highly emotional. Her strength lies in the fact that she admits it. . . . Her stubbornness is that of a centipede, which keeps the same direction in spite of any attempt to take it off its course" (Chapman 1989, 107). Ngoyi puts in an appearance later on in Mphahlele's novella "Mrs Plum."

Rive, Mphahlele's protégé, in his well-crafted story "African Song" comes closest to emulating Mphahlele in his depiction of a protagonist who exhibits strength and commitment to African values, both nationalistic and humanistic. Muti has come to the city for employment, but lacks a pass. He attends a meeting where the ANC national anthem is sung—"Nkosi Sikelel' iAfrika": "God Bless Africa . . . the sun-scored Karoo and the green of the valley of a Thousand Hills. . . . This Africa of blue skies and brown veld, and black and white." Muti knows police will come to break up the meeting and may arrest him for not having a pass, but he is carried away by the song and by a sense of nationalistic pride. The plot is skillfully woven into the song and its poetic lyrics, just as feelings of fear and pride achieve an effective, tension-producing counterpoint.

The liberal Afrikaner writer, André Brink, in his book of critical essays *Writing in a State of Siege,* conducts an anguished interior dialogue on the ethics of a white writer like himself choosing not to exile himself from a country in which codified racism, censorship, economic exploitation, and police brutality are the order of the day. He explains that he remains where he is—a decision not without considerable risk since he as a dissident Afrikaner is perceived as a dangerous threat to the closed wagon circle (the *laager*)—because "I must be here: because I love this land with a deep and terrible love: because not being here would be spiritual death" (1983, 35).

Many of the *Drum* writers who, in the late 1950s, fled South Africa as a result of political harassment, banning or worse threats, surely felt much the same close identification with the land that Brink describes, but had very little choice in the question of political exile versus remaining in South Africa. Writers such as Alex La Guma, whose works depended so greatly for effect on naturalistic evocation of landscape, must certainly have felt as spiritually cut off at the roots in exile as did Mphahlele and many of his *Drum* colleagues.

Thus, it was in the years from 1955 to 1965, during the "Drum decade," that such a flowering of black talent occurred, only to be prematurely blighted by "a torrent of restrictive legislation," including censorship in the form of banning, gagging, and muzzling, that N. W. Viser has referred to "as the Renaissance that failed" (1976, 118). Just as blacks were beginning to define a national myth and political consciousness embodied in literature, that literature was dealt a mortal blow, a form of spiritual alienation that continues even to the present.

Critic Ursula Barnett states that Mphahlele's *Drum* stories are as "rich a source of information about black city life in South African in the 1950s as are the works of Dickens and Gorky about their period" (1976, 47). In the "Lesane" series and other stories of that era, Mphahlele had begun "to exorcise the African's image of himself as the perpetual imitator and underling, the 'non-white' in a white world," enabling "Africans to find a new sense of cultural identity" by placing "their own history, achievements, and standards of beauty and worth at the center of the psychological universe" (Gerhart 1979, 201).

In 1956, Mphahlele departed South Africa for Lagos to take up a teaching position. For the next decade, he would not publish another work of fiction.

Chapter Four

The African Image

MAKING THE LABEL STICK

My body itches from the labels that have been stuck on it.
—Es'kia Mphahlele

In 1961, under the Suppression of Communism Act, after Mphahlele had departed for Lagos, he received the ultimate coup de grace as a writer in his own country. Under this act any action was outlawed that "aims at bringing about political, industrial, social or economic change within the Republic by the promotion of disturbance or disorder, by unlawful acts or omissions." In other words, "any political action by the disenfranchised non-whites constitutes a crime" (JanMohamed 1988, 80).

Mphahlele's "crime" was that he had lobbied actively against the promulgation of the Bantu Education Act. Anyone under banning orders was prohibited from entering educational institutions and could not be quoted in the country. Mphahlele notes, in his collected essays, that by 1968, more than five hundred people, black and white, were under banning orders (1972, 205). For more than three decades all of Mphahlele's important works, including *Down Second Avenue* and *The African Image,* were published and read abroad. Not until 1980 did Mphahlele publish again in South Africa. Thus, was he twice-alienated: first as a teacher, then as a writer.

Mphahlele's pan-African travels as well as his admiration for such black American writers as W. E. B. Du Bois, Langston Hughes, and Richard Wright helped shape his thinking on questions concerning the African personality, negritude, and Black Consciousness. Indeed, Mphahlele's entire intellectual and spiritual life became in itself an *oeuvre* in progress. It was, at times, a fragmented lonely journey in which his sense of "the tyranny of place" drove him in efforts to recover "an effective identifying relationship between self and place" (Ashcroft 1985, 9). In the end, however, Mphahlele was able to contribute significantly to the struggle to "move the center," a struggle that was most dramatic in African countries and the Caribbean "where the postwar world saw a new literature in English and French consolidating itself into a tradition. This literature was celebrating the right to name the world. . . . The new tradition was challenging the more dominant one in which Asia, Africa, and South America were always being defined from the capitals of Europe by Europeans who often saw the world in color-tinted glasses" (Ngugi 1993, 3). In his memoir *Afrika My Music*, Mphahlele, an active participant himself in this celebration, observes that he left one literary renaissance behind him in South Africa to find himself in the midst of another, "a west African one, which was in full swing." In Lagos, Mphahlele worked with such writers as Wole Soyinka and Amos Tutuola (Mphahlele 1984, 23). He also helped establish the Mbari Centre for writers and artists. Here in Nigeria he found freedom exhilarating and Africa being "revived for me" (Makgabutlane 1990, 36).

Shortly after his arrival in Lagos, Mphahlele completed his well-known autobiography *Down Second Avenue*, which not only constitutes community history, but stands as an affirmation of the great "I am." Like Chinua Achebe in his fiction, Mphahlele had begun to transform "the African's status from that of an object to that of a subject" (JanMohamed 1988, 273). This process was taking place at both the literary and personal levels, where Mphahlele was celebrating not only the right to "name the world" through literature but also to name himself. To name a thing is to invest it with being and "once a man's identity is denied, a struggle is initiated which cannot end before he has found his place and his name again" (Brink 1983, 47). In his sometimes painful struggle to resolve the tension-inducing dialectic between his more individuated persona steeped in the Western humanities and his more communally oriented, spiritually inclined, poetic self, Mphahlele eventually stuck a new label on himself. He did this despite his numerous protestations earlier on to the effect that so many labels had been stuck on him that he "itched all over" (Thuynsma 1989, 7).

Unlike past labels, however, which were mostly negative and told blacks what they were not and could never aspire to be, this new label was positive, upbeat, and held moral clarity. It was shaped by Mphahlele's pan-African travels and by his scholarly and academic pursuits. It acquired a voice of authority through such works as his volume of essays, *Voices in the Whirlwind* (1972), gaining even clearer definition in *The African Image* (revised 1974). While Mphahlele's life provided raw material for the evolution of this concept, his literature became for him a "building block for identity" (Bates 1993, 215).

The mythic label was not based on a tribalized folklore nor did it draw on tyrannical, unpredictable gods and superstitions that could hold people in thrall. Neither were its precepts so particularized that only a small community could agree on them. Its recovery was guided by precepts that Fanon in Algeria was simultaneously giving voice to in *The Wretched of the Earth*—that is, that the Third World should not "define itself in terms of values that preceded it," but rather should seek out and define its own values and a "new humanism" (1963, 99, 246).

The label was, of course, that of "African humanist." Although a tiger (to paraphrase Wole Soyinka) may not feel a need to declare its "tigritude," the African humanist did feel compelled to shout back his essential humanity in the face of colonialism, the white liberal establishment, and the brutally dehumanizing system of apartheid. In his formulation of a sociopolitical and aesthetic philosophy that is the theoretical equivalent of Julius Nyerere of Tanzania's *Ujamaa* (family-based) socialism, Kenneth Kaunda's Zambian humanism, Biko's Black Consciousness, and Leopold Senghor's negritude, Mphahlele joined the ranks as a standard bearer and "cultural liberator," scoring against the self-alienating forces of Eurocentric cultural imperialism operating out of Western capitals.

On March 21, 1960, three years after Mphahlele fled into exile, the historic Sharpeville shootings took place in which white police fired into a crowd of unarmed Africans gathered in an anti-pass protest demonstration outside Vereeniging. Sixty-seven Africans were killed, most shot in the back. Of the 186 wounded, many were women and children. This event, combined with the banning of political parties, such as the ANC, and episodes of police raids, terror tactics, brutality, detentions without trial, and jails filled to bursting, further convinced black resistance movements that violence not peaceful protest was the only effective means to bring about change (Thompson 1990, 210). Sharpeville proved to be a historic watershed in black politics as well as in black literature, transforming resistance into active protest.

In the post-Sharpeville era, Mphahlele had begun to search for more forcible ways of affirming black values and community culture. His monumental critical work, *The African Image* (1962), was an attempt to portray images of Africans: who they are within the context of a brutal history and an ancient humanism and how they give artistic expression to their ontology. Mphahlele's endeavor to "re-create an image" of Africans "from the disparate elements of their culture . . . [and] the debris of their shattered pre-colonial past" is sometimes, states Lewis Nkosi, "too joyous an affirmation, it seems to me—that such an image has been fragmented almost beyond recognition" (1983, 129). Yet it is through Mphahlele's conceptualization of African humanism that he is eventually able to impose a meaningful organizing principle on the chaos of the shattered pre- and postcolonial past. Mphahlele, in his critical pan-African review, initially distances himself from negritude—because of its tendency to oversimplify, to "not tell us the whole truth," to falsify and to overlook the need for modern solutions in Africa (Mphahlele 1974, 80). Mphahlele by way of example quotes the following stanza by poet Jacques Romain from Guinea:

> Your heart trembles in the shadows
> like a face reflected in troubled waters.
> An old picture rises from the tomb of the night,
> You feel the sweet magic of yore;
> A river carries you away from the shore,
> Carries you away into ancestral fields.

Negritude poetry, as in the passage cited, is, Mphahlele states, nothing more than "sheer romanticism, often it is mawkish and strikes a pose" (1962, 27). Mphahlele later wrote a poem about rivers and ancestral fields titled "Death" (1987, 274–77). But, in its concrete allusions to historical context, it does not ignore the harsh political realities of modern Africa, and specifically of the "painful South." Hence, it avoids the pitfalls of "sheer romanticism" and of striking a pose even while utilizing nearly identical imagery.

Mphahlele in his search for meaning and a sociological aesthetic initially found negritude and the African personality distinctly wanting, particularly in the South African context. In similar vein he examines white liberalism in both *The African Image* and in his essays, *Voices in the Whirlwind* (1973), and likewise finds it wanting. The alienation Mphahlele feels toward white South African liberals is doubtless frustrating to him, since under more normal circumstances such thinkers, writers, and educators would be among his natural peer group. (Indeed, some of his best friends and most admired mentors, such as Norah Taylor and Professor Edward Davis of University of South Africa to whom he dedicated *The African Image*, were white liberals.) This element of Mphahlele's growing political alienation is doubly ironic since Mphahlele is himself a liberal. Yet, in chapter five of *The African Image*, Mphahlele feels compelled to begin with a categorical denial that he is a liberal since in the South African context to be called a liberal would be "to describe a white man who believes in redressing political wrongs by constitutional means" (1962, 67). Mphahlele's liberalism (in the broadest sense) is, however, clearly manifested in the high value he places on individual free expression, his dislike for arbitrary authority and violence, and his belief in the right of man by reason of his humanity "to order his life as seems good to him" within the framework of the community.

As Mphahlele continues to make plain in *The African Image,* as well as other works, there were significant drawbacks to white liberalism in South Africa and with the Liberal party itself. Founded in 1953 by white liberals such as Alan Paton, the Liberal party boasted a multiracial membership, but was cautiously gradualist and frequently elitist in its approach. Such gradualism is best illustrated by its advocacy of only a limited franchise for blacks, a qualification that was not dropped until 1959 (Lodge 1990, 87). It was entirely possible prior to 1959 in South Africa to be a self-professed liberal while not being a true democrat. Mrs Plum, in the story by that name, is the paradigm of such a "bossy" white liberal—a voluble advocate of a limited franchise who presumes both to speak on behalf of blacks and also to tell them what is best for them. In his revised *African Image* Mphahlele, by now giving full vent to his disillusionment, states that he finds it galling, for example, that such advocates of "enlightened" liberalism as Professor Alfred Hoernle urged blacks to "accept statutory councils [set up by the apartheid state] as a training ground in democratic processes" (1974, 51).

In *Voices in the Whirlwind,* Mphahlele questions the moral courage of the white liberal press for failing to take an unequivocal stand against apartheid, observing that it "hardly requires moral courage if he [the reporter] merely reports the facts, or protests within the law." Mphahlele avers that "This is in the true tradition of South African white liberalism, which has always accommodated itself in the safe capsule of legality, and that means white legality, since the laws are made by whites" (1972, 200).

Indeed, it was arguably the ideological incompatibility between black and white liberals, as much as apartheid itself, that led Mphahlele in works such as *The African Image* to search out a new world vision. As Themba Sono states, "Black Consciousness has its roots located primarily in the African liberals' disenchantment with (white) liberalism . . . which could be looked upon as the creation of black liberals shorn of their 'white liberalism'" (1993, 6). As the pendulum began to swing to the extreme limits of alienation, there was an even greater need for a counterweight to restore balance. The limits of this alienation were being plumbed in such works as

The African Image, where an African nationalist world vision was being defined and a new aesthetic was also taking shape.

In both original and revised editions of *The African Image,* we see a unique narrative voice that functions on several planes: autobiographical, anecdotal, literary, socioeconomic, and political. In the first edition of *The African Image,* the increasingly self-aware political voice states the need to evaluate "the sense and nonsense that is often said and thought by whites and blacks, top dogs and underdogs, about each other and about themselves" (1962, 16). Next, the critic's voice analyzes the treatment of black characters in English fiction by white writers who deal in such stereotypes as the "Noble Savage," "Degenerate," "Man with the Halo," and "Menacing Servant." Ironically, certain trace elements of these very stereotypes outlined by Mphahlele are identifiable in his own first collection of short stories. The character Zungu in *Man Must Live,* for example, falls rather neatly into "the degenerate" mold. Last but not least, the communal voice in *The African Image* affirms values and beliefs consonant with African humanism—the very same that are vividly documented and come to life in *Down Second Avenue.*

There is also in *The African Image* a persona, sometimes Westernized and individuated, other times, an African elder, who portrays himself often and well, and, not infrequently, from the inside out as well as the outside in, with whom the reader feels a warmth of rapport that is quite unexpected in a work of literary criticism. Jane Watts describes *The African Image* as an "intellectual autobiography" (Watts 1989, 62). Ursula Barnett suggests that it is an "emotional autobiography" (1976, 117). British critics charged Mphahlele in his analysis with "isolating character from context" and others suggested he "was practising unorthodox literary criticism" (Mphahlele 1974, 10). *The African Image* is incontestably both autobiographical and unorthodox. Perhaps it is best described as an "aesthetic autobiography," with its roots in Africa, that combines anecdote, scholarly style, gnomic insights, and warmth of tone in a manner that sets it apart in an uncatalogued genre of its own. Far from being a "transplanted fossil of European literature" adhering to standardized critical norms, it has broken out of the "straitjacket" and stands in its own right as an Africanist statement against Eurocentric literary imperialism (Chinweizu et al. 1983, 239).

Even in his works of literary criticism, the African humanist narrator never loses sight of the human in the critic's play of abstract thought. One arresting example of the personal used to make a political point in the literary and critical occurs in "Black and White Cameos" in the final chapter of the first edition of *The African Image.* Mphahlele is at a social function in

London where he encounters Afrikaner South Africans connected with the Dutch Reformed Church and the South African Bureau of Racial Affairs, "who cause so much suffering among non-whites" (1962, 222). Mphahlele is torn between wanting to say something hurtful and wanting to project a friendly but assertive presence, to show that he is "out of reach of the government." He is also besieged with guilt for even talking to the Afrikaners. Suddenly in a "neurotic tremor" he sees everything in split images and immediately leaves the party. Later he analyzes the episode and his own response to it and decides "after that bit of therapy, I was quite all right. Another of my failures to live with freedom? I've tried to read Britain—or what part of it I've seen—letter for letter, like a child learning how to read. Each letter has been a huge impression, and the sum total has left me a bundle of agitation. How long freedom is going to intensify my hatred of those who have denied me it, I don't know" (Mphahlele 1962, 223). Here the alienation documented is psychological as well as political. It reflects the Black Consciousness emphasis on a move from the "exterior manifestation of oppression, to the interior psychology of that oppression" (Ndebele 1991, 64). The fragmented self is brought forward by the humanist narrator and given preeminence over the realm of abstract thought. Mphahlele thus documents the fragmentation and the psychological oppression that Steve Biko later identifies as being central to black oppression. With remarkable candor in a work of literary criticism, Mphahlele describes his personal experience of "an acute sense of radical disparity" between self and consciousness and the external world. The loss of identity is "reflected back" in "the loss of a live sense of a relationship between himself and the world" (Irele 1990, 172).

In the literary act of his therapeutic confessional, Mphahlele's fragmented self is once again recreated. The inclusion of such an unorthodox human cameo in a critical work not only is proof of Mphahlele's psychological oppression, but also confirms his observation that "Africans have always been more interested in human relations than in gadgets. . . . [they] have always gravitated towards people, not places and things" (1962, 91). In this example, the personal experience of the human narrator is showcased as being of greater value and significance than purely theoretical concerns of abstract critical thought.

The painful cameo stands out in dramatic relief, drawn all the more sharply in its sincerity and poignancy by virtue of its contrast to earlier passages of the text in which is projected the voice of the inclusive, wry-humored African humanist narrator. Mphahlele, for example, had earlier stated that in his nonracial, democratic liberal definition of "African nationalist," he includes "everyone born in Africa, who regards no other place as his home . . . be he black, white, Coloured, or Indian. Even the self-styled 'Afrikaners' in South Africa [are included]—for their own good, if not mine as well" (73). Again, this tongue-in-cheek political statement, serving as an African humanist counterweight to themes of racial bitterness and alienation, is like the highly personalized cameo sketch itself an unorthodox addition to literary criticism.

Between the first and second editions of *The African Image*, Mphahlele's narrative voice shifts across the political spectrum from that of the educated, African, middle-class, Christian liberal to the position of "deviant from the Christian Liberal frame of reference." This shift is characteristic of black thinkers, writers, and political leaders "who have been essential catalysts of change in black politics" (Gerhart 1979, 39). The shift, as seen in Mphahlele's critical work, in the broadest sense is one from negritude, emerging in the first edition of *The African Image*, to a more hardened political stance (and one might add, a more acerbic tone) of Black Consciousness in the revised edition (1974). Moreover, in the revised *African Image* there is far greater emphasis placed on "black nationalism as an instrument for freedom and fulfillment" (Barnett 1976, 116). In what Fanon characterizes as the stages in the evolution of the black writer, Mphahlele has moved to the fighting phase where "he turns himself into an awakener of the people" (1963, 222–23).

In his chapter "The African Personality" in the revised *The African Image*, Mphahlele clearly redefines his terms, managing to illuminate and clarify several philosophic complexities with a few deft strokes, observing that:

> The African Personality or negritude: the distinction is unimportant. Each concept involves the other. They merely began at different times in different historical circumstances. But they share the same mood, the same utopian fervor. Negritude claims the whole of the black world, the African Personality refers only to Africa. Historical negritude laid emphasis on the arts and *"l'ame noir,"* the African Personality began as a sociological concept and moved on to political liberation and presence. (67)

In the revised *The African Image*, Mphahlele, writing in the post-Sharpeville era, overhauled his thinking. He no longer speaks of negritudinist "creepy-crawlies" or dismisses the movement's practitioners as "jungle boys," as he did in the 1962 edition, albeit he remains "critical of the literary positions of historical negritude" (1). Nor does he view negritude as a "form or degree of black consciousness" or the African personality as necessarily irrelevant to the needs of an urbanized black culture. Instead, he "accepts the social thought" such movements and concepts "claim[s] to inform," viewing them as positive insofar as they make a valid historic contribution through self-affirmation to black empowerment.

Before turning the spotlight on African humanism, it is instructive briefly to compare and contrast it with other African nationalist, humanist movements to which it is related. Negritude emphasized stylistics and its locus in the Caribbean and West Africa; the principal founders were Aime Cesaire, Senghor, and Leon Dumas (Kesteloot 1991, xiv). Black Consciousness emphasized political content and links with America and South Africa, while African humanism claims ties with both Africa and the West. All three are fundamentally humanist movements. A major difference is that African humanism does not share either negritude's or Black Consciousness's preoccupation with blackness as a defining attribute of its ideology. Thus, it avoids either movement's divisiveness or potential for reverse racism. Indeed, it was "the brutal contact with the West since the fifteenth century . . . [that] modified original negritude" (and what today is still in America referred to as "soul") and added to it "the idea of race." Jean Paul Sartre, moreover, sees in negritude the antithesis of white supremacy, working in turn, toward a dialectic synthesis that by definition is not racist (108, 111).

This line of thinking suggests that the intent of negritude is not to renounce whites, but rather to affirm with equal zeal black culture and black pride in order to effectively counter the impact of white supremacists. When oppression disappears reconciliation and synthesis will be possible. Negritude according to the dialectic outlined by Sartre "exists in order to be destroyed." Nevertheless, the black "awareness of self is . . . a definitive conquest" (111). Negritude, in short, answered the needs of assimilated Francophone Africans and a major thrust of the negritude movement is stylistic, whereas a major thrust of Black Consciousness, as articulated by Biko, is political and was addressed to the South African Realpolitik. In this respect, African humanism with its broader social and historic scope, its awareness of self and unifying human focus, will theoretically outlast either of the other two movements in the dialectics of history.

By the time the revised *The African Image* was published, Mphahlele had already been living in exile for nearly two decades. As time went on and the clampdown in South Africa of state apartheid grew increasingly violent and iron fisted, his bitterness against whites grew and festered. Not surprisingly, then, in his revised edition, Mphahlele both anticipates and articulates ideals of Black Consciousness that were concomitantly being voiced in

South Africa in the early 1970s by Biko. The direct link between Black Consciousness and psychological oppression forms an integral part of Mphahlele's experience of alienation as delineated in all of his works, including *The African Image,* and that range from the Jamesian "divided personality" to the "segregation of imagination [that] has as its starting point the division of races" (James 1990, 161; Parker 1978, 93). As with Western alienation, an increasingly pessimistic note creeps into Mphahlele's documentation of his own alienation as a writer and teacher in political exile. But whereas Western alienation reflects an often solitary, nihilistic, cold, and even antihumanistic landscape (elements not uncommon in works by such white liberal writers as J. M. Coetzee and Gordimer) the opposite is true of African writers "whose works are created from the perspective of the struggle of the people for social justice [which] will always have an inner buoyancy and hope denied the writer who feels himself entirely isolated from the people" (Nkosi 1981, 74). Mphahlele also makes a distinction between the alienation of the "indigenous self and the one that is superimposed by the new culture" that all colonized people experience and the Westernized, lonely, existential alienation of the individual. The alienation experienced by the colonized people in Africa is not the same, says Mphahlele, because in Africa there are always the many "voices" of the community (Mphahlele 1986, 24).

Yet at the same time Mphahlele believes that from the 1950s "industrialization and migrant labour have played havoc with traditional values. We have lost sight of the myth that could stabilise our spiritual and mental life and save it from the religion of the desperate, the poor, the helpless, the downtrodden that the missionaries left us hanging on to while a pretty noisy and powerful segment of the western world was asserting a completely different set of claims for Christ from what we had been hoodwinked into believing" (Chapman 1992, 57). Mphahlele then goes on to say that "as present-day writers we need to go out in search of the myth and redefine it" (57). As a writer and an exile Mphahlele, however, was for long years separated from the source of that myth. This is why Mphahlele's phrase "tyranny of place" has such meaning. Places have a way of defining an author and of determining the content of writing; of assigning roles. We know, for example, that after Mphahlele left South Africa, much of his work was devoted to literary criticism such as *The African Image* in which he did "go out in search of the myth and redefine it," but perhaps in a more abstract, less concrete fashion than he might have done had he not been cut off from its source. In a review of *The African Image,* Lewis Nkosi movingly and perceptively writes: "Ezekiel Mphahlele is a black South African writer now living in Paris. To be a black South African is to be both unspeakably rich and incredibly poor: and also, it means to live in perpetual exile from oneself, which is worse, since to know who one is today one must be able to relate oneself in a dynamic manner to what one was yesterday" (Nkosi 1983, 129). Africanist and writer Gerald Moore also bears eloquent witness to the tragedy of forty years that "alienated every South African writer of any compassion or sensitivity from the society developing around him. Most . . . have taken refuge in exile, others are prematurely dead, banned or in prison" (1969, xi).

Wole Soyinka, the Nigerian Nobel Laureate, supports both the view of Mphahlele and Nkosi when he asserts, with disarming simplicity, that the difference between European alienation and African is that one is located within its subject and the other is seen as external and is recognized in the form of an oppressor (De Wall 1991, 29). To this external schism, experienced by the colonized and Westernized Africa, Mphahlele devotes an entire chapter, titled "Dialogue of Two Selves," in the revised edition of *The African Image.* In this chapter, Mphahlele rather humorously describes the colonized self and the indigenous selves as being "apt by turns to fight, quarrel, despise each other, hug each other, concede each other's roles" (281).

From 1972, as Mphahlele was about to bring out his revised *The African Image,* Biko began to articulate his views on Black Consciousness, stating that the black man lives in a state of alienation due as much to psychological oppression as to such external factors as exploitation of labor and unequal education which keeps him powerless (Davenport 1989, 418). Some thirty years previously, in *Man Must Live,* Mphahlele had already begun to depict characters living in a "state of alienation" due to psychological oppression. In the "Lesane" series, such characters as Fanyan and Diketso are prime examples of black men and women living in a state of alienation that starts with external causes and becomes internalized. The black man "rejects himself," said Biko, "precisely because he attaches the meaning white to all that is good" (1979, 22). Mphahlele recognized this self-rejection right from the start, devoting his Unisa dissertation to the debunking of white stereotyping of black characters in English literature which promotes such Manichean self-rejection.

Biko stated that "the most potent weapon in the hands of the oppressor was the mind of the oppressed"—to counter which it was crucial to raise black pride and help blacks "attain the envisaged self" (Arnold 1979, xx). By documenting community history in his short stories, novels, and autobiography and memoir and by defining a black aesthetic and a nationalist vision in *The African Image,* Mphahlele was enabling blacks both to rediscover and to "attain the envisaged self." All of Mphahlele's works reflect an increasing degree of black consciousness in the broadest sense, which eventually formed part of his conceptualization known as African humanism. The revised *The African Image* not only reflects Black Consciousness values, it goes beyond describing and documenting the problems of colonialism, racism, and impoverishment to proposing solutions—moving from a mode of peaceful protest to a mode of active resistance in the most positive sense. Written in the post-Sharpeville era marked by increasing repression in South Africa and after long years of exile, it is a work that bears the imprint of its "historical conditions." Metaphysically as well as socially, it extols African thought and values as providing useful tools for overcoming white oppression and political and psychological alienation.

In the revised *The African Image,* for example, Mphahlele states that Africa was "ambushed" by Muhammad and Jesus. He asserts that spiritual colonization and conversion was the price paid for schools and hospitals. He suggests that African humanism can fill the spiritual vacuum since it is true that "No man is complete in himself. No Man is a palm nut, [a fitting use here of African imagery to supplant the standard 'no man is an island'] self-contained. . . . Ancestors will keep you and carry your wishes . . . to the Supreme Force" (44). Already having defined the problem of black oppression, political, economic, and psychological, Mphahlele proposes solutions. He discusses, for example, the need of "our humanism . . . to try to deal with the problems of power, of a national army, of education, the arts, land and land ownership, poverty, medical care and so on" (36). He asserts the need to teach African literature, music, and history in the schools and to develop "traditional African humanism" for the benefit of blacks (30–36). Two decades later, Njabulo Ndebele notes a desperate need in modern education for South Africa to produce a "viable home-grown humanistic ethical tradition."

Mphahlele's political alienation from both white liberals and Afrikaners in South Africa takes on new levels of awareness and articulation in the revised edition as compared to the original edition. In the first edition of *The African Image,* as previously noted, the white liberal, for example, is criticized by Mphahlele for his gradualist approach and his insistence on "making use of statutory bodies" within the apartheid state to bring about change. But Mphahlele ultimately lets the white liberal off the hook by saying he is "at least sincere in his own screwy fashion" (1962, 67). In the revised *The African Image,* Mphahlele, by contrast, expresses deep frustration and despair over what he describes as "garden-party liberalism" and asks what those same liberals were doing when blacks "fought 'Bantu education,' removal of whole communities away from the fringes of city centers, all unjust laws, liberals were telling us that we should accept what we were given and work for reforms from within. That we should not break the law. We had seen this for the wretched idealism it was" (1974, 27). This anger, bitterness, and frustration, no doubt leavened by guilt since many white liberals were Mphahlele's friends and benefactors, found its most productive outlet in the writing of "Mrs Plum." Written a full decade earlier, "Mrs Plum" both anticipates and typifies Biko's call to Black Consciousness in the early 1970s and his statement that white liberals were the worst racists of all because "they refuse to credit [blacks] with intelligence to know what we want" (Biko 1979, 299).

Similarly, in the revised and subsequently banned edition of *The African Image* several passages were perhaps considered sufficiently incendiary to constitute a threat to the republic (although history has recorded no known cases of revolution brought on by literary criticism). Doubtless some of the text might well have qualified as being, at the very least, objectionable, particularly when seen through Afrikaner eyes. The Censorship Board, which banned the revised *The African Image* some nine years after its publication in England, was made up of nine members of which a quorum consisted of four, none of whom required to have literary training and all of whom presumably claimed strong ties to the Dutch Reformed Church (Gordimer 1988, 6). Such a board would not have taken kindly, for instance, to the sharp criticism leveled at Christianity by Mphahlele for keeping blacks powerless by teaching them to be submissive and to turn the other cheek. Mphahlele scoffs at the proposition that the poor and meek shall inherit the earth, dismissing it in a single deft line that says more than volumes of bombastic protest: "Though many are invited, few are chosen" (1974, 45). Furthermore, Mphahlele several times in the text extols an African ethos that involves prayer to ancestors as intercessors to the Supreme Force to which even progressive white liberals might take strong exception. The revised *The African Image,* in several key passages, positively vibrates with the fresh, assertive, bitter stridence that is one of the hallmarks of Black Consciousness thought and writing. One riveting and unexpected example is a passage which is essentially a dream sequence (again a literary device not standard in criticism). The passage begins with Mphahlele's dream that he has returned to South Africa. Arriving at the Johannesburg airport, he tells a "Boer" official he is surrendering because he wants to teach in South Africa. He promises not to make trouble and to stay out of politics. Then, he signs an agreement as the "Boers" wave goodbye smiling "like mannequins." The rest is interior dialogue in which Mphahlele says: "I'll poison the minds of our youth, I think. I promise you that you stinking

Boer bastards. You can take that agreement I've just signed and tear it up into pieces enough for you to stick a few pieces up each of your pink and purple asses. I fought your stinking educational politics in the fifties and I'll fight them again" (43). The foregoing passage reflects the Black Consciousness shift from "moral indignation to anger: from relatively self-composed reasonableness, to uncompromising bitterness" (Ndebele 1991, 64). Moreover, there is no alienating disjuncture here on the part of the author. External action or expression mirrors internal reality. The need for pretense to being, feeling, expressing something completely opposite from what is going on inside has been suspended. In this way self-alienation is overcome. Writing permits Mphahlele to express interiority at least in print, even though he was unable to do so when he confronted Afrikaners at the party in London. The dikes are breached in this assertive, bitter flood of vituperation and mockery. It is a Black Consciousness outpouring that any black audience could easily relate to and feel empowered by. Its message is clear. The humiliation, dishonesty, and powerlessness of being forced to live the lie the apartheid state tells itself violates one's sense of personal integrity; fragments one's sense of what is real and what is not and destroys hope itself. As Ndebele states, "that is the point at which protest literature turns into a pathology: when objective conditions no longer justify or support an entirely emotional or moral attitude" (64). Although the censors could not have been happy about such a passage, if they troubled to read it, they might at least have resonated to its fundamental earthiness and humor that serves in an African humanist sense both to highlight the burning pain and bitterness and to make it seem all that much more real.

Finally, Mphahlele in the revised edition of *The African Image* makes still one more pointed political statement surprising for a work of literary criticism. He throws down the gauntlet and engages in fighting talk, asserting that one day the tables will be turned and the white man will have to choose "to quit or adopt the majority African culture or be marooned by history, go the way of the Saan [*sic*], those poor victims of benign neglect" (Mphahlele 1974, 35). Mphahlele, again anticipating and echoing Black Consciousness, concludes that in a world where "might makes right" and people are treated as units of production, in short, "in a world in which power operates on assumptions that resist traditional humanism, we need to develop this humanism for Africa, for our own edification" (35).

Thus, the dialogue of two selves and between themes of alienation and African humanism "never ends. The pendulum swings between revulsion and attraction, between the dreams and the reality of a living past and the aspiration, the imperatives of modern living. Ambivalence" (41). In this case, the swinging of the pendulum is measured by Mphahlele's keen insights, humor, and his gift for the epigrammatic turn of phrase. It is measured by the intimacy of the dialogue between African humanist narrator and reader, and the bursts of poetic lyricism amidst prosaic analysis. It is also measured in the radically unorthodox nature of both content and structure of *The African Image.* The pendulum's swing is finally measured by events such as Sharpeville, movements such as Black Consciousness and the need to let go of the anger and frustration of the dispossessed in order to live. One way to restore balance, Mphahlele suggests, is to reaffirm and practice an African humanist ethos, with its greater spiritual, moral, and historic meaning and relevance than is found in Western materialism, especially in South Africa, where its profoundest expression took the form of pure capitalist exploitation, power politics, and greed. In an otherwise chaotic and alienating universe, African humanism can act, as Mphahlele demonstrates, as a unifying principle—be it in literature or in life.

In Mphahlele's retrieval of a national myth, rebellion becomes a force not "directed against . . . but aimed towards" (Brink 1983, 62). In an age that is aggressively anti-myth, myth ironically has the power to restore man to his "'place' in the world, neither as mere observer nor as victim, but as creative participant" (216). In a sense myth for Mphahlele becomes the "word," that, itself, is dialogic in nature, in turn possessing an unlimited capacity to generate discourse. Dialogically, *The African Image* is both provocative and a landmark work, just like Fanon's *Wretched of the Earth. The African Image* has continued to generate a diverse range of responses from an equally wide assortment of sources. Even its silencing by Boer censors represents a considered response to its discourse. In the pendulum's swing, the arc encompasses other literary critics whose stance comes nearly full circle along the continuum of Black Consciousness ideology. Their "ideologemes" or points of view on the "word," in turn, range across the spectrum from Louis Nkosi, who often sounds defiantly Eurocentric in his criticism, to the Black Consciousness of Mongane Wally Serote, who spent nine months in solitary confinement in a South African prison and who, exiled in London, served there as cultural attaché of the ANC. Serote, in his book *On the Horizon,* shifts from a position of Black Consciousness that relied heavily on anger, bitterness, and cynicism to one which sees no further need for those days when expletives "such as 'fuck off' and 'shit' became poetical terms" (and he is speaking from experience as one of South Africa's most gifted and politically outspoken black poets).

In 1990, it is time, says Serote, to move beyond such "screaming" poetry, just as Njabulo S. Ndebele asserts it is time—as suggested by the title of his critical work, *Rediscovery of the Ordinary*—to forswear as subjects the brutal ugliness of the Boer, the spectacular "hypocrisy of the English speaking liberal" and the melodrama of the South African political situation in general (1991, 40).

Although Serote's writings are saturated with political ideology, with signs that a disengagement is taking place, Ndebele wishes to see art reclaim some of its autonomy from politics. Mphahlele, Ndebele, and Serote are all critics and writers who have chosen to return to South Africa, while Nkosi, on the other hand, has chosen, as of this writing, to remain abroad. His critical approach is the antithesis of that of Mphahlele. Thus he writes:

> With the best will in the world it is impossible to detect in the fiction of black South Africans any significant and complex talent which responds with both the vigour of the imagination and sufficient technical resources, to the problems posed by conditions in South Africa.
>
> If black South African writers have read modern works of literature they seem to be totally unaware of its most compelling innovations; they blithely go on "telling stories" or crudely attempting to solve the same problems which have been solved before—or if not solved, problems to which European practitioners, from Dostoevsky to Burroughs, have responded with greater subtlety, technical originality and sustained vigour; and black South Africans write, of course, as though Dostoevsky, Kafka or Joyce had never lived. (1983, 31)

Nkosi, unlike Mphahlele, appears to be viewing African literature through exclusively Eurocentric eyes, when, "he ought to be afrocentric." Such critics "if at all they are aware that African culture is under foreign domination . . . seem to think that it ought to remain so" (Chinweizu et al. 1983, 3).

Ironically, Nkosi takes Mphahlele to task for "being the spearhead of a whole attack on negritude" and for treating negritude "as another version of the racist ideology of the Afrikaners" (1981, 14). In fairness to Nkosi, perhaps, when he wrote those words in 1981, he had not yet had a chance to read Mphahlele's revised *The African Image,* despite the fact it had been published abroad in England a full decade earlier. Even a superficial reading of the revised *The African Image* makes abundantly clear that Mphahlele had already seriously reconsidered his own position on the question of negritude. But, perhaps, Nkosi cannot be faulted for his oversight. After all, it took the censors themselves several years to discover the literary work's subversive content and to place it safely under wraps in the extensive and well-stocked banned section located in the basement of at least one major university library in South Africa, which is where the author of this study eventually, with special permission, uncovered it.

As can clearly be seen in any comparative study of the original and revised versions of Mphahlele's unprecedented critical work, his inner and outer discourse is ongoing, "multifaceted and multidirected. It reflects both forward and backward in time and space." The "word" or in this case "words," African humanism, live "at the intersection of all past and present intentions with which" they are "permeated" (Danow 1991, 40). With Mphahlele's publication of *The African Image*, the first major critical overview of South African literature and a provocative and timely Black Consciousness manifesto, the discourse had been officially launched.

Chapter Five

Down Second Avenue

THE AUTOBIOGRAPHY OF
AN AFRICAN HUMANIST

The traveler has to knock at every alien door to come to his own.
—Tagore

*Down Second Avenue is a masterpiece . . . written
out of an authenticity of (human) experience.*
—Gerald Chapman

*One of the least self-indulgent autobiographies one can find. Considering
the facts of the life reported, that achievement is indeed genius.*
—Robert Pawlowski

Mphahlele once wrote that autobiography in South Africa "has emerged naturally from South African conditions, and in fact, we are seeing it emerge all over Africa as a literature of self-definition. It has become a peculiar genre in Africa, a genre that depicts the very social conditions that have given rise to it" (Lindfors 1976, 28). N. W. Visser describes autobiographical writing in South Africa, a trend started by Peter Abrahams with his publication *Tell Freedom* (1974), as being "South Africa's most singular contribution to black literature" (136). Not only did Mphahlele help pioneer the black South African township autobiography, with its novelistic textures and elements of social and community history based in an urban setting—but, as Visser and other critics have suggested, *Down Second Avenue,* "is the most widely known autobiography by a black South African writer" and is quite possibly Mphahlele's most successful work to date (127). *Down Second Avenue* was followed in 1963 by Bloke Modisane's *Blame Me on History,* the third in an historic triptych of some of the best-known works in the canon.

Both the short story and autobiography were literary forms particularly well suited to the "special circumstances" of black South Africans writing in the 1950s, for whom leisure, comfort, privacy, economic security, and even safety (in short, all those conditions that lend themselves to the production of a lengthy work of fiction) were at a premium. But the genre is also a natural choice for a professed humanist and dedicated educator. The underlying assumption of humanism is that man is at the center of being. Thus, the very act of writing an autobiography is a humanistic one, placing the author squarely at the center of his own "self-discovery and self-creation," shouting "I am" (Eakin 1985, 3). In addition, according to Ashcroft, Griffiths, and Tiffin, there is a need in postcolonial society to affirm "a valid and active sense of self [that] may have been eroded by dislocation" or "destroyed by cultural denigration" (1989, 9). What renders this process uniquely African is that the "I" is inevitably deeply rooted in the community. On the anvil of pain, necessity, and tradition were forged two of South Africa's best, most original gifts to English literature in Africa.

The flowering of autobiographical writing in South Africa among black writers in the early 1950s occurred at a time when the National party government had begun to practice "applied apartheid in a plethora of laws and executive actions" (Thompson 1990, 190). All three autobiographies just cited describe the authors' "special circumstances," detailing lives of poverty and privation, hurt and abuse suffered while growing up in the black ghettos and locations during the heyday of apartheid, and culminating in flight into exile in search of political freedom and a new life. All three deal with certain recurring motifs and themes of alienation, such as a rejection of the Christianity that was used by authoritarian whites, who have set themselves up as demigods, to rationalize their power in terms of a Calvinist covenant with God (Olney 1973, 272). All three also document and describe the community in such a way as to constitute an act of cultural and literary biography.

James Olney notes that while black writers were "oppressed by politics" they have written "not political manifestoes but literary autobiographies" (42). The fact that *Down Second Avenue* is, indeed, a literary and cultural autobiography concerned with people and community, and not a political manifesto, further defines it as humanistic. Its method and purpose is to educate, rather than propagandize, through a social and political message embodied in art. *Down Second Avenue* is both the autobiography of Mphahlele, as "panel-beaten by the community" and that of the urban black slum of

Marabastad, where Mphahlele spent his youth (Thuynsma 1990). It represents the definitive statement of an avowed African humanist insofar as it is
reflective of such things as strongly held community values, caring, compassion, and reverence for (as opposed to worship of) ancestors as a source
of strength and moral guidance—those same values that were absorbed
early on in Mphahlele's boyhood when he was herding goats in the countryside near Maupaneng and imbibing the wisdom of African sages and
storytellers around the communal fire.

   Yet *Down Second Avenue,* like the works of Abrahams and Modisane,
also comprises an individual narrative that, in the more traditional autobiographic mode, is "essentially an exploration of consciousness" (Watts 1989,
109). This individuated self never lapses into sheer vanity or egoism because
it is balanced against the narrator as witness (124). The narrator interprets
life in the black slums and townships for, among others, the uninformed
Western reader, but equally importantly fulfills a need on behalf of blacks
"to respect and preserve, at least in record, a fast-disappearing past of
unique glory" (Olney 1973, 330). Such a reverential attitude toward the
communal African past, toward community history is a key element in
Mphahlele's humanism. The fusion between the "I-am-us" and the more
individuated narrator echoes and parallels the dialogue between two selves
in which a Western consciousness joins with an African sensibility to produce the structural synthesis of a fresh, innovative genre, "the township autobiography" (Chapman 1992, 228).

   In autobiographic writing the overlap between history and literature
has subsequently resulted in an understanding of truth defined best by the
statement that "every fact has its fiction." As James Olney states in *Studies in
Autobiography,* before the 1950s, autobiography as a literary form was regarded as a mutant of biography, itself the poor "stepchild of history and literature" (1988, xiii). Although the novel is usually considered to be closer to
art than autobiography, there are works, such as *Down Second Avenue,* which
in their unique blend of art, history, and social document "must be called
works of art while being, nevertheless, autobiographies" (Olney 1973, 20).

   As both historic record and act of imagination, autobiography arises
out of a concept of the evolving self and of self-discovery based on received
models of selfhood from the surrounding culture. When that received
model involves the African humanist communal voice, then certain events
or people, while true-to-life, may also serve as dramatic representations of
the group experience (Watts 1989, 125). Thus, one finds in *Down Second
Avenue* an individual like Ma-Lebona whose character looms novelistically
larger than life, who engages in extended dialogue and who is involved in

dramatic events, much like in a novel. Ma-Lebona is also a believable and authentic spokesman of communal values, giving voice to ancestral beliefs, the need to preserve rituals and customs such as weddings and funerals, the offering of assistance to a neighbor, and showing respect for elders.

White readers encountering Ma-Lebona for the first time might label her correctly as a gossip, busybody, and mischief-maker or incorrectly as a practitioner of witchcraft in her meddling, idiosyncratic ways, rather than understanding her role in a more nuanced sense. Such generic labeling is inevitable when racial divisions exist and leads inevitably to the stereotypes of a divided imagination, characterized by political, social, intellectual, and artistic alienation. The tendency to think in sweeping generalities and deal in generic labels feeds into Manichean dominated allegories of "white and black, good and evil, salvation and damnation, civilization and savagery, superiority and inferiority, intelligence and emotion, self and other, subject and object" (JanMohamed 1988, 4). Thus, Mphahlele could be labeled a communist simply because he resisted the implementation of the Bantu Education Act.

Historic realities have served further to solidify and strengthen the barricades of the divided imagination. Corroborating this view, Tim Couzens quotes De Kiewiet as stating that "at least two generations of settlers grew up in ignorance of the ingenuity and appropriateness with which the natives in their tribal state met the many problems of their lives, in ignorance of the validity of many of the social and moral rules which held them together" (Parker 1978, 67). Furthermore, what little whites did see of blacks and what most often caught their attention was largely the negative side— such as ignorance, superstition, and witchcraft (67). This statement is equally valid for the 1950s, in the heyday of apartheid, when the Pass Laws and Group Areas Act meant that whites saw Africans only as domestics in their own homes and a majority of whites rarely, if ever, set foot inside an African township. Even as recently as 1994, it was still possible for a white Afrikaner living in Verwoerdburg to say of her black domestic, "I have had a maid for nineteen-and-a-half years, and I think of her as family; but I still don't know what goes on inside her head" (Taylor 1994, A1).

This form of alienation, the division of races leading to the divided imagination, also affects Mphahlele's knowledge of and ability to depict white characters because as he says, he "first came to know the white man at the point of a boot and then at the point of an index finger—as a servant to him. I know there is much more to him than his fear of me, and I want to explore this other side. But then he won't let me!" (1962, 29). Very few white characters of lasting import appear in *Down Second Avenue* and those who do, such as Ma Bottles, Mrs. Reynecke, and Mr. Goldstein, do not leave a favorable impression. At the same time, much of what is of value and adds cohesion to traditional black society including an ancient and indigenous humanism is being eroded away by state apartheid, poverty, industrialization, and a proliferating culture of violence. By documenting life in the township and its foundation of community values, Mphahlele has served to bridge the alienating gulf of ignorance. He has added to the understanding of enlightened but uninformed white and black readers whose interests transcend mere matters of skin pigmentation. These include, over the past several decades, readers in German, Hungarian, Czech, Serbo-Croatian, Bulgarian, French, Swedish, Japanese, and several African tongues (Barnett 1983, 220). Clearly this unique South African account of the "author's special circumstances," with its recurring motifs of alienation and African humanism has captured the imagination of listeners well beyond the African communal fire. Both endeavors on the part of the author—to preserve community history for black youth who are in danger of losing touch with their cultural heritage and to enlarge the understanding of readers everywhere—with their implicit reverence for the past and desire to teach, are humanistic undertakings.

Not only in intent, but also in style and structure, *Down Second Avenue* is a quintessential expression of African humanism, utilizing as it does colloquial banter, African myths, tales, and proverbs, and distancing itself from the Victorian prose and conventional romantic plots that characterized Mphahlele's earliest published work, *Man Must Live.* Structurally, *Down Second Avenue* has a circular jazz-like contrapuntal form, relying heavily on five fugue-like interludes written in the present tense that recapitulate poetically and philosophically the main body of the text which is set in the past. This structure replicates the African view of life as a cycle in which events and ancestors are reincarnate in the present that is "a ritual repetition" of the past and "a precise rehearsal of the future" (Olney 1973, 28). The five innovative chronological breaks in the narrative, at once lyrical and reflective, examine meaning while advancing the narrative. These stream-of-consciousness and poetic ligaments serve to connect episodic chapters that like folk tales could very nearly stand alone as individual, well-crafted, semi-autonomous units. The break in style and structure from Western models represents an affirmation of Mphahlele's African voice in which "African literature has its own traditions, models and norms" against the alienating forces of apartheid and Eurocentric cultural imperialism (Chinweizu et al. 1983, 4).

Down Second Avenue helped establish certain literary conventions that later came to be regarded as hallmarks of the township autobiography such as description of the local bioscope, of police raids on illegal home distilleries, and of communal life around the local water tap. There is also frequent and effective use of extended dialogue, character description, rendered thought, flashbacks, foreshadowing, use of story line with motifs and thematic juxtaposition, and strong characterization in a manner reminiscent of the novel. Barnett states that *Down Second Avenue* was, in fact, originally conceived as a novel (1976, 51). Nevertheless, this does not detract from its credibility as social document. With scenes and events reported in realistic and accurate detail and "characters" presented in the round (there are good whites and bad blacks) the authenticity of the narrative itself is never in doubt, despite the book's novelistic textures and larger-than-life characters.

Down Second Avenue, as the autobiography of the community of Marabastad, a slum that grew out of the rural to urban migration caused by the 1913 Land Act, introduces a colorful cast of memorable characters, each of whom manifests aspects of African humanism and most of whom are strong women. These women, including Mphahlele's mother Eva, aunt Dora, maternal grandmother Hibila, and a host of others, work tirelessly to hold the fabric of the community together. South African historian Leonard Thompson has written that "there is a story to be told by social historians of the ways in which black people not only survived under apartheid but also created their own social and economic worlds" (1990, 201). *Down Second Avenue* is that story—although the work may not be as widely recognized as it deserves to be, primarily because it was banned in South Africa between the year of its publication in 1959 and the time of Mphahlele's return in 1977, some two decades later. Of the many women who create "their own social and economic worlds," Mphahlele's mother was an outstanding example. Working her way to an early grave while still in her mid forties, she was the sole support and provider for her family on a meager income earned as a dressmaker, domestic, and producer of "illegal" home brew: "Mother did dressmaking for an African tailor just outside town. In the evenings she brewed beer out of corn malt to sell. The family's budget was all on her shoulders. She was hard-working and tough. She never complained about hard work" (1959, 24). Tough resourcefulness, along with a viable community support network based on a deep humanistic concern for one another, was one of the secrets to the survival of the oppressed majority under state apartheid. There was compassion, caring, and love amidst struggle—of which Eva's back-breaking toil stands out as but one of the many silent, yet eloquent statements of a heroic nature.

Because Eva must work in the city and be away much of the time, Aunt Dora and grandmother, Mphahlele's uncles and teachers, Mathebula (the

Shangana witch doctor), and even Ma-Lebona, who takes the children from time to time, provide the daily support and guidance Mphahlele and his siblings need growing up, operating on the principle "that it takes an entire village to raise a child." In *Down Second Avenue* the author bears witness to the importance of the formidable African network as well as the centuries-old development of "social forms and cultural traditions that colonialism, capitalism, and apartheid have assaulted, abused, and modified but never eradicated. One cannot understand how Africans have endured the fragmentation of their family life by migrant labour unless one has knowledge of their customary social values and networks" (Thompson 1990, 2). What is of interest is not only that such social forms and cultural traditions exist—all of which are manifestations of the philosophy of African humanism—but how well they worked in the face of that constant assault, especially when on top of it there is a dehumanizing and punishing overlay of poverty of unprecedented magnitude. This poverty is fully documented in vivid, realistic detail in *Down Second Avenue,* which serves as a running indictment of such facts as those outlined in the Second Carnegie Inquiry into Poverty and Development in South Africa. The inquiry conducted in the early 1980s (when conditions presumably should have improved over the 1950s when Mphahlele was writing) mentions, for example, that two-thirds of Africans were living below the Minimum Living Level, with conditions even worse where large numbers had been relocated, particularly in the homelands. In 1978, in Soweto up to twenty people were found occupying the crowded rows of small, individual four-room box houses under conditions similar to ones Mphahlele describes in his own childhood home on Second Avenue (202).

One can best appreciate Mphahlele's autobiography as social document and work of art by examining the socioeconomic and historic context that provided its genesis. Before proceeding further it is essential briefly to review certain historical details, major pieces of repressive legislation, acts of government and news-making events that have changed and disrupted countless black lives from the early part of the century to the present and that figure in all of Mphahlele's prose works, both of fiction and nonfiction. *Down Second Avenue* as the biography of a community gains in poignancy and meaning, for example, when it is read in the light of the slum clearances and one realizes that Marabastad had long since been obliterated even as Mphahlele was bringing it to life again in his autobiography.

Mphahlele's autobiography was published ten years after the Nationalist party came to power in 1949, putting an end to any hopes of extinguishing racial discrimination. Apartheid policies implemented by the Nationalist party in effect codified and enforced the racism and segregation that already existed. The Natives Resettlement Act (1954), an offshoot of the Urban Areas Act (1923), led to the rezoning and bulldozing of townships in the Western Areas such as Sophiatown where blacks had once owned their own land (194). The Suppression of Communism Act (1950), with its sweeping definition of 'statutory communism,' "spearheaded the state's sustained attack on civil liberties" (Chapman 1989, 185). Under this act, Mphahlele was banned as a teacher for his opposition to the Bantu Education Act. With the subsequent passage in 1965 of the Suppression of Communism Amendment Act, Mphahlele and fellow *Drum* writers Bloke Modisane, Can Themba, Todd Matshikiza, and Lewis Nksoi were "silenced as 'statutory communists,'" and their writings and speeches prohibited (185). The superstructure of apartheid was further secured with the enactment of such legislation as the Population Registration Act (1950), the Prohibition of Mixed Marriages (1949), the Immorality Act (1950), and the Separate Amenities Act (1953). Because there would have been a time lag between passage and full implementation of these draconian acts and because Mphahlele left South Africa in 1957, after which he completed his autobiography, it was arguably the era of segregation as much as that of apartheid that affected his writings up to and including *Down Second Avenue.* Moreover, as much as three-quarters of Mphahlele's autobiography is concerned with his childhood, youth, and young adulthood. Since at the time of the book's writing, Marabastad had already been bulldozed under, one must look back further in history to the "segregation era" in order to place the evolution of this location and community in its proper historic context.

Mphahlele was born into an era in which segregation (a precursor of apartheid) was the rule of the day—and as much a product of British officialdom as of Boer generals. According to historian T. R. H. Davenport, in the Botha-Smuts period from 1910 through 1924, both the South African and the Unionist parties were in total agreement on their fundamental views regarding "native policy." "Both disapproved of racial miscegenation; both regarded the idea of a black political majority as unthinkable . . . both desired to see the restriction of African land ownership to the Reserves, and both wished to see African urban immigrants segregated in locations." The overriding motive in the controls exercised over the level of wages, the freedom of labor to organize and bargain, and the ownership of land by blacks was, on the part of both politicians and the white electorate that supported them, to preserve and "to safeguard their supplies of black labour" (1989, 258).

The amalgam of racism and economic exploitation that helped determine government policy was blatantly and crudely spelled out by Sir Godfrey Yeatman Langden, who headed the South African Native Affairs

Commission. Arguing in favor of the policy of establishing separate reserves for blacks in which there was an artificially created shortage of land "in order to force more and more rural Africans into the service of white industry and agriculture," Langden said: "A man cannot go with his wife and children and his goods . . . on to the labour market. He must have a dumping ground. Every rabbit must have a warren where he can live and burrow and breed, and every native must have a warren too" (Oakes 1988, 313). Several laws passed during this period were of such far-reaching effect that in the judgment of Davenport the "'Botha-Smuts period' was the most formative until the era of Verwoerd." As previously noted, the Natives Land Act of 1913, which preceded Mphahlele's birth by six years, effectively ended African land ownership and share-cropping with whites and enforced the segregation of Africans onto reserves where they could be recruited for labor in the mines (Davenport 1989, 259). Another important piece of legislation was the more benign sounding "Natives (Urban Areas) Act"—an act that was much amended through the early 1970s. The act was "a portmanteau law covering a great variety of issues. One of its objectives "was to clear Africans out of the mixed residential areas that had grown up in some of the larger towns, notably Johannesburg, and re-house them in locations" (548). Initially, its intent was to "promote public health" through the control of endemic diseases such as tuberculosis, but "alongside the clearance of slums, there developed a campaign to keep urban areas in white hands" and to eliminate what later came to be known as "black spots" (260).

Such acts were the beginning of the psychological oppression of blacks that Fanon had noted, stating that "for a colonized people the most essential value, because the most concrete, is first and foremost the land: the land which will bring them bread, and above all dignity" (1963, 44). In the case of urbanized blacks living in South African slums, locations, and townships, the urban community arguably had supplanted land as "the most essential value" and to obliterate it was to destroy its history and its soul.

The forms of political, psychological, and spiritual alienation blacks had begun to experience included the taking of the land, obliteration of the community, and government control of black movement in order to implement the Urban Areas Acts. Influx control resulted in a series of Pass Laws whereby blacks were restricted to the impoverished "'homelands' (in which 80% of the population occupied 13% of the land) unless black labour was required in the cities" (Thompson 1990, 93). Between 1937 and 1976, the Pass Laws had been tightened and refined to such a degree that blacks were not allowed to visit "urban areas for more than 72 hours without a special permit." This in effect made aliens and criminals out of thousands of otherwise law-abiding blacks who were arrested for not having a pass (known as the "dampas" or "damn pass"), thus rendering them stateless, illegal visitors in their own country (193).

In his "Lesane" stories, Mphahlele had already begun to address the theme of blacks as stateless aliens and the related issue of the much-hated passes, specifically in the case of the character Fanyan, whose entire course of action was dictated by the fact he was living in an urban area without a pass. As a jobless black male, his sole reason for being in the city was perforce to work as a laborer. According to the law, without either a pass or a job he had no right to be in a "country" not his own, regardless of whether his family lived there or not. Similarly, Mphahlele's work of juvenile fiction *Father Come Home* deals directly with the conditions that were set in motion by the Natives Land Act. His first novel, *The Wanderers,* concerns the fact that an abundance of cheap labor in reserves and of unemployed jobseekers in the cities put blacks in a position of great vulnerability. Such jobseekers then became prime targets for exploitation by unscrupulous straw bosses and white farmers. Issues such as slum clearance, which disrupted families and obliterated entire communities and their histories, as well as the illegal brewing of traditional beer by women to supplement incomes in households where men were often unemployed or absent are also dramatically portrayed in vivid tableaux and poignant vignettes *in Down Second Avenue.*

The alienation between self and place described by Mphahlele in all his works can be traced back to the original loss of ancestral land, with the slum of Marabastad growing out of rural to urban migration caused by the 1913 Land Act and subsequent legislation. The aforementioned Natives (Urban Areas) Act—which reached the statute books when Mphahlele was still a goatherd in Maupaneng—not only restricted land purchase by blacks and allowed for racial segregation of urban communities, it also failed to provide for middle-class blacks and it "placed the whole cost of black housing on black communities through rents and fines" ("Autobiographies" 1989, 63). The massive rural-to-urban black diaspora brought about by demands for labor in mining and manufacturing industries parallels Mphahlele's childhood move from rural Maupaneng to urban Marabastad in the fall of 1924. Three decades later, in 1957, Mphahlele moved out of South Africa altogether as a result of his political banning and the "progressive alienation that, forced to the extreme, became spiritual and physical exile" (Olney 1973, 20). In commenting in one of the final "interludes" of *Down Second Avenue* on the obliteration of Marabastad, wiped out like so many other "black spots," Mphahlele says: "Marabastad is gone but there will always be

Marabastads that will be going until the screw of the vice breaks. Too late maybe, but never too soon. And the Black man keeps moving on, as he has always done the last three centuries, moving with baggage and all, for ever tramping with bent backs to give way for the one who says he is stronger" (1959, 157). The razing of Marabastad becomes a powerful symbol for the author's and the community's spiritual death as well as for the history of black Africa in the colonial and postcolonial eras in which dislocation and exploitation (in the name of land and labor) are primary themes. The picture of the stateless alien, the political exile, the disenfranchised, and dispossessed—of the black man who is beaten down, but not defeated—is sketched out in a few lines. The prose is at once muscular and lyrical. The narrative with its unique format of chapters clustered around events or characters like folk tales, interspersed with philosophic and poetic interludes, gathers momentum with its inevitable movement down Second Avenue—a street itself serving as metaphor for life as it is lived by impoverished blacks in rural slums and townships throughout the country.

What adds to the irony and poignancy of this inexorable denouement is that, based on substantial internal evidence, it is clear Mphahlele was just beginning to find his African voice, in the process of decolonizing the already detribalized, Westernized African (as the author has frequently described himself). Like a python shedding its old skin of colonialism, the author emerges in a new, shiny African humanist skin that is self-confident, marked with artistry, and a far better fit. Thus, Mphahlele presents conclusive supporting evidence for J. M. Coetzee's case on behalf of the necessity of an African idiom to describe the "real Africa." Mission press and Victorian English with its European metaphors, imagery, and vocabulary is frequently inadequate and inappropriate in its efforts to capture an African landscape. It is rather like trying to use a palette and techniques better suited to the romantic pastoral landscape school of English art (Coetzee 1988, 163–77). Nothing could be more alienating thus than the artist standing outside himself to describe a scene that seems unconnected to any sense of immediate reality in place, time, and idiom.

Down Second Avenue, which was begun in South Africa, with the last two chapters completed in Nigeria, illustrates how well Mphahlele was beginning to put into practice the literary dictum Coetzee articulated some years later. By comparing the opening descriptive paragraph from his autobiography with a similar passage from one of Mphahlele's early short stories from *Man Must Live,* it is possible to see the dramatic transformation the author underwent, as it were, from the English painter of the romantic school to an effective and original African writer describing a real African scene, drawing on a lively palette of colors better suited to the terrain. The veracity of the latter description can never be in doubt. As opposed to gentle, lyric, and ideal, the landscape at times is harsh, threatening, and impoverished, set against the ominous backdrop of apartheid and of a grim fate symbolized by Grandma and by the mountain, on which "the village clung like a leech," that is a dark and brooding presence but never totally despairing and that has the ring about it of unvarnished truth.

The first passage is taken from the story "The Leaves Were Falling" and describes a rural town, in all its "rustic simplicity" to which the central character, Rev. Katsane Melato, a city-bred and educated man, is sent to work:

> The cows were lowing for their calves; the goats were bleating for their young. The Reverend Katsane Melato felt he was on the very edge of the world. Further than this, he felt there could be no other peace, no other joy. These streams, these trees, these valleys, those interlocking spurs seemingly stretching away and further away from him. Yet how calm and firm they were in their never-ending beauty! Eternity, in all its mystery, he thought, had painted a portrait of breath-taking marvel here, on a canvas of golden sunset. (1946, 14)

The foregoing lines might have been composed a few miles above Tintern Abbey and have a Wordsworthian, romantic aura to them, reflecting, no doubt, Mphahlele's earlier training in the English classics. It should be noted here that it is not entirely fair to these early stories to isolate such descriptive passages without giving due credit to the stories' stronger points, which include a promising facility to depict character—a reflection, perhaps, of Mphahlele's perennial interest in the human element. Later on in his autobiography, Mphahlele uses the rural image of "the muted lowing of a cow" humorously to describe his snoring uncle (1959, 44). Nevertheless, the opening lines of *Down Second Avenue*, which are strikingly different in tone, with the description so closely identified with place, reveal how successfully the author has overcome the colonial alienation of an exclusively Eurocentric focus:

> My grandmother sat there under a small lemon tree next to the hut, as big as fate, as forbidding as a mountain, stern as a mimosa tree. She was not the smiling type. When she tried, she succeeded in leering muddily. But then she was not the crying type either: she gave her orders sharp and clear. Like the sound she made when she pounded on

the millstone with a lump of iron to make it rough enough for grind-
ing on. (1959, 11)

This passage could have been taken as easily from a work of fiction as nonfiction. What it illustrates is that Mphahlele has effectively used an African
idiom to capture the flavor of a precolonial African past that is neither romantic nor exoticized in the manner of a Rider Haggard, but, instead, is real
and alive. Grandmother is a grim presence, "big as fate," incapable of a smile
that is more than a muddy leer. Far from being a source of comfort, grandmother symbolizes a menacing fate defined by chaos and meaninglessness,
bitter as the lemon tree beneath which she sits. The theme of alienation, of
fear and displacement, is further suggested by the ominous hills and by
"mountain darkness, so solid and dense" (11). Nature is, indeed, not gently
pastoral and worthy of romantic contemplation, but unpredictable and
threatening like the nearby Leshoana River in spate that carries away the
heathen girl with whom the Christian boy Thema is in love (17) in a tragic
tale that has the ring of a folk story or ballad to it. Hence, the cruel harshness and unpredictability of nature accentuates the need one has of people,
of reliance on others, and of community support. With fate as a stated and
apartheid an implicit backdrop, people are foregrounded even in natural
settings. In keeping with Mphahlele's African humanism, any given scene
"always has a human content" (Watts 1989, 44).

In terms of content, idiom, and identification with place, Mphahlele
has clearly found his own voice, and a highly original and gifted voice at
that. In the dialogue of two selves between the West and Africa, the author
has managed successfully to face down the problem of colonial alienation.
It is ironic that he managed this feat at precisely that juncture when a new
form of alienation awaited him—that of political exile. One wonders what
course Mphahlele's writings might have taken had it been possible to remain in South Africa under circumstances other than those obtaining at the
time. As it was, however, his choices were, simply put, between "a rock and
a hard place," between external or internal exile.

The closing scene of Chapter One and the opening of Chapter Two in
Down Second Avenue is set at the village fireplace with such sages and storytellers as Old Modise and Old Segone (14–16). The fireplace is an evocative
symbol of African humanism and helps establish the warmth of the narrative. Just as the choice of autobiography as a medium of self-expression is
consistent with the stance of a self-professed African humanist, the authorial stance and tone is in keeping with the same aesthetic and philosophic

world view. The "I" is not only deeply rooted in community, but there is no sense of the more highly educated and, hence, superior outside observer of that community looking in. Instead, there is warmth, compassion, identification—the presence of a man, at once sensitive and brave; of uncompromising principle, but invariably down-to-earth and approachable—even though the narrator is himself an educated member of the small, elite, black intelligentsia. (In 1935, only 193 Africans were registered in standards nine and ten of missionary-run schools countrywide [Thompson 1990, 172].) This close identification with community as well as with the African oral traditions of storytelling are arguably themselves structural expressions of a deep-seated African humanism.

At the fireside, as Mphahlele describes it, the reader can also observe the African humanist philosophy as it is lived. There is a historic sense of ancestors as a source of strength and moral guidance. While listening to the African sage one imbibes his collective wisdom through proverbs, tales, and the recounting of tribal history and myths. Gossip is exchanged and manners and morals are imparted in such a way as to confirm James Olney's statement that "In African autobiography . . . the ancestral-descendant motive is something infinitely deeper than curiosity [and] . . . the present repeats the past and rehearses the future" (1973, 27–32). References to "The Tribe," as one manifestation of the ancestral-descendant motive, are elaborated on in both Chapters One and Five, where we learn of Mphahlele's Mopedi origins as well as the extended family and community of some five thousand inhabiting Maupaneng village. These are among the "social relationships [that] constitute a formidable network in Africa" (Mphahlele 1986, 9). Furthermore, there are strong women and cultural carriers such as Mphahlele's mother, Eva, and his maternal grandmother, Hibila, who always checks on Es'kia's friends and sends them off if she does not approve. His aunt, Dora, in an amusing and lively encounter, takes on "Big Eyes," Mphahlele's school principal, when the young "Eski" is not allowed to participate in a concert for the Prince of Wales because he missed choir practice as a result of having had to pick up white people's laundry for his aunt. Above all, this network of kith and kin is not only a leading precept of African humanism as it is actually lived, but it represents stability and a defensive bulwark against the alienating forces of apartheid and the poverty that accompanies it.

If the warmth and kinship experienced at the village fire is a metaphor for African humanism, the "brutal" Leshoana River "carrying on its broad back trees, cattle, boulders; world of torrential rains" symbolizes the divisive and alienating impact on indigenous culture of a harsh and aggressive colonial culture as well as the larger conflict all colonized peoples may experience between traditional ways and Western modes of thought (1959, 18). The resulting conflict between Christian and "heathen" communities is seen at work in the stark vignette of Christian boys beating up "heathen" boys in the school. Gerald Moore put it most eloquently when he observed of this passage: "As if their poverty and ignorance were not enough, Mphahlele's companions were so bigoted by mission teaching that they would not step in a pagan footprint, let alone live within reach of the 'heathens'—their own brothers of a saner day" (1962, 94). Such Christian-inspired alienation, conflict, and cruelty stand in dramatic contrast to the serene and peaceable gathering at the communal fire where standards of conduct are imparted through the African oral tradition of talk and storytelling. As a spokesman himself for African humanism, Old Modise consistently advocates tolerance and compassion in human conduct, for "We all have our secret little gods, Christians or none" (1959, 14).

Furthermore, the communal fireplace illustrates the cooperative nature of African humanism. Here men and boys gather. Even the man whose wife is sick is given food, while the women tend to the sick wife. The boys, however, if they wish to sit at the fire must bring back wood from the veld when they return with their goats. Shirkers are not tolerated. Those who are "too lazy to carry wood" are told to return home: "We learned a great deal at the fire-place, even before we were aware of it: history, tradition and custom, code of behavior, communal responsibility, social living and so on. 'When the Swazis clashed with Bapedi. . . .' 'As things were when we lived under Boer rule'" (15). Old Modise, in turn, suggests the African habit of mind that connects all living things as a part of a unifying vital force (Mphahlele 1986, 13). For example, he commences his storytelling with a reference to spring as a time when "You know you are part of that which dies and yet doesn't die" and thus he continues dispensing wisdom around the fire to the next generation (1959, 16).

In dramatic contrast to the community spirit felt around the village fire, the contrasting chill of the Leshoana further serves to dramatize and make palpable the alienating racial conflict between the Christian whites and their black brothers and sisters. In a brief monologue of less than a paragraph, there is a searing indictment of apartheid with its codified racial discrimination as well as cold-blooded economic exploitation and Christian hypocrisy when Thema says that it cannot be true that "Christ died for us all, and he was our brother" for in the cities men are not brothers.

> The black man must enter the white man's house through the back door. The black man does most of the dirty work. When a white man who hasn't gone far in school is given such work he says *I'm not a kaffir!* Black man cleans the streets but mustn't walk freely on the pavement; Black man must build houses for the white man but cannot live in them; Black man cooks the white man's food but eats what is left over. Don't listen to anyone bluff you and say Black and white are brothers. (16–17)

This brief, damning indictment of apartheid and the Christian Nationalist state is lightened by the quick humorous rejoinder, "You read too much . . . and believe too little." At this juncture, we catch a brief glimpse into the self-alienation experienced by the author, himself. Although the rejoinder is addressed to Thema, it equally could apply to Mphahlele, as does the following description which foreshadows the progressive alienation we see the author undergo as the autobiography unfolds: "We were afraid for Thema's mind. Something seemed to have happened to him in the city. Something terrible and dark" (17). A poignant part of Mphahlele's early personal history of self-alienation is that of a sensitive young man who grew up virtually without a childhood. His was not the idyllic childhood made up of loving parents, sibling rivalries, innocent schoolboy pranks and lazy summer days spent on fishing expeditions that many of his white peers would have experienced. Mphahlele instead looks back over the first thirteen years of his life and sees them as wasted years with "nobody to shape them into a definite pattern" (8). Herein lies another theme of alienation—with the autobiographer writing in the present moment from the perspective of someone who has been shaped into something quite different from his childhood self by the forces of history as well as by a Western education and who perceives in this earlier self no one with whom he has any immediate sense of identification.

One of the most dramatic episodes in *Down Second Avenue* occurs when Mphahlele's alcoholic father, Moses, in a drunken rage, throws a heavy pot of boiling curry at Mphahlele's mother, Eva. The event is recounted in a perfectly crafted episode that utilizes place setting, dialogue, a flashback, and mounting tension. It also appeals strongly to the senses in the use of sensual, realistic detail. Thus Moses shouts, "I'll show you who I am!" and then the highly charged action scene unfolds:

> "What is it with you, Moses? What are you standing up to do?"
> "Get up!"

"I can't—I can't—my knee!"

"This is the day you're going to do what I tell you!"

He limped over to the pot on the stove. In no time it was done. My mother screamed with a voice I have never forgotten till this day. Hot gravy and meat and potatoes had got into her blouse and she was trying to shake them down. . . . Only then did I have the wits to go and ask for help. I came back with Aunt Dora. An ambulance had already been and carried my mother to hospital. . . . That was the last time I ever saw my father, that summer of 1932. The strong smell of burning paraffin gas from a stove often reminds me of that Sunday. (28)

Thematically, the scene not only underscores Mphahlele's early sense of self-alienation but painfully compounds it with his experience of "father-lessness." To add to the feeling of powerlessness and impending doom, both father and son are hopelessly entrapped by broader socioeconomic forces beyond their control. Like so many others their lives have been affected, directly or indirectly, by such draconian laws as the aforementioned 1913 Natives Land Act, the notorious Pass Laws, and the much-amended Natives (Urban Areas) Act as well as subsequent legislation such as the Bantu Education Act (1953), which limited work and educational opportunities, controlled the movement of blacks, determined in which "warrens" they could live and which placed strict controls on land ownership and sharecropping by blacks and increased the size of reserves in order to guarantee farmers, industry, and the gold mines of Johannesburg a plentiful source of cheap labor (Davenport 1987, 259).

With jobs scarce and wages low, with exploitation rampant and large numbers of blacks migrating into cities, a breakdown in social norms and family structure was all too predictable. This is seen at work in Mphahlele's own family. Eva, the author's mother—hard-working, tough, uncomplaining, and someone who would "fight like a tigress to defend her cubs"—became the family bread winner (1959, 26). Mphahlele's father, Moses, on the other hand, drinks away his income and is prone to fits of violent anger. Hence we have the beginning of the father-son alienation that reaches a climax when Mphahlele's father picks up the heavy pot of curry boiling on the paraffin burner and assaults Eva with it. The hatred and fear aroused by Mphahlele's father, together with the related themes of father-son alienation and breakdown of the family structure, is balanced by the nurture and love provided by Eva, the archetypal strong African woman. Eva's story, indeed, bears out Leonard Thompson's observation that "by 1936 the disruption of African families meant women were beginning to assume responsibilities as head of the household" and that as a result of the migratory labor system and its negative impact on family life, large numbers of black South African men experienced "social powerlessness" and "a frustrated rage that all too often manifests itself in domestic violence, particularly against women" (1990, 172, 202). Eva and Moses are classic examples of Thompson's observation.

Mphahlele continues to draw comparisons between his present life in the urban slum of Marabastad and his early years in rural Maupaneng, offering a commentary on the ways in which urbanization has altered the lifestyle and fundamental humanism of city dwellers. In urban Marabstad people relieve themselves in buckets, rather than in nearby fields. Houses are lined up in a straight row rather than in a circle. People no longer visit back and forth nor do they sit around the "communal fire" and tell stories. Nonetheless, Mphahlele avers, people still speak "with a subtle unity of voice. They still behaved as a community" (1959, 34). Thus, urbanization has eroded certain traditions, but it has not destroyed the strong sense of community.

As an urbanized member of a dysfunctional family and the eldest son in an African family being educated and living in the city, Mphahlele finds himself under tremendous pressure to succeed. But in the beginning as he starts school in Marabastad he thinks of himself as being merely a "backward" child—evidence of the urban alienation he experienced as a country "skapie" (sheep) coming to the town (40). "The class teacher said I was backward. The principal said I was backward. My aunt said I was backward. So said everybody. Mother didn't know. I had no choice but to acknowledge it" (47). Mphahlele, however, despite this humble, humorous, and slightly rueful sketch, soon proved everybody wrong. Not only was he the eldest son in an African family, but he was unusually gifted and hard working. He possessed all the qualifications to play the "hero" role in his dysfunctional family: striving to excel, to help his mother, to make something of himself; and to be everything his father was not (Gravitz 1985, 23). At the same time, the entire family was dependent on Mphahlele's success and his mother had virtually given her life's blood to educate him. The combined pressure on Mphahlele of his need to succeed and the guilt he felt over his mother's burden and his father's failure result in a breakdown at St. Peter's where he "lost the half-yearly tests." Nevertheless, he made a rapid recovery and went on to obtain a first-class pass in the 1937 examination.

The reader can observe in Mphahlele's early life an insidious ripple effect in the forms of alienation generated by the system, affecting first the society, then the community, next the family, and finally the individual. A careful reading of the text suggests that Moses' alcoholism had another effect on the temperament of his already shy and sensitive son. It may be that Mphahlele was afflicted by the fear of intimacy that is still another, highly personalized form of alienation typical of adult children of alcoholics (Gravitz 1985, 72). For example, during visits to his home in Marabastad while employed at Enzenzeleni Institute for the Blind, Mphahlele found that his mother, with all her great sacrifice and love, overwhelmed him so much that he was unable to express his own deeper feelings and that "I felt most bitter about my inability to thank her substantially for all she had done for me and the others. Her abundant love made me wish we could quarrel. Meantime, I noticed her strength was flagging" (1959, 153). Clearly the pressures of living in the midst of poverty, under state apartheid, and with the scars of alcoholic behavior, placed enormous burdens on even the most loving of relationships. Mphahlele's inability to communicate his gratitude to his mother for the magnitude and heroism of her sacrifice represents another form of interpersonal alienation that has its roots in historic and socioeconomic conditions as well as in personal and psychological ones.

From an individual focus, the narrative shifts back to a communal one as, in Chapter Four, the citizens of Marabastad parade past the communal water tap. Indeed, in this chapter Mphahlele helps establish what became one of the better-known conventions of the township autobiography—that of the communal gathering at the water tap. Even the water tap on Second Avenue, however, serves to reflect the polarity of the themes of alienation and African humanism. On the one hand, it is a lively community gathering point; on the other it symbolizes a life of deprivation under a harsh and discriminatory system where "Time ran out with the same slow, relentless and painful flow . . . [and where] . . . we all waited with dry patience" (30).

Poised at its center, skillfully wielding the artist's brush, Mphahlele paints a moving cameo of African humanism in its most humanized form. The gathering at the tap allows Mphahlele to introduce such notorious township types as Boeta Lem, the *tsotsi* (thug) about whom Old Rametse remarks, "'You can light a match on his big red eyes'" (31). Ma-Lebona also puts in an appearance as does Ma-Janeware, who claims to be the widow of a Portuguese trader. In a crosscultural exchange that reveals racial and skin biases within the black community itself, Ma-Janeware ironically refers to the others as being as black as soot when she herself is as "'black as Satan's pit'" (3). Mphahlele's sharp eye and his broad-based humanism lend balance to his observations and prevents him from falling into the Manichean trap. His portrayal of cross-cultural, interracial bias and bigotry makes a significant point—that is, that there are no easy black-white, urban-rural,

Western-African dichotomies. Life is both richer and more complex than that. Here at the tap gossip is traded, along with news of local witchcraft, and one gets the sense of a "sacred organic unity" in which "I am because you are, you are because we are" (1984, 9).

The dialogue bristles with colloquial banter, rendered proverbs, broken English, literal translations, Afrikaans and Sotho words, all tossed into a rich broth that bears little resemblance to the stilted dialogues and Victorian English found in Mphahlele's earlier writings such as *Man Must Live*. Mphahlele no longer, in the words of Mikhail Bakhtin, "ignores the social life of discourse outside the artist's study, discourse in the open spaces of public squares, streets, cities and villages, of social groups, generations and epochs" (1981, 259). Such "heteroglossia" indeed become the unique voice of Mphahlele's African humanism. In breaking away from the cultural imperialism of the West by way of an English that has been tamed and "domesticated," and by replicating the "heteroglossia" of Second Avenue, Mphahlele is not only affirming African values, he is coming into his own as a writer. Yet despite the humanism, the abundant humor, and the strong sense of community, life on Second Avenue is a constant struggle for the Mphahlele family, crowded into a two-room hut with bucket toilet and no heating. This tableau is brought fully to life on a Saturday night as described in the following impressionistic interlude that balances the lyric and ideal against harsh reality:

> I know the cold air coming through the hole in the flooring boards will whip us out of sleep. . . . My sister also on the floor is kicking the leg of the table. . . . Grandmother and three of Aunt Dora's children are lying quiet on the old double bed. With two frayed blankets on us it's good to feel hot. . . . And then the boxes containing old handbags and hats and trinkets given by some long-forgotten missus. . . . A police whistle, the barking of dogs . . . heavy booted footsteps, it's sure to be a person running away from the law, the police cells, the court and jail. Saturday night and it's ten to ten. I can hear the big curfew bell at the police station peal 'ten to ten, ten to ten, ten to ten.' . . . Black man must run home and the Black man must sleep or have a night special permit. (1959, 44–55)

In this passage, the degradation and deprivation of poverty is highlighted by the kind but utterly futile gesture of the white "madam" who gives the family her useless trinkets. The oppression of the apartheid state is emphasized with whistle, curfew bell, and heavy booted footsteps. We can hear it, just as we can smell the dust, feel the heat and cold and the frayed blanket.

The law reaches out into the black man's life and controls his every move, even at 9:50 on a Saturday night. He is constantly being pursued by the law that exists not to protect but to prosecute. The black man, in short, is on the run. In this page-and-a-half interlude of stream-of-consciousness prose, we have an entire *cinema verite* picture of life as it is lived on Second Avenue. Marabastad is a slum with a soul, but it is nonetheless a slum where "dirty water and flies and dead cats and dogs and children's stools owned the streets" and where whites are seldom seen and only then if they are the location superintendent, police or a white minister serving in some official capacity (33).

Mphahlele concludes his interlude on "Saturday night" with the statement "I feel so weak, inferior, ignorant, self-conscious" (46). He tells his psycho-biographer, N. Chabani Manganyi, that the tyranny of poverty and police brutality under which black people lived resulted in the lost childhood of a forced precocity. Mphahlele states that he thinks he felt more than most the anxiety and fear, not only of adolescence, but of adolescence for a black growing up in an apartheid state. Moreover, he is tormented by self-consciousness about his smallness and other perceived inadequacies, particularly around women. Thus, when he meets at school one of the loves of his life, another strong woman, Rebone, he is overwhelmed with shyness. Because of the importance of strong women in his life, Mphahlele attributes his preoccupation with "compassion" as an "important value" to the fact that all his role models were women. He concludes that, "At the end of the tunnel of time, I see the women of Marabastad and say to myself: there was a noble chance for a feminine identification on my part" (1983, 46–49).

One of the strongest, most insistent, even shrill, voices in *Down Second Avenue* is that of Ma-Lebona, a figure who is full of complex ambiguities and contradictions. One of the subtexts of *Down Second Avenue* is the theme of change. Although Mphahlele validates the philosophy of African humanism and the lifestyle that goes with it, he is not averse to change itself, nor does he ever intimate that all African traditions, customs, and values are by definition "good." He is much too balanced to fall into this Manichean trap by reversing old stereotypes. Ma-Lebona is an example. She is a spokesman for community values and customs and in her personage and interaction with others can be seen the conflict between old ways and new; African and Western in the process of urbanization. She is the sort of African woman who acts as a self-appointed, "unpaid social worker" and ombudsman, articulating traditional values and advising anyone who will listen on such matters as how to clean the house and prepare food, particularly such unwilling listeners as her assorted daughters-in-law, whom she manages thoroughly to antagonize.

At her best, Ma-Lebona's involvement recalls a time when Africans still behaved in traditional African humanist ways—offering condolences in a death, supporting young women in childbirth, and preparing food for a wedding (Mathiane 1990, 99–100). At her worst, Ma-Lebona is a professional busybody, but in both instances she embodies one of the chief tenets of African humanism. Of her it can be truly said: "'She's there!' When Africans say a person 'is there,' they mean you cannot but feel she is alive; she allows you no room to forget she was born and is alive in flesh and spirit" (1959, 59).

The ambiguities and conflicts of the life and times of the author find expression in Ma-Lebona's character in various ways. She is first and foremost a strong personality, like so many of the women in Mphahlele's life. She has that "unsinkable" quality that Mphahlele also attributes to his wife, Rebecca, in his memoir. Like grandmother Hibila, she is "clean as a cat in a white man's house" (64). She is preoccupied with education and the cachet it gives her like Mphahlele's mother. She is also very controlling, in the manner of aunt Dora. For example, she manages to drive away her son-in-law and describes him and her daughter, Nkati, as being "just hippo-headed" because they refuse to live with her in the traditional African way. Her first husband left after three years when "'the bell rang for stopping work', as Africans say when relations are severed." In another case, Ma-Lebona "kept a rough twig between the husband's buttocks long enough to drive him mad and out of the house" (61).

It is quite clear that living together with the traditional mother-in-law is not an African custom Mphahlele would necessarily celebrate or want to preserve and by implication Mphahlele is suggesting that preserving old customs for their own sake is not always desirable, nor is change itself necessarily bad. Sometimes change is necessary and good. Beyond that, it is entirely possible, given his own innately shy, reflective, and sensitive nature, that at times in his life Mphahlele felt himself to be something of a slave to the strong-willed women he was surrounded by and that at times he even felt himself to be hen-pecked, driven, and emasculated by their "thereness." If so, perhaps some of that frustration was vented in the creation of the character of Ma-Lebona who is a multidimensional and memorable composite of the many strong women Mphahlele had known.

Another manifestation of alienation that is vested in the persona of Ma-Lebona is between educated and uneducated blacks. Although

Mphahlele professed to feel no such alienation when the author of this study interviewed him, nonetheless, it is hard to imagine that he never experienced some of its ramifications as he himself describes them. For example, Ma-Lebona was forever mentioning that she was a schoolteacher (like Mphahlele, himself) trained at Kilnerton Institute. Such references, invariably, provoked among the other women sentiments at once "jealous, envious, annoyed and humble" (60).

Ma-Lebona, in short, contributes dramatic tension and textual balance by providing the focus for the dual themes of urban alienation and African humanism. In her articulation of the conflict between the modern present and traditional past and in defining and elucidating the individual's right relationship to society Ma-Lebona sometimes gets it right, but quite often, too, she gets it entirely wrong. In her militantly traditional insistence on playing the old-fashioned mother-in-law who demands that the daughter-in-law be "obedient" and in her contemptuous dismissal of modern daughters-in-law as being "thick-headed and stubborn," Ma-Lebona further serves to dramatize the conflict between the old generation and the newly urbanized, modern youth (59). This alienating conflict reaches a climax when her daughter-in-law Anna does the unthinkable. Rather than displaying veneration for elders in the traditional African humanist manner, Anna, instead breaking all strictures, slaps Ma-Lebona on the cheek. This shocking development symbolizes the breakdown in relations between the two generations, another theme of alienation.

Finally, Ma-Lebona calls down the wrath of the ancestors on her daughter Nkati and husband. Here the author breaks into the narrative, defending Ma-Lebona's gesture with a recapitulation of one of the precepts of African humanism that is intended for an audience who may not fully understand, explaining that "about eight out of every ten educated Africans, most of whom are still professed Christians, still believe firmly in the spirits of the ancestors. We don't speak to one another about it among the educated. But when we seek moral guidance and inspiration and hope, somewhere in the recesses of our being, we grope around for some link with those spirits" (64). Even the gods (and ancestors) are reflective of a "precolonial Africa [that] was essentially humanistic. . . . [the] existence of human society was the pre-condition for existence of religion and gods." Gods "were imbued with humanistic attributes." They "in turn influence social action in a dialectical process" (Amuta 1989, 39). In short, the gods are approachable and human-centered, tied by the "umbilical cord" of past and present generations to the here and now. They derive attributes from people in society striving after the highest good. People perceive in the gods the best they are capable of combined with self-knowledge. Having imbued the gods, or what Mphahlele refers to as the "Vital force," with such humanistic attributes people are in turn influenced by these same attributes. Mphahlele speaks of a "pipe-line" to the ancestors who are a source of "moral guidance and inspiration and hope" which suggests two-way reception—in short, a metaphysical humanistic dialogue in which the gods are not in the Islamic or Christian sense abstract, monolithic, and authoritarian, occupying some unknown fourth dimension.

An essential part of Mphahlele's humanism, in addition to his quest for meaning in the midst of chaos, his awareness of the larger picture beyond black and white issues in the human condition, his poet's vision that lifts the text to the level of art rather than mere reportage and the value he places on people and community as well as on ancestors as a source of moral guidance and inspiration, is his fireside gift as a storyteller. Direct, down-to-earth, and accessible, he has a feel for dramatic action and an eye for the telling detail and picturesque turn of phrase that befits an African elder and *griot*—that is fresh, original, earthy, and uniquely African. Thus, the woman next door is vividly described with wry humor as being "fat, like a bag of mealie-meal spreading over the back of a donkey" (78).

Although Marabastad and Second Avenue are repositories of African humanism, the alienation its inhabitants experience is not always external or directly attributable to black/white racism and/or the segregationist rule of whites. Within the township itself there is rampant thuggery and a proliferation of gangs due in part to unequal administration of criminal law, economic disparities, and the inability of the churches to stop them. There is also underlying racism and bias exhibited in the cross-cultural conflicts between African and Asian communities and further aggravated by such conditions as rapid urbanization, ignorance, overcrowding, and poverty.

Although black-white alienation is one of the paramount albeit unstated themes of *Down Second Avenue,* Mphahlele in his broader awareness of the human condition does not hesitate to shine the spotlight on the darker side of life in Marabastad. We see the ingrained humanism of an ancient culture afflicted by a tragic, urban blight in the form of township thuggery as "boys of our age were getting rough and knife-happy." For such youths, Boeta Lem (Brother Blade) who "collected a nice bunch of hangers-on" who "hero-worshipped him as an ex-convict" serves as a prototype (90). Boeta Lem, the township *tsotsi* who victimizes his own people and who breaks his father's heart, symbolizes a generation of lost, brutalized black youth and a proliferating culture of township violence. So destructive and alienating is this culture of violence that it ultimately begins to destroy the very humanism Mphahlele records, preserves, and celebrates.

Rebone's father, Dinku Dikae, the vegetable seller, stands as the ultimate tragic metaphor, almost a case study, of brutality triumphing over humanism. Dikae's daughter, Rebone, is Mphahlele's childhood sweetheart—the memory of whom is "like lace of a petticoat . . . [which] is all right as long as it doesn't show" (155). Like Ma-Lebona and Grandmother Hibila, Rebone also symbolizes the conflict and "the dialogue between . . . the present and the living Past."

Initially, Rebone displays customary respect for and support given African elders by children in that she behaves like a dutiful, caring daughter, even to the extent of teaching her father to read and write. But later she fails altogether to show this respect, becoming more modern in her defiant attitude. Going against her father's wishes, she scandalizes both grandmother Hibila and Ma-Lebona by attending dances at the Columbia Dance Hall and, although a good student, she also begins to skip classes.

Dikae, in the meantime, has a deeply ingrained fear of the police that goes back to a riot during a slum clearance when he watched a policeman shoot a boy (117). One night a white policeman forces his way into Dikae's hut and hurtles brutal and indecent insults. In a moment of sudden, violent rage and fear, Dikae kills the policeman. So alienated has Dikae become, in short, that the only means of self-actualization he can find is through violence. After the murder, he appears "more composed, stronger and surer than I have ever seen him" (141–42).

Thus does the system not only reinforce economic and social inequities, but it also fosters a culture of violence and of self-alienation that reaches across racial, ethnic, and geographic barriers into black townships, destroying the very ethos of African humanism. Dikae is a repository of the definitive form of alienation in which violence against others is ultimately violence against oneself.

Unlike Dikae, Aunt Dora is in charge of her own destiny. She is caring, but she is also tough. The polarity in temperaments between Mphahlele's paternal and maternal grandmothers—one representing forces of fate and alienation and the other the caring and compassion of African humanism—is echoed in the dramatic contrast between gentle, quiet Eva and big, strong, boisterous, domineering, meat-eating, life-loving Aunt Dora. A presence to be reckoned with, she is "there," in the African sense, fully inhabiting and engaged in the archetypal ghetto world, with no past and no future: "For

Aunt Dora the past never seemed to hold any romantic memories; she never spoke about the future; she simply grappled with the present" (107). Aunt Dora's knockdown, drag-out battle with Abdool, the Indian shop-keeper, over money owed for goods, provides comic relief and reveals Mphahlele's remarkable ear for dialect, but it also has its darker side in that it illustrates still another theme of alienation—the antagonism felt between Asians and blacks. Although this conflict can, in part, be traced to socioeconomic inequalities built into the apartheid system of economics insofar as Indians and "coloureds" often enjoyed better prospects for education and employment as well as significantly higher wages than their African counterparts, it is also clear that lack of understanding, racial prejudice, and cultural biases enter in (135).

For example, when she tackles Abdool, Dora gives free vent to her own prejudices, and bars no holds, either physically or verbally. As for Abdool, he proves himself a worthy adversary, able to give as good as he takes:

> "Stamp that book I say, coolie! You come from India to make money out of us, eh!"
> "Aldight aldight I come from Hindia what he's got do with book? No-no-no a-a-a!"
> "Abdool I don't want any dusty nonsense!"
> "If hum coolie ju Kaffier ten-times ju-self." (109)

As an African humanist writing about alienation, Mphahlele remains fair-minded and objective, never losing sight of the broader human canvas. Blacks may be oppressed, but they are not by virtue of their oppression automatically blameless. Boeta Lem, for example, perpetrates violence against his own people as Moses does against Eva and Dora against Abdool. Unlike apologists for negritude, Mphahlele does not omit the potential for "violence in the African character" nor does he simplistically present only "warm, loving, caring, socially-oriented" black characters as opposed to the "cold technology-oriented whites" (Watts 1989, 75).

Characters such as the two grandmothers, maternal and paternal, are also used to symbolize and counterpoint themes of alienation and African humanism as well as to heighten dramatic tension and advance the narrative. On the one hand, Mphahlele's paternal grandmother is as "grim as fate" and is a reminder of the hostile and alienating forces in his early life in Maupaneng. His maternal grandmother, Hibila, is a more complex figure. She is a "consummate combination of the toughness associated with the rural peasantry and the defiant cheek of the semi-literate grand old ladies of

African townships" (Manganyi 1983, 49). In addition, she is the perfect exemplar of *ubuntu*, the spirit of generosity, compassion, and sharing that defines African humanism.

In a sense she is a living practitioner and role model of the synthesis Mphahlele seeks in two streams of consciousness: African and Western. A woman of uncompromising principle, Hibila is perfectly at ease in her own skin, and entirely comfortable holding on to some of the old beliefs while praying to a Christian God daily. Indeed, she had a "fetching way of talking about the Christian God and the gods of the ancestors in the same breath" (Barnett 1976, 61). She frequently invokes the name of her deceased husband, swearing "by Titus who lies in his grave" (1959, 91). She may be a Christian herself, but she feels no compunction about offering hospitality to Mathebula, the witch doctor. It is true, of course, that Mathebula as an herbalist can, in return, offer his medical services to the family. So there is a good deal of pragmatism in Hibila's *ubuntu*.

Grandmother Hibila, like Eva, and in the best tradition of classical Western humanism, also entertains a fierce belief in the redeeming power of education. Even as the family is being raided by police for selling home brew and a white policeman strikes the youthful Mphahlele, forcing him to the ground and calling him a "stinking kaffir," Hibila continues to implore God to help her "make money to send my children to college" (43). She does succeed in educating three sons. The dedication to family and community exhibited by these strong-willed, resourceful women in Mphahlele's life provides the necessary counterpoint in an alien and hostile world to enable him to survive and endure, and, eventually, to realize some of Eva's fondest dreams.

Although there is friction and bickering amongst the denizens of Second Avenue, with Dora and Abdool, for example, exchanging racial epithets as freely as blows, the black community stands in stark contrast to the isolated whites in their posh suburbs. Treating Mphahlele "like a tool" and with a certain grim impersonality, Mr. Goldstein works at the museum with Aunt Dora's husband but never thinks to carry the laundry there himself. Self-absorbed Miss Foster or "Ma Bottles" is the white counterpart to Mphahlele's father, preventing Moses from being typecast a "degenerate" since drunkenness is clearly no respecter of race or gender. Then there is the Singer family, who give the dog tea, and fire "the girl" for beating the dog. Mrs. Singer is hence "christened . . . Chobolo (shrew)" (68–69).

In short, the isolation and alienation of Pretoria whites from their own humanity and that of their fellows is profound, providing a commentary on the suffering of blacks who may be poorer materially, but are ahead of the game spiritually. This is not to suggest that "poor blacks are the 'authentic' blacks [because] fearsome poverty has granted them deeper truths and wisdom" (Staples 1994, D2). None in this cast of characters, black or white, is free from defects. All are unforgettable, in keeping with Mphahlele's humanism, where people matter more than things.

In the meantime, a building series of episodes shows Mphahlele's progressive political alienation based on harsh personal experience and his mission-school education at St. Peters. First, there is his skirmish with some white boys in Pretoria with whom he collides, after losing control of his bicycle, which was loaded down with laundry. The boys, in turn, thrash him soundly and with all the self-righteous indignation befitting demigods who are a law unto themselves. "'Bastard!' shouted the boy who had fallen first. His friends came to me and about three of them each gave a hard kick on my backside and thighs. And they cursed and cursed and then rode away, leaving me with the cold, the pain, the numbness, and a punctured and bent front wheel" (1959, 39–40). Then, there are the continual slights and humiliations he suffers at the hands of such Pretoria whites as Mrs. Reynecke, the Afrikaner woman who addresses him as "boy"; the whites he encounters working as a messenger for a law firm who either put on "superior airs" or are coldly distant, such as the firm's proprietor, a "tall forbidding colossus" whom Mphahlele comes "to regard . . . as a machine who generates power but only from somewhere on the fringe of one's awareness"; the "anemic" secretaries with long red nails who send him on private errands and address him with a string of "You hear? You hear? You hear?" and the heavyset typist who sits knitting and makes him "think of Madam Defarge." Throughout the day Mphahlele is "Jim'ed and Johned to death" and is subjected to constant affronts which cause him to wake up at night in a cold sweat (136–43).

In the revised edition of *The African Image,* Mphahlele says of the white man: "I wanted my portrait of him in my fiction to be fuller so I myself could begin to understand him. . . . Over the last ten years I have ceased to care. It is not worth the trouble. The white man's inhumanity in South Africa has proved that much to me." Frequently Mphahlele comments on the racial alienation that has prevented him from getting to know the white man except at the "point of a boot or the point of a gun." This being the case, Mphahlele suggests that if he merely succeeds in caricaturing whites that will, at least, constitute some form of "poetic justice." Finally, he declares: "If any critic tells me my white characters are caricatures or only monsters, he is welcome to the opinion." Although it may be true that

Mphahlele's pen and ink sketches of Pretoria whites lack "light and shade, angles of vision, images and symbols," they nonetheless cleverly and believably depict plausible types while mildly satirizing them (Mphahlele 1962, 15). The truth of the matter is that in real life certain "types" fit the description, right down to the painted red nails. In playing out assigned roles these "types" master their parts so well they become caricatures of themselves. State apartheid provided a milieu that readily fostered such extremes in manners and morals associated with caricatural behavior.

The antihumanistic indifference and lack of compassion of Pretoria whites who appear to be "clean, quiet but either dead or neurotic" in their separate suburbs stand in dramatic contrast to the humanism of Mphahlele's family members (1959, 174). They may be members of the oppressed majority but they are never mere helpless victims. They exhibit hope and caring, rather than impersonality and a sort of disgruntled and existential despair, often seen in their white counterparts. Dora, Eva, and Hibila are, on the contrary, active, alive, energetic, fiercely determined people who take charge of their own destinies. Even as they sacrifice and suffer from hard work and deprivation, they are expressive of their African humanism. That is, they are not like whites "all bottled up." Rather they and others on Second Avenue "sing, dance, touch and laugh" and they live very much in the "now," which is a vital part of their humanism (Thuynsma 1991).

Although African humanism is the common thread that holds the fabric of the text of *Down Second Avenue* together, the themes of rootlessness, fragmentation, literary exile, and alienation slip over the seams of the text into its very structure, into what James Olney refers to as the "shape" of an autobiography—"because any autobiography is in one sense a psychological and philosophical imitation of the writer's personality" (Olney 1973, 52). *Down Second Avenue* does not unfold so much as it develops and is shaped by "historical contingency" (Shear 1981, 41). This helps explain why, for example, there is a marked and unsettling change of mood midway through the book. Those chapters composed on home soil, which the author states comprise the first half of the book, reflect, in turn, the author's sense of immediacy and closeness to his subjects as opposed to later chapters that reflect more his state of mind (1959, 218). Initially, the narrative crackles with action and the characters are "there" in an African humanist sense—larger than life and believable. By contrast, the mood of the final chapters written during Mphahlele's exile in Nigeria are brooding, ruminative, and, at times, bitter.

This disjuncture in mood and structure is echoed in the narrative itself. The chapter on Mphahlele's schooling at St. Peter's represents a critical turning point in his increasing political awareness and hence alienation from the white liberal establishment with its humanistic and Christian leanings. St. Peter's is in itself the very statement of a liberal, humanist approach, teaching a liberal arts curriculum based on Western classics that implicitly endorse the "commitment of a set of methods and policies that have as their common aim greater freedom for individual men" and the "spread of attitudes hospitable to individual enterprise and the creed of individual responsibility" (Smith 1968, 276–77). At St. Peter's, Mphahlele and his peers were being taught about civil liberties, egalitarian principles, the right of an individual to realize his highest potential, but the students were not, as Mphahlele remarks, encouraged to put these precepts into effect beyond the walls of the school. Increasingly, Mphahlele began to see the self-alienating discrepancy between the ideal and the real—between what he was being taught (and at the same time told not to apply) and the harsh illiberal, nondemocratic reality of the world beyond the cloistered halls of academe. Furthermore, none of these grand Western liberal humanistic principles which had helped raise the level of his own political awareness seemed to hold out the promise of effectively changing the current order. Thus, at St. Peter's, Mphahlele, whose predilections were not naturally toward politics, began to put all his past experience in its proper historic context—from the poverty his family suffered to his "mother's resignation, Aunt Dora's toughness, grandmother whose ways bridged the past with the present . . . the police raids; the ten-to-ten curfew bell; encounters with whites; humiliations" (1959, 128). Ultimately, however, Mphahlele's humanities-steeped liberal education would equip him with the tools to fight as a liberal for the egalitarian civil liberties he was being denied.

Mphahlele also began to realize that while debate on political issues was encouraged inside St. Peter's there was a double standard on just how far these principles of liberal individual free expression and responsibility should be carried beyond its gates. At the same time, there was an enormous and unsettling difference between the whites on the faculty with whom Mphahlele and his fellow students, such as the noted writer Peter Abrahams, "enjoyed complete harmony" and those on the outside whom Mphahlele was learning to hate. (Eccentric Brother Rogers, for example, seems to have been an unforgettable favorite, despite his hard canings. He comes amusingly and dramatically to life in a manner various generic Pretoria whites do not.) Thus, a white tram driver might abuse Mphahlele and a school chum trying to ride into the town of Johannesburg, forcing them to walk the four miles back from town because it was, after all, a "white" tram. It was a difficult and frustrating dichotomy continually to bridge—particularly since the respected and even likable whites on the inside of St. Peter's professed an idealism that had much to recommend it but seemed to have little practical applicability in the real world.

But there was to be no recourse, no outlet for Mphahlele's anger and humiliation, and no support either from that, in many ways, admirable bastion of white liberal Christian humanism. The reality was that no one on the faculty was prepared directly to confront the issue of how their young charges should behave in the brutal world of racial segregation and poverty outside the cloistered halls of St. Peter's, aside from keeping a low profile (126). For example, when Mphahlele curses a pair of white motorcyclists who try to run him off the sidewalk, hurtling the expletive "Voetsek" at them like a bullet, the Yorkshire headmaster of St. Peter's reprimands him, saying, "Do you want us thrown out by the European people from this place?" (127). The Western humanism and liberality of the headmaster and faculty appear a pale thing in comparison to the African humanism of Hibila, Dora, and Eva, who are willing to stake their very lives on their commitment to those they care for. At St. Peter's humanism and liberal thought apparently stopped at the gates. Mphahlele reluctantly concludes that the liberalism espoused in school does not "extend to the attitude they [the faculty and administration] thought we should adopt towards whites and white authority outside school. Slowly I realized how I hated the white man outside St. Peter's" (126).

Mphahlele's progressive political, spiritual, and racial alienation provides the foundation on which he first makes a break from the Anglican Church (paving the way to seek out a spiritual and philosophic ethos to fill the void), and, second, takes a brave and unequivocal stand against Bantu education and the syllabus it prescribes—one that he, as a trained educator, immediately recognizes has been deliberately designed to create "a race of slaves." It is supremely ironic that Mphahlele, a dedicated teacher steeped in the humanities and Western classics and by implication in Western humanism itself, which implicitly subscribes to "the belief in the unity of the human race and man's potential to perfect himself by his own efforts," was required to teach a syllabus founded on the counter-humanistic premise that blacks are inferior and that the education they receive should be commensurate with that inferiority (Fromm 1965, viii). Furthermore, the texts by which these insidious goals should be achieved were not designed to enlarge understanding and bring truth to light, according to liberal-humanistic principles, through scientific and scholarly inquiry, but instead they consciously distorted truth. These included, among others, such examples as "a history book with several distortions meant to glorify white colonization . . . [and] Afrikaans grammar books which abound with examples like 'the Kaffir has stolen a knife; that is a lazy Kaffir'" (1959, 167).

Long before the passage of the Bantu Education Act in 1953, legislation such as the so-called Hertzog Bills in 1936 had been passed, removing black voters from the rolls, providing them with communal representation by a single white, and restricting the purchase of land by blacks (138). Yet it was the Bantu Education Act that caused Mphahlele, as an educator, to revolt. It was because of the Bantu Education Act that South Africa's 4,500 mission schools fell "under the hostile gaze of the National Party Government. At these schools, ideologues claimed, 'dangerous, liberal ideas were being fed by outsiders into untrained minds.'" Hendrik Verwoerd, minister of Native Affairs, said that school must prepare the Bantu for his "proper place." There was no point, for example, in teaching a Bantu child mathematics "when it cannot use it in practice" (Oakes 1988, 379). Mphahlele, as secretary of the Transvaal Teachers Association, "travelled during school vacations to the districts to crusade against the recommendation of the Eiselen report." Shortly thereafter, Mphahlele was summarily dismissed from the teaching that was his "first love," with no reasons being given for his discharge (1959, 168).

Political and professional alienation was followed by spiritual. In 1947, Mphahlele decided no longer to attend church. Christianity, Mphahlele believed, was being used to encourage blacks passively to accept their lot, meekly to turn the other cheek and endure. Mphahlele felt vindicated in his decision not to attend church any longer when, in 1947, the Nationalist party came to power. After this event, Mphahlele states, his belief in such humanistic and liberal values as "fellowship," "love," and "obedience of the law" were challenged. "Suddenly I did not know what these meant in terms of my place in society" especially as white voters had voted into parliament "a bunch of lawless Voortrekker descendants whose safety lies in the hands of sten-gun-happy youngsters" (163).

In his efforts to lobby against the Bantu Education Act, Mphahlele took positive action in a manner for which his education had prepared him: in short, he attempted to put into effect liberal humanist precepts of individual responsibility and free speech. He actively committed himself to the classic liberal endeavor of bringing peaceful change about through education and persuasion, campaigning against the Bantu Education Act in his elected capacity as secretary of the Transvaal Teachers Association. Ultimately, he was fired for his good faith efforts and forbidden to teach in all government schools. By that time Mphahlele was also married to Rebecca and the couple had a young family to support. When he discovered he was dismissed as a teacher at Orlando High for "subversive activities," he writes, "bitterness ate into me like a cancer" (169). As a black and despite his education, Mphahlele is able only to find a job as a factory invoice clerk. He then had to live in fear of the pass laws "and [at] the risk of being whisked off to a Bethal prison farm, I decided to go and queue up for a reference book" (170).

At a time when Mphahlele was subsequently very short of personal funds and when a black youth who sought his advice had been severely beaten by white police, an Anglican priest appeared on Mphahlele's doorstep to remind him of a sum owed the church and to bring up the subject of Mphahlele's attendance. Mphahlele had already begun, however, to question the double standard of Christianity—used on the one hand to justify the position of the apartheid government and on the other to ensure that blacks remain meekly, passively, and humbly in their place. Mphahlele makes an eloquent and definitive statement of his alienation from Christianity and the "longings" that that sense of loss triggers:

> Just now, I don't think it's fair for anybody to tell me to expect a change of heart among a bunch of madmen who are determined not to cede an inch or listen to reason. It is unfair to ask me to subsist on mission school sermons about Christian conduct and passive resistance in circumstances where it is considered a crime to be decent; where a policeman will run me out of my house at the point of a sten gun when I try to withhold my labour. For years I have been told by white and Black preachers to love my neighbour; love him when there's a bunch of whites who reckon they are Israelites come out of Egypt in obedience to God's order to come and civilize heathens; a bunch of whites who feed on the symbolism of God's race venturing into the desert among the ungodly. For years now I have been thinking it was all right for me to feel spiritually strong after a church service. And now I feel it is not the kind of strength that answers the demands of suffering humanity around me. It doesn't even seem to answer the longings in my own heart. (178)

By the late 1940s, Mphahlele's progressive spiritual alienation continued to build as he began to see, not only the church, but also the parliament and the white press as among the white liberal institutions that have "become a symbol of the dishonesty of the West" (221). All of them "babbled their platitudes" about the "native emerging from . . . primitive barbarism" and of "white guardianship" while the church, in particular, continued to teach the non-white to love his neighbor and while the white preacher "felt committed to an ethic he did not dare apply to the necessity of group action against the forces of evil in a setting where such forces have worked themselves up into a savage national attitude said to be based on a Christian sense of justice" (163). At the same time, the church practiced an insidious cultural imperialism in which African customs and religious practices were deemed primitive and inferior and where black Christians themselves were treated as second-class citizens. Thus, Mphahlele came to realize that "my outlook on the church has decidedly changed" (179).

The painful forces of spiritual and political alienation had for the moment won out, setting in motion "a terrible conflict" whose resolution would come in the form of a decision that would give meaning to all that had preceded it and that of itself lacked meaning. Mphahlele would feel compelled to exit the prison of self-alienation in which he believed he had given life nothing; and where it seemed even life "resented your efforts" (202). There appeared to be only one choice for someone with so much to give and yet so tormented by his inability to do so—and that was political exile.

In the meantime, death hangs like a pall over the narrative. We learn, in one of the final interludes, that Marabastad had been razed; but the black people kept moving on with "bent backs" (down Second Avenue, out of the "painful South" and finally out of Africa altogether). Siki, the tubercular guitarist, has died as has Mphahlele's mother, Eva. Ma-Lebona also dies, a symbol of the harshness of ghetto life and its spokesman even in her death. She does not receive the burial she had hoped for. Instead, there are thorn trees, no tombstone and an ant-eaten cross and the smell of "poverty from far away . . . More mothers will come and pass on but the African sage will tell you pain defies comparison. There are many more second avenues with dirty water and flies and children with traces of urine running down the legs and chickens pecking at children's stools" (158–59). In the end, there is the angry, bitter, and frustrated self-alienation of a teacher who cannot teach, of a writer who cannot write; and the alienation from a world that rejected all your "strivings and desires," but that "continued to torment you" until "you knew it was your soul that was imprisoned" (202). There was no hope of putting those skills to work on behalf of the poor, undereducated blacks on the many second avenues throughout the country. Perhaps, of the multiple forms of alienation Mphahlele the teacher, writer, and scholar undergoes and describes in *Down Second Avenue* and other works, that which is most cruel, most ironic, and ultimately most meaningless is that Mphahlele's "whole life had been an unrelenting struggle to achieve the way of life for which his urban upbringing and liberal education had prepared him. But to achieve this life he had finally to become an exile" (Moore 1962,

93). Thus, the themes of alienation embrace the dehumanizing effect of life for blacks under apartheid; the philosophic and cultural conflict between Christian and African modes of thought; between old ways and new; the breakdown of the family structure and father-son alienation; political, socioeconomic, and racial alienation, and finally, the lonely and bitter self-alienation of the exile and writer separated from the very community that forms an integral part of his unique humanism. Herein the groundwork is set for Mphahlele's quest for a philosophic approach that will fill the spiritual vacuum, that will reaffirm black values, and that will provide an answer to the inadequacies and hypocrisy of white liberalism.

The object of the quest driving this African Odysseus, however, was there all along. Strong women like Eva, Dora, and Ma-Lebona are the walking, talking, living, breathing manifestos of the abstract ideal of African humanism—a concept that was simply waiting to be named and articulated. African humanism as seen in Marabastad lived out on a daily basis is not so much "a philosophic contention that has been argued . . . as a way of life. The African lives it and does not stand outside it to contemplate the process" (Mphahlele 1986, 10). It is a working philosophy that, like African art, fulfills a purpose within the community. In its fundamental humanism and *ubuntu,* it made life supportable for blacks in slums and townships like Marabastad throughout the "painful south," providing stability against chaos, humor and love against denigration and hate.

State apartheid valued power, affluence, and privilege more than people. African humanism valued people more than places and things. Where apartheid oppressed, African humanism shared and showed compassion. Apartheid fostered guilt; African humanism gave evidence of sacrifice and courage. It afforded hope and an ability to savor what life has to offer in the now.

There is more to life, the author tells us, than the white man's technological achievements and there are truths that the white man (and woman) could learn from Mphahlele's forbears if he, the white man, would but keep an open mind:

> I admire the white man's achievements, his mind that plans tall buildings, powerful machinery. . . . [But] I think now the white man has no right to tell me how to order my life as a social being, or order it for me. He may teach me how to make a shirt or to read and to write, but my forbears and I could teach him a thing or two if only he would listen and allow himself time to feel. Africa is no more for the white man who comes here to teach and to control her human and material forces and not to learn. (218)

Nigeria, where Mphahlele landed in September 1957, with its rejuvenating freedom and its Africanness, afforded fertile ground on which he could embark on his spiritual quest. It enabled him, in short, "to be African, to rediscover the real dimensions of my selfhood" (Manganyi 1983, 169). But Mphahlele also discovers that life in exile can lead to a profound sense of dislocation, especially if alienation is defined as having no roots in the community. This sense of being rootless and thus of being no one can obtain even in another African country. Mphahlele told his biographer that writing *Down Second Avenue* helped him to "clear the air," to "take stock," to place life in exile on a "firmer foundation," and to bring "coherence where chaos had raged" (Manganyi 1983, 163).

Even while uprooted and exiled, Mphahlele, however, remains strongly tied to the land of his birth. He still feels the African connection and the responsibility to a people he has left behind in a condition of "collective spiritual exile" (163). He says of himself as a writer and educator separated in space and time from his own community, "You are not an outside observer; you are committed to the very society you criticize and commend, the tragedy and comedy of its thought and action are *your* tragedy and comedy" (Mphahlele 1974, 77).

Through the writing of an extended praise poem that celebrates his people, Mphahlele is able to replenish his own roots, reaffirm his commitment, feel the connection. *Down Second Avenue,* in short, becomes for Mphahlele a "literature of self-definition" (Lindfors 1985, 28), the theme of which is the search for the lost and alienated self within the framework of his own community—where the alien and the exile find meaning and affirmation through a humanism that is uniquely African.

In order better to appreciate Mphahlele's unique achievement in terms of his contribution to an "anticolonial movement" based on restoring "confidence in the native culture and tradition" and his efforts "to revive submerged mythologies . . . resurrect dead languages and . . . restore old habits of . . . behavior," it is instructive to compare his autobiography with Abrahams's *Tell Freedom* and Modisane's *Blame Me on History* (Obiechina 1990, 68). A brief comparative glance at the three writers will serve to support my contention that Mphahlele is more concerned with documenting what Charles Larson calls the "group-felt experience" (1972, 116). At the same time, he is more profoundly engaged in an aesthetic and philosophic sense with resurrecting "submerged" myths and reviving African humanistic black culture and traditions with the implicit objective of reclaiming alienated black youth, unifying the community, and reviving black pride, thereby helping to pave the way for Black Consciousness in South Africa.

Autobiographical writing in the 1950s in South Africa reflects both in content and form a fragmented reality and a journey toward meaning in which the search for self and its remaking is pivotal. Although the choice of autobiography as a genre of protest was dictated to large extent by historic contingencies, in a literary and cultural sense it was also arguably an appropriate and natural choice. It is perhaps more than coincidental, for example, that in African folktales, the "quest hero" is a popular character. In a sense each of the three autobiographic narrators fits quite naturally into the traditional mode of the African quest hero "who goes in quest of something or some ideal (in this case freedom) and usually undergoes harrowing ordeals before attaining his objective. . . . He owes his escape from disaster and defeat to personal courage, chance, divine intervention or magic" (Obiechina 1990, 27). In the case of the three autobiographers under consideration, personal courage is the common denominator and the harrowing experiences documented include descriptions of police brutality, denial of fundamental civil and human liberties, state-sponsored oppression and violence, white cruelty and indifference, cross-cultural conflicts, and premature death of friends and loved ones. All three autobiographies also resort to novelistic devices such as flashbacks, dialogue, and characterization while simultaneously evolving what later became accepted conventions of the township autobiography, including descriptions of the local bioscope, *shebeens,* and the communal tap, as well as such major township events as weddings and funerals.

In each autobiography the narrator represents in both an allegoric and dialectic sense the larger community—whether it be Vrededorp in the case of Abrahams, Marabastad in the case of Mphahlele, or Sophiatown in the case of Modisane. Each of these townships was bulldozed, symbolizing the spiritual and cultural demise of the community itself. The narrator personalizes and refracts the losses suffered by the community in an ongoing dialogue. Each narrator, to some degree, documents an increasing political awareness combined with a growing sense of alienation—starting at one end of the spectrum with Peter Abrahams and ending at the other with Bloke Modisane. Political, spiritual, and intellectual alienation culminates in a tension-filled flight out of South Africa either by boat, train, or air and thence into political exile.

Similarly, all three autobiographers are concerned with related socioeconomic themes of alienation—ranging from fatherlessness and the breakdown of traditional values and family structure to the utter meaninglessness of a society in which the final arbiter in each and every human endeavor and relationship is that of skin pigmentation. The theme of fatherlessness is related to the parallel theme of psychological oppression and self-alienation. Fathers, it would seem, are invariably missing. For example, Mphahlele's father is an alcoholic and abandons the family; Abrahams's father dies when he is a child. Modisane's is killed in a meaningless act of township violence, although for all practical purposes, his father dies as a person in his son's eyes when he, powerless to resist or fight back, is treated with contempt by a much younger police constable during a pass raid. Modisane in a sense becomes his father in this symbolic act of emasculation by the police constable in which the father is reduced in his son's eyes to a nobody. Modisane sees this as the death knell of the father-son relationship that ultimately climaxes in his father's equally meaningless and violent death in a township murder so brutal that his father's face bears no resemblance to the man Modisane once knew. When the funeral takes place, Modisane's own name by mistake appears on the coffin. This becomes for him the definitive symbol of his own lost identity:

> The de-personalization of the African has been so thorough that I have no name, none of them care to know whether I have one, and since there was very little point in having a name—in any case, I have no name, the only one I had was buried on the coffin of my father—I adopted the label Bloke; it was a symbolic epitome of the collective thing I was made to be. The African is a collective which cannot be classified and distinguished apart, or hated apart, as an individual.
> (1990, 242–43)

The very title of Modisane's autobiography, *Blame Me on History,* differentiates it in degree and focus, if not in actual substance, from that of either Abrahams or Mphahlele. Modisane sees his fate as historically determined. In his irony and bitterness, he takes the self-obliterating realities of life in a black township a step further. It puts him as an educated black with an appreciation for Western culture at odds with other blacks, with himself and with his unfulfilled dreams. With Western nihilism that stands as the antithesis of Mphahlele's African humanism Modisane declares himself a faceless, nameless "bloke"—a nameless pawn of history, an invisible man. Modisane takes the "I am nothing" and turns it into "I am invisible."

His divided self is in essence a profound split between his intellectual, self-analyzing, self-aware persona and that of the African community. Modisane's "individuated intellectual self yearns to be accepted in the world of white culture, but finds it impossible to sever connections completely with a subcultural ethos characterized by the jazz, bioscope and shebeens" (Ngewenya 1989, 71). This theme of the culturally colonized divided self is also played out in the works of Mphahlele. Nevertheless, the split in Mphahlele's work is rarely so profound, self-analytical and de-spairing (in the more Westernized sense of the alienated hero) as it is in Modisane. Mphahlele manages to bridge the crevasse, turning negation into self-affirmation. Returning to the community for self-identification and for a vision that can offer redemption both to self and community, Mphahlele begins by affirming "I am" and eventually completes the state-ment with "an African humanist." Modisane's mental, physical, and spiri-tual annihilation is, by contrast, equated with the leveling of Sophiatown with which he opens his autobiography, stating that "Nothing . . . seemed to have any meaning, all around me there was the futility and the apathy, the dying of the children, the empty gestures of the life reflected in the seem-ingly meaningless destruction of that life, the demolition of Sophiatown" (1986, 117). Thus, there is a major difference between Mphahlele and Mod-isane in tone and emphasis—which, in turn, indicates an increasing degree of alienation and bitterness, both psychological and historic, on the register of black consciousness, with Modisane representing an extreme in anger, self-loathing, and alienation.

Although Peter Abrahams in *Tell Freedom* describes a more intact com-munity of nuclear and extended family than does Modisane in *Blame Me on History*, neither the community, the place, nor the people are as vividly or memorably portrayed as are those in Mphahlele's *Down Second Avenue*. Because the place setting shifts in Abrahams's *Tell Freedom* from urban to rural, from Vrededorp to Cape Town and District Six, the canvas in Abrahams's work is neither so crowded nor so immediate and central as Mphahlele's. More significantly, there is in *Tell Freedom* no sense at work of a black aesthetic. For example, there is scant evidence in the text of African metaphoric speech, proverbs, or dialect. Traditional activities and practices, such as the cooking of mealie pap or the wearing of a *doek* (woman's head scarf), are documented, but little else is suggested of underlying customs and values whether of the black or of the "Cape Malay" community from which Abrahams's mother sprang. Abrahams describes the problems of apartheid well and affectingly, but ultimately his solution is to go into exile in order to write books to change the minds of the white oppressor. He ex-presses the liberal humanist view "that perhaps life had a meaning that tran-scended race and colour. . . . There was the need to write, to tell freedom, and for this I needed to be personally free" (1981, 311).

Unlike Mphahlele, Abrahams does not advocate the retrieval of black myth (although he does take considerable pride in his Ethiopian heritage through his father's line) or the affirmation of black culture and values to empower blacks. In terms of "home" as community, it is significant that Mphahlele's title *Down Second Avenue* is exclusively place-centered. It does not embrace such sweeping abstractions as either history or freedom. Because of Mphahlele's intense focus on his early years in Marabastad, the community on Second Avenue takes on a vibrant life of its own. The past becomes present in a fresh, innovative way that enables the reader to learn from it.

Although one of Modisane's preeminent themes is historic determinism, one of Abrahams's is the liberal humanist message that change will be brought about through persuasion. Abrahams believes that by telling the story of the gross inequities and human rights abuses perpetrated by white supremacists, his predominantly white liberal audience will rally around the cause of freedom. Although both Abrahams and Modisane document, Mphahlele puts the most human face on the outrages perpetrated in the name of racism, colonialism, and apartheid. Indeed, it is this human face given expression by such superb communicators as tough Dora, "she [who] could be midwife to a lioness, we say in Sesotho," Hibila, and Eva that gives *Down Second Avenue*'s protest message its power (Manganyi 1983, 21). Although Mphahlele as African humanist narrator merges harmoniously and unselfpityingly with community, Modisane, despite his protestations of being nameless and invisible, is an ever-present, highly individual, and deeply anguished narrative voice who stands apart.

Mphahlele sees the need for something more than decrying one's history or telling freedom. That is what defines his autobiography, and adds balance, depth, and sweep to the pendulum's swing, distinguishing it from the others. Mphahlele's deeply rooted African humanist stance, his vivid, realistic documentation of community history, and his sense of a black aesthetic are the magnets that keep the pendulum swinging back and forth. They maintain the tension and drive the plot. They add depth to character portrayal and interest to text. This contributes to the polarity between negation and alienation and affirmation and hope in the continuing dialogue of two selves.

Whereas in Modisane's *Blame Me on History* the pendulum, by contrast, tends to get stuck at the negative pole, in Abrahams's *Tell Freedom* the pendulum simply lacks the power of a black aesthetic. Although Abrahams's writing commands a certain old-fashioned, stately dignity in its biblical style, reliance on parallel structure, very much in the manner of Paton's *Cry, the Beloved Country*, and echoings of mission-press prose, it is more beholden to Eurocentric modes. Thus, Abrahams describes the meeting and marriage of his parents: "To this street and this house came the Ethiopian. There, he wooed my mother. There, he won her. They married from that house. They found a house of their own further down the street. They made of it a home of love and laughter. From there they sent their boy and girl to the Coloured School above Vrededorp. From there the Ethiopian went to work on the mines each morning" (1988, 11). Abrahams, however, must be credited for helping to pave the way in the evolution of a new literary genre, the black township autobiography. Writing a full decade before many of his contemporaries, Abrahams "has been acknowledged as an obvious influence on subsequent African writers."

Nonetheless, some critics (perhaps unfairly) do not regard Abrahams as "a part of the African literary tradition," viewing him instead as a writer who "sought only to meet Western literary demands." He is seen, instead, as someone who, unlike Mphahlele, "was hardly interested in traditional African aesthetics," and who furthermore was a "champion of Western liberalism" (Ogungbesan 1992, 166–67).

Abrahams clearly had not undergone the decolonization process Mphahlele underwent. Yet thematically and structurally in the use of certain conventions and literary devices in the development of an entirely new genre, Abrahams was an important forerunner. Moreover, there are far too many similarities in episodes and conventions between the works of Abrahams and Mphahlele to overlook the indebtedness of the latter author to the former. For example, like Mphahlele's mother, Eva, Abrahams's mother also suffers a severe burn—in this instance from boiling water while doing laundry. Her heartless white employers subsequently send her home alone without proper medical attention and with no pay. We are reminded at once of the episode in which Eva is severely burned when Moses heaves the scalding pot of hot curry at her. Although these events are true, it is with their selection and retelling that I am concerned. Both episodes are tied in with subsequent separations and with resultant breakdown of the family structure, one of the strongly interwoven themes of alienation documented in both the works of Modisane and Mphahlele. Indeed, it is at this juncture that Abrahams comments: "it seemed to me there is no meaning in life. Things happened and no one seemed to know why" (1988, 72).

Modisane, as we have seen, has already commented on such meaninglessness. His narrative is heavily underscored by his anger and self-hatred, serving as evidence of psychological oppression in the sense of Black Consciousness—a type of self-alienation largely missing in Abrahams's autobiography, and only sporadically in evidence in Mphahlele, who continues to insist that blacks are not just victimized, impassive objects, but are also subjects who enjoy a rich meaningful life of their own beyond apartheid. Since Modisane is writing a decade after Abrahams, we can see proof herein not only of progressive alienation in a intertextual sense, but in an extratextual sense as well. The progression—as "history" continues to wreak its havoc—applies as much to the narrators as to the texts themselves.

Accordingly, we become far more intimate with Modisane's psychological landscape than with that of either Mphahlele or Abrahams. Furthermore, while the prospect of community offers inspiration and succor to Mphahlele, one sees in Modisane's intense ambivalence toward whites, his promiscuity, and his profound bitterness a form of self-alienation from which even the community itself seemingly cannot rescue him. Modisane's alienation strikes the reader as being ultimately too lonely, isolated, debilitating, and potentially self-destructive for community to operate as an effective counterweight in the same way it does for Mphahlele. When Modisane thinks about his past, he says, "Remembrances of that life made me feel dirty, I longed for Christ and Fiki to come and wash the corpse of my body before it is finally lowered into the grave, so that I could appear before my God clean and sanitary" (1990, 285). Modisane's alienation is both more Western and existential in its interiority and psychological cast than Abrahams's or Mphahlele's.

Modisane, unlike Abrahams, however, does show evidence of a black aesthetic at work in his writing. His description of his discourse with Ma-Bloke over the need to pay lobola (bride price) when he and Fiki plan to marry is lively, funny, and steeped in a black aesthetic and ethos. It documents one of the themes of alienation informing Mphahlele's work—that is the conflict between contemporary youth and traditional society. Thus, Modisane tells Ma-Bloke: "There's no lobola, Mama, Fiki and I don't believe in [it]. . . . Ma-Bloke, Fiki is not a cow; I won't buy her, we don't think it's right. Besides, I haven't got the money" (256). Sadly Modisane's marriage, like everything else in his life, also breaks down. Ultimately, when he finally decides to leave South Africa for good, he turns his attention to questions of human rights and justice, much as Abrahams did. His position in the concluding passages of the text, like Abrahams's, is to define the problem in an abstract (as opposed to a concrete human and humanitarian) sense and to address its political inception. He asks: "Does a wrong become less immoral because it is written into the constitution? Am I to believe that only white men are created equal?" (310). Thus, he defines the problems pointedly, eloquently, and even unforgettably. Unlike Mphahlele, however, Modisane does not move beyond the level of protest to that of resistance. Although Mphahlele criticizes, he also affirms and his affirmation is in the form of a black aesthetic and a vision which he chooses to call African humanism: a vision that has ramifications in every realm of human endeavor—the arts, education, and politics itself.

Ultimately, Mphahlele says that the white man "may teach me how to make a shirt or to read and to write, but my forbears and I could teach him a thing or two if only he would listen and allow himself time to feel" (1989, 218). By unequivocally affirming the spiritually redemptive and healing power of a black ethos, Mphahlele, unlike either Abrahams or Modisane, takes a significant and even (for the times) radical first step forward beyond that of merely defining the problem of black oppression.

As poet Mongane Wally Serote has suggested is necessary in the struggle for liberation, Mphahlele has developed "two tongues, one to expose and fight against the fallacy which the oppressor creates in order to justify his position of dominance . . . another to inspire the oppressed" (1990, 8). Mphahlele has developed two tongues, but neither is forked. Such a development is a major step forward in the affirmation of Black Consciousness. Whites, moreover, are also invited in the inclusivist spirit of African humanism to come along on "the journey," if they are willing to listen, learn, and feel. Critic Charles Larson eloquently interprets the passage from the epilogue with which Mphahlele brings *Down Second Avenue* to a close as meaning that: "Only when the white man is willing to learn as well as to teach can he reap the benefits of cultural syncretism" (1972, 218). Accepting the invitation to do precisely that is one of the primary aims of this study.

Chapter Six

"Mrs Plum"

THE AUTHORITARIAN PERSONALITY
AND BLACK CONSCIOUSNESS

The violence with which the supremacy of white values is affirmed and
the aggressiveness which has permeated the victory of these values over the
ways of life and of thought of the native means that, in revenge, the native
laughs in mockery when Western values are mentioned in front of him (43).

For a colonized people the most essential value . . . is first and foremost
the land: the land which will bring them bread, and above all, dignity (44).

Perhaps unconsciously, the native intellectuals, since they could not stand
wonderstruck before the history of today's barbarity, decided to back further
and to delve deeper down; and, let us make no mistake, it was with the greatest
delight that they discovered that there was nothing to be ashamed of in the
past, but rather dignity, glory, and solemnity. The claim to a national culture
in the past does not only rehabilitate the nation and serve as a justification
for the hope of a future national culture. In the sphere of psycho-affective
equilibrium it is responsible for an important change in the native (210).
—Frantz Fanon

Next to *Down Second Avenue,* Mphahlele's novella "Mrs Plum," first published in *Corner B* in 1976, is his best-known work and unquestionably one
of his most effective and memorable pieces of fictional protest writing. It
has appeared in at least three anthologies, including the collection *African
Short Stories* edited by Charles Larson (Hodge 1981, 33; Barnett 1976, 110). It
was written in the post-*Drum,* post-Sharpeville era after the author had left
Nigeria for Paris. In its searing shock tactics and scathing depiction of the
white liberal establishment in the person of Mrs. Plum, it illustrates the
point that: "Exile released me from bondage: the knot of bitterness that had

always stuck in my throat. Wholesome and purer emotions like anger became possible. I was free to be angry" (Manganyi 1983, 195). Although "Mrs
Plum" may represent, in Mphahlele's words, a "fragile bridge" between his
short stories and the novel, it is strong enough to sustain the full force of
Mphahlele's anger in the fiery, eloquent crossing (218). "Mrs Plum" is considered by many to be "Mphahlele's most serious attempt to explore the relationship between white and black in South Africa" (Barnett 1983, 176). The
fact that the chief white protagonist is in this instance a high-minded, well-
meaning liberal, symbolizing a group and movement that at one time
"seemed to provide an answer to South Africa's problems. . . [and] represents the culmination of the heyday of white liberal optimism and confidence" adds enormous irony to a story already fraught with tension, a breakdown in communication, and fundamental alienation (Watson 1982, 232).

One of the failures of vision of white liberalism that resulted in
black/white alienation and set liberals of the Mrs. Plum school up as worthy
objects of derision, mockery, and satire, as Mphahlele states in *Voices in the
Whirlwind,* is that "protest within the law . . . . is in the true tradition of
South African white liberalism, which has always accommodated itself in
the safe capsule of legality; and that means white legality, since the laws are
made by whites only" (Mphahlele 1972, 200).

The sanctity of the law, Mphahlele suggests, is logically called into question when its sole purpose is to uphold, validate, and perpetuate a racist, authoritarian regime that denies people their fundamental human rights.
Lending further irony to this failure of liberal vision is that despite a theoretical overlap between white liberalism and black humanism where one
might normally have expected a meeting point between the races, one finds
instead only bitterness, anger, and alienation. The dynamics of this alienating and tragic disconnect are explored in "Mrs Plum," not only politically
and culturally, but in greater psychological depth than in any of Mphahlele's
previous works.

Mphahlele uncages a lion in the drawing room by relaxing the censorship regnant or ego, in Freudian terms, and deploying grotesque realism
with its focus on material, bodily functions of eating, drinking, urination,
and copulation "to jolt us out of our normal expectations and epistemological complacency" (Gardiner 1992, 47). The fact that this particular lion is
uncaged in a Puritan-Calvinist setting makes it all the more effective. The
author/narrator also vents his own frustrations through the intergenerational voices of the African past—represented by Chimane, her aunt, Dick,
and later by Karabo's parents; the ideological present for which Mrs. Plum

is spokesman; and the yet unrealized promise of the future, symbolized by Karabo. Stripping the arrogant liberal of divine-white status, Mphahlele shows to his white readership the potential settler in each. The subtext of "Mrs Plum" echoes Jean Paul Sartre's words: "Let us look at ourselves, if we can bear to" (Fanon 1963, 24).

The novella opens with a humorous, satiric cameo, sketched out in three short, punchy, introductory sentences. Immediately, the reader is apprised of what sort of patronizing liberal Mrs. Plum might be and where her priorities lie. What the author says and what he leaves unsaid gives this mocking portrait its power: "My Madam's name was Mrs Plum. She loved dogs and Africans and said that everyone must follow the law even if it hurt. These were three big things in Madam's life" (Mphahlele 1981, 216).

Although it is not unreasonable to expect that a professed African humanist might give the white liberal a more sympathetic hearing and vice versa, this cannot be the case when the liberal, like Mrs. Plum, is so incredibly myopic that she fails to recognize that the law she insists one must follow "even when it hurts" is morally bankrupt (216). In her insistence on the need to follow the law, Mrs. Plum articulates an important precept of liberalism—in that "anyone who breaks the law has no right to the benefits—security, respect, recognition in an ordered world—that the law confers, since breaking the law threatens everybody else's right to those benefits. However, this axiom has an important corollary—that everyone should have equal access to the same law" (Ruth 1986, 78).

Laurens van der Post best describes this "classic liberal double-bind" (78). In his novel *In a Province* he writes, "We [whites] forbid them [blacks] the sort of life their law demands, and give them our law without the sort of life that our law demands" (191). The juxtaposition of dogs, Africans, and the law, in the order of values cherished by Mrs. Plum, underscores van der Post's observation and is pointedly suggestive of both a patronizing attitude on the part of the white liberal and the absence of any true understanding and compassion, let alone sense of equality, particularly when it comes to the individual person as opposed to the abstract group or principle. How far Mrs. Plum's caring (and by extrapolation that of all white liberals) extends remains an implied question throughout the story and is one of the important subthemes of alienation.

Although Mrs. Plum is not as rounded a character as the story's narrator and chief black protagonist, Karabo, who is employed by her as maid, she is nonetheless plausible. One is tempted to label Mrs. Plum a "flat" character. As E. M. Forster observes in *Aspects of the Novel,* when a writer wants "to strike with direct force it is convenient for him to use 'flat' characters; characters who can be easily labeled and therefore managed" (Mphahlele 1962, 131). Mphahlele's undisputed aim in his narrative is "to strike with direct force." On the other hand, Mrs. Plum does successfully pass one of the critical tests, according to Forster, for qualifying as a "rounded" character in that she is "capable of surprising in a convincing way" (Chinweizu 1983, 115). Here again we have the problem of the divided imagination. In a society that labels and catalogues people by pigmentation, in effect assigning roles, writing scripts, and predetermining destinies by something as arbitrary and meaningless as skin color, people, in turn, have a tendency to become typecast.

The geographic distances set up by the Group Areas Act, and the educational distances and mind control reinforced by the Bantu Education Act, further lent themselves to racial stereotyping and white paranoia. Thus, it might be argued, Mrs. Plum is believable precisely because she is something of a caricature of herself. She is markedly similar to such real people as the English-speaking mother of South African writer Rian Malan, about whom he says: "She loved blacks, but she loved dogs, too, and I am not sure the distinction was all that clear in her mind" (Malan 1990, 238). For white liberals like Mrs. Plum, self-deception and hypocrisy are raised to an art form—ultimately becoming an insidious form of psychological self-alienation leading to anxiety, guilt, and paranoia in addition to raising roadblocks to friendships with and serving to alienate the very blacks whom she wishes to befriend.

Although Mrs. Plum's character may be flat insofar as it is an ideological construct, it does possess psychological complexity—just as the narrative, itself, possesses incredible linguistic richness. On the one hand, Mphahlele's novella deserves to be read in terms of what Bakhtin would see as an embattled arena in which opposing world views are dialogically engaged in a struggle. At the same time, "Mrs Plum" requires to be examined through the hermeneutics of psychological criticism, with primary emphasis placed on the neo-Freudians. Experts in the fields of psychiatry and psychology such as Linda Brown and H. I. J. van der Spuy agree. Brown states: "It seems impossible to understand Mrs. Plum adequately from an individual, intra-psychic perspective" despite the fact her "most outwardly shocking behavior is sexual" (Brown 1996). South African–born psychologist van der Spuy also prefers "to understand her [Mrs. Plum] as being shaped by her times rather than to slap a pathological clinical label on her." In the early 1930s, Karen Horney propounded the neo-Freudian theory that: "Cultural conditions not only lend weight and color to the individual experiences, but in the last analysis may determine their form" (Horney 1937, viii). Behavior in turn is affected, states Horney, not only by "standards of culture," but also by "class, gender, time," as well as external dangers, social relationships, injustice and "enforced dependency" (13–18). Accordingly, conflicting values, life conditions and cultural influence can give rise to anxiety-induced neurotic patterns of behavior.

Regardless of cause, Mrs. Plum, insofar as she is narcissistic, is filled with self-loathing; insofar as she is neurotic, she "is a suffering person" (26). She is in imminent need of psychological attention. Since it would be well-nigh impossible to bill a fictional character, van der Spuy generously agreed to provide such a consultation without fees. In the early 1970s, he conducted an exhaustive survey of white South African youth which found that on the chart of authoritarian personality traits and neuroses, they scored highest in the world, significantly higher than other national test-case groups including Australians, Ghanaians, Americans, and British. Van der Spuy states that the common denominator of these psychological maladjustments was "a higher level of anxiety." He concluded that "legally enforced racial discrimination is just as harmful to those who discriminate as those who are discriminated against" (1974, 197). This seminal study into the "Psychology of South Africa" lends credibility to Mphahlele's psychological probings of his white protagonist and tallies with the text's register of Freudian/neo-Freudian implications.

The author/narrator's grasp of the human psyche as relates to the classic conflict-anxiety-neurosis cluster of maladjustments is impressive, suggesting he has a far better understanding of whites than he intimates. He appears to have had 20/20 vision while peering through the keyhole, and is not surprised to find no one on the other side returning his gaze. As an educator and scholar, as well as someone who has had a psychobiography written about himself, Mphahlele is undoubtedly versed in Freudian/neo-Freudian psychology. In his memoir *Afrika My Music* (1984), Mphahlele twice refers to ideas concerning the paranoid, authoritarian personality based on Eric Fromm's theories. Still, his perceptive handling of his characters' psyches tends to bear out Freud's own disclaimer to the effect that he, Freud, father of psychoanalysis, was not the *de facto* discoverer of the subconscious. Rather, it was the many great writers and poets who preceded him.

Although the themes of alienation and African humanism are the glue that add cohesion, "Mrs Plum" can stand on its own as a well-crafted tale, unified by time, place, and point of view as well as by the author's creative use of linguistic narrative devices. As a *Bildungsroman*, "Mrs Plum" is made up of entire "character zones" in which the narrator/author either imitates or parodies the speech of another. Mphahlele's use of Karabo as first-person narrator adds an intensity of focus that helps further connect various episodes and serves to heighten the reader's emotional involvement. Mphahlele uses the technique of "carnivalesque laughter" in the case of Dick, the garden "boy," to overcome fear or to point out the absurdity of a situation. The discourse also draws on quoted Sesotho phrases, syntax that replicates African dialect, colloquial epithets of the "marketplace," such as the assimilated Afrikaner "voetsek" (a word forbidden by Mrs. Plum), "sies," "ach," "shame," and African exclamatory utterances, such as "woo," "oho," "hei," "hau"; ritualized greetings and folkloric idioms, such as "God sees you true," "daughter of the people," and turns of phrases that idiomatically comment on socioeconomic conditions, such as "the smell, you could fill a hungry belly with it, the way it was good"; and hierarchical forms of address including the ubiquitous "madam." Even the transliterated sound from Sesotho a kicked dog would make lends a realistic touch. Thus, Malan is heard to cry: "tjunk—tjunk—tjunk." As a trilingual narrator (fluent in Sesotho, Afrikaans, and English), Mphahlele is able to draw on these rich linguistic resources in a way neither an Afrikaans nor an English speaker could do. Karabo's self-reflective speech types are democratic and open, in contrast to Mrs. Plum's, which are monologic, patronizing, closed, and self-deceptive. Behind her pious utterances, Mrs. Plum conceals her true state of mind. Her anxiety is hinted at by the fact her eyes are always swollen and she smokes too much. She also argues with her daughter. The tragic detail of her husband's suicide is something van der Spuy would like to explore in greater depth before psychologically labeling Mrs. Plum.

Through her parodied, stylized speech, the narrator's hidden polemic is to persuade true liberals of Mrs. Plum's blatant hypocrisy and moral bankruptcy. Mrs. Plum does not, as a rule, engage in dialogue, but rather she lectures. She is given to addressing Karabo with the patronizing, "you people," denying Karabo her personhood while classifying her in terms of group (as opposed to community). Karabo's speech, embedded throughout with social and cultural values, is presented without "formal markers," allowing for complete identification among narrator/character and reader. Mrs. Plum's authoritarian speech type, by contrast, serves constantly to remind the reader that hers is the voice of the colonizer (a polyphonic effect here in which the author consistently manipulates another's speech to comment on the worldview she symbolizes) addressing the colonized. When Karabo uses the word "boy" to refer to Dick, the gardener, because she learns it from whites, she is treated to a horrified monologic lecture about this politically incorrect usage by Mrs. Plum, the irony of which cannot be missed. The following passage is but one example of the technique of imaging characters through their heterogeneous, multilingual speech styles, without markers, so that we seem to be inside the narrator/character's head. The dialogue includes the use of African oral narrative technique of repetition of certain phrases that signal reported speech. Here Karabo reports her reprimand from Mrs. Plum to her friend Chimane: "I said 'garden boy'. And she says to me she says Stop talking about a 'boy', Karabo. *Now listen here,* she says, *you Africans* must learn to speak properly about each other. And she says *White people won't talk kindly about you* if you look down upon each other. . . . . You'll learn, *my girl.* And you must start in this house, *hear?*" ([emphasis added] Mphahlele 1987, 224). Under such verbal-psychological assaults on her intelligence, adult status, and personhood, Karabo might be expected to question, as she eventually does, "Who am I?" and, more damagingly, to internalize the humiliating mask of submissiveness and inferiority demanded of her while simultaneously being lectured about her rights to equal treatment. Instead, Karabo emerges as a dynamic character, strong and believable, who in the course of the narrative, as she herself says, "grows up." Drawing the reader immediately into the narrative, Karabo is presented from the inside out as well as the outside in as opposed to how black characters, primarily servants, in the past were frequently portrayed by white, liberal writers of the stature of a Nadine Gordimer. As Mphahlele writes in his dissertation: "Miss Gordimer's characters do not talk or think about these relations [with whites]. They simply feel the little world around them narrowing and crowding in on them as a result of their class prejudices, fears and doubts" (1956, 75). Gordimer was not happy about this verdict rendered by Mphahlele on, among other works, her short story "Six Feet Under." When he received "a stinging and indignant letter" from Gordimer expressing her displeasure, Mphahlele, ever the humanist, was sufficiently concerned about the friendship that he lets "scholarship . . . wait in abeyance" while he took time out to write "Nadine" in order to explain (Manganyi 1984, 40).

Petrus, the black "farm boy" in *Six Feet of the Country* rarely speaks unless spoken to and then only in rather laconic one- or two-sentence responses and takes concrete action only once, when he collects money for his deceased brother's exhumation (Gordimer 1987, 7–20). Karabo, by contrast, is a multidimensional personality whose interiority is made accessible through her first-person narrative of the story. The reader is able to get inside Karabo's head, seeing things through her eyes—an African story, told by an African. Not only does Karabo embody the tenets of African humanism, she speaks with its voice. Possibly because of the close identification between her and the author, and the views and values she represents, Karabo is arguably one of Mphahlele's most interesting and successful fictional characters. Her character is successfully developed through the skilled use of idiomatic as well as interior dialogue and in the course of the narrative she undergoes plausible growth and change.

The multicultural critic likes Karabo for her strength and for her distinctive brand of humanism—which includes examples of community involvement, respect for elders, loyalty, and compassion—and admires her for the fact she is also a thoroughly modern woman. Karabo learns, for example, how to assert her economic needs and is inspired early on by the leadership of her sewing teacher Lilian Ngoyi—one of the genuine heroes (profiled earlier by Mphahlele for a *Drum* magazine story) and real-life organizers of the Federation of South African Women (Thompson 1990, 209). Karabo comes to realize the truth of Ngoyi's words in a hard-hitting and realistic talk in which she tells her listeners, "A master and servant can never be friends" (Mphahlele 1987, 227). Karabo also shows a growing political and social awareness and is interested in Ngoyi's vision of what the political future might hold for the majority black population. Despite her hard-headed pragmatism, Ngoyi's vision reflects the inclusiveness and generosity of African humanism as opposed to what might be viewed as a justifiable position of reverse racism on her part (had she taken such a stance) that excluded whites at the helm of government altogether.

If "on one level Lilian Ngoyi serves as a mouthpiece of Mphahlele—her social and political goals may be taken as his," then it is an indicator of Mphahlele's prescience and wisdom that Ngoyi's vision is an almost identical blueprint for what later became the remarkable democratic constitution, freely negotiated by all parties, for the new South Africa (Hodge 1981, 35). Indeed, Ngoyi's words give voice to ANC policy as outlined in the Freedom Charter, which states that "South Africa belongs to all who live in it, black and white, and that no government can justly claim authority unless it is based on the will of all the people" (Benson 1987, 66). Thus, Ngoyi, echoing the aims of the ANC Freedom Charter, says:

> the world would never be safe for black people until they were in the government with the power to make laws. . . . We asked her questions and she answered them with wisdom. . . . Shall we take the place of the white people in the government? Some yes. But we shall be more than they as we are more in the country. But also the people of all colours will come together and there are good white men we can choose and there are Africans some white people will choose to be in the government. (Mphahlele 1987, 226)

By contrast, Mrs. Plum's objective is merely to allow a "few" of the black majority into the government and to insure that they get "more money to do what they do for white men," which, despite her liberal stance, strikes one as being far more feudal and patronizing than truly egalitarian (221). Mrs. Plum, although a self-declared liberal, is in reality not a true democrat. Like the Liberal party itself, which did not change until 1959, she advocates a qualified franchise (Lodge 1990, 87).

In his characterization of Karabo, Mphahlele breaks from stereotypes that grew naturally out of the South African situation. He presents his reader with a character that is neither *shebeen* queen nor standard domestic. His hidden polemic, in this case, is to persuade the black reader of a new aesthetic, a new kind of man or woman that they can become. Karabo represents the "common man" [or woman] in whose "ordinary everyday life" and in whose folk and fundamentally democratic rural roots one can find "the real African personality." In Karabo's essential being, in her compassion and respect for the humanity of the other, is expressed a dynamic "dialogue between two streams of consciousness: the present and the living past" (Mphahlele 1974, 70). Karabo is also an example in her life of what Mphahlele means when he says in his most pragmatic voice: "Our humanism must bring about the second productive revolution. . . . Instead of shouting about African values, we should translate them into educational and economic planning" (Mphahlele 1974, 36).

Although Karabo serves as the female counterpart to the theme "Jim goes to Johannesburg," unlike either "Jim" or even Sylvia Direko in Mphahlele's earlier story "Unwritten Episodes" from *Man Must Live* (1946), she is no naïve, hapless victim from the rural areas whose morals are corrupted and who fails to make a go of it in the city. Although employed as a domestic, she is not conventional in the sense of being "obsequious and almost inconspicuous" (Hansen 1989, 248). Instead, Karabo "is a vital part of the continuum from past to future in Mphahlele's African Humanism, an "answer" to the severe problems involved in the clash of traditional—modern, rural—urban values" (Hodge 1981, 37). Despite the risks involved, Karabo finds opportunity early on to affirm her self-respect while asserting her economic independence. She has, for example, already left two previous jobs in the white suburbs of Johannesburg, once in Parktown North where her employers drank too much and forgot to pay her, making it difficult to contribute to the support of her aging parents in Phokeng, and; a second time in Belgravia where she was sexually harassed.

The first part of "Mrs Plum" details Karabo's life in Johannesburg over a period of three years, while the latter half of the narrative shifts from the painful, and sometimes humorous episodes of daily life to the tragic mode of loss and suffering. Perhaps one of the most frightening and anxiety-generating of the many forms of alienation confronted by either blacks or whites in this conflicted tale is what Mphahlele identifies as the "consuming fear of annihilation" or "spiritual extinction" (Manganyi 1983, 132). Several key factors contribute to this sense of being annihilated or swallowed up, a fear Mphahlele is able to describe vividly because he has personally experienced it. Among them is the fact that Karabo "is a migrant labourer and faces the fragmented sensibility of an exile." Furthermore, as a black migrant worker she enjoys almost no worker's rights. Even though she has had previous work experience she is, nonetheless, in madam's home—in an alien space with unfamiliar routines, "unknown artifacts and procedures and [the need] . . . to cope with a different classification of reality" (Ruth 1986, 83). At the same time, the Madam has even less knowledge of Karabo's home and her cultural and personal ways of being. Thus, there is no chance of finding "myself in another by finding another in myself (in mutual reflection and mutual acceptance)" (Danow 1991, 59).

This, then, is the sociopolitical, cultural, and psychological context in which the story's conflict arises. Karabo receives a letter from home informing her of her uncle's death. She requests leave, but is refused and is told if she does take leave it must be without pay. Why, Mrs. Plum asks, must Karabo go, since the uncle died three days previously. Because, responds Karabo, "My uncle loved me very much. . . . [and] to take my tears and words of grief to his grave and to my aunt, madam" (255). Karabo in this statement personifies the African humanist showing compassion for her aunt and respect for her ancestors as well as love for her uncle. Karabo's humanism stands in dramatic contrast to Mrs. Plum's materialism and her concern, like that of so many others in the exploitative South African economy, for the trinity of "power, prestige, and possessions," a concern first identified by Horney as defining the neurotic. Displaying little interest in understanding Karabo's culture or personal needs, Mrs. Plum's chief concerns are her own personal convenience and the issue of money. Although Mrs. Plum espouses equal rights and respect for blacks as a group, she fails to apply this value at the individual level. Yet as an activist she is all the while writing books, attending meetings, and doubtless "verbalizing all the complaints of the blacks beautifully while skillfully extracting what suits [her] from the exclusive pool of white privileges" (Gerhart 1979, 264). In her inability to recognize Karabo's cultural, spiritual, and psychological needs to grieve in ways that are both traditional and community based as well as her

rights to reasonable pay and leave as a valued employee, Mrs. Plum is denying Karabo a separate identity other than one of inferiority and dependency. Mrs. Plum suffers from a moral blind spot which enables her to
espouse liberal ideals with great conviction on the stump while behaving
like a feudal lord at home. She is an example of the failure of white liberal
vision insofar as "it could never provide a solution because it failed to take
into consideration the African's spiritual plight" (Gerhart 1979, 271). To
quote van der Spuy:

> Mrs. Plum appears to me to be a typical product of her time and a
> good example of the so-called liberal South Africans of the 50s, 60s
> and 70s. These people were usually rich capitalists and not really liber-
> als at all. In Britain they probably would have been right-wing conser-
> vatives. It was only in the rather weird South African political
> spectrum that they were called liberals. Although they wanted to get
> rid of the more repressive aspects of apartheid, there was a definite
> limit as to how far they would accept blacks as fully equal humans: the
> possibility of her [Mrs. Plum's] daughter marrying a black was quite
> unacceptable to her. The daughter of course was of a younger genera-
> tion with the resulting generation gap and clash. (1997, 1)

The absence of mutual respect and lack of equality in the relationship,
both at the employer-employee and personal levels, is indicated by Mrs.
Plum's failure to listen. In the first instance, Mrs. Plum's denial of Karabo's
request for leave time to attend the funeral of her much-beloved uncle illustrates Mrs. Plum's ignorance of kinship practices in the African community network, which reflects an underlying lack of interest in blacks as
people, despite her stated interest in promoting their well being. Since this
favored uncle is also Karabo's mother's brother, he occupies an important
position in the extended family structure. Moreover, in African society, such
funerals are an important rite of passage. Mrs. Plum, however, refuses to listen or understand, turning a deaf ear to Karabo's request for leave. A narcis-
sist, Mrs. Plum experiences as real only what exists within, while external
phenomena have no reality for her. Confronted with Mrs. Plum's inflexibil-
ity, Karabo then does the unexpected. She leaves.

Thus alienation takes the form of cross-cultural conflict, the self-
centered materialism of the white liberal, and a total breakdown in understanding and communication. In the end, however, it is Karabo who triumphs, for Mrs. Plum in an unprecedented gesture drives herself all the way
to Phokeng, finding a villager to guide her to Karabo's house. Mrs. Plum

then swallows enough of her pride to ask Karabo to return to work, although she offers no apology. Although her motives are, no doubt, to some extent self-serving, there is a glimmer of humanity in Mrs. Plum's implicit need, after the mysterious disappearance of her two dogs Monty and Malan, for human companionship. At the same time, she is beginning to see Karabo in a different light as Karabo commences to establish boundaries in their relationship.

Karabo's self-empowering departure and Mrs. Plum's drive to the village are important first steps in the promise of a changing new relationship. When Karabo eventually agrees to return, Mrs. Plum "was very much pleased and looked kinder than I have ever known her" (261). But Karabo does not agree immediately. First, she establishes a set of guidelines, thus asserting her own human needs and employee rights and managing the negotiation. Then, she consults with her parents as a courtesy and in the manner of a well-brought-up African showing respect to elders. Finally, she negotiates both a higher salary and more liberal leave time.

"Mrs Plum," therefore, is a story not merely of alienation and suffering under a brutal system, but of survival and hope. Karabo overcomes alienation by affirming African values and adopting some Western ones. For example, she identifies and clearly states her needs and rights, and advocates for her own economic empowerment. Through her and other liberated characters, such as Lilian Ngoyi, Mphahlele gives flesh, bones, and voice to a form of political resistance involving cultural affirmations and education. Indeed, the episode just described is illustrative of Mphahlele's belief stated in his own dissertation that

> there are a great number of things in the traditional social codes of the African—also reflected in his political organization—which it would be a pity to lose. There are beautiful behaviour patterns within the family, in public gatherings, during festivals like communal harvesting and so on. These, together with . . . the whole structure of African traditional life which places the accent on "being"—could tone down and supplement the white man's highly acquisitive urges. (1956, 45)

Mrs. Plum would benefit from greater knowledge of African traditional life, by having her "acquisitive urges" toned down and by placing the accent on "being" rather than doing. Apartheid has robbed her of her Western humanism. In its place she has donned a mask of unfeeling pride, her discourse marked by cant and sanctimony. It has also warped her moral fiber. As Bakhtin has observed, there is little chance of full spiritual realization of self without "other": to be is to communicate. Karabo, on the other hand, has obviously profited by learning both from Lilian Ngoyi and Mrs. Plum to be a bit more acquisitive; to articulate her needs, both personal and economic. It is a promising symbiotic exchange that stands to enlarge both participants. Ideologically, it might even be viewed as a recipe for a national melting pot in which the whole is greater and richer than the sum of its parts.

As a story charged with bluntness and anger, "Mrs Plum" anticipates and affirms Black Consciousness through the linking of Karabo's consciousness of self with black pride and emancipation, while affirming the black community's "value systems, their culture, their religion and their outlook on life" (Thompson 1990, 212). Black Consciousness, according to Biko, "implies a desire to engage people in an emancipatory process, in an attempt to free one from a situation of bondage" (1979, 141). Biko believed that part of this process called for making a break with white liberals, especially those pressing blacks for dialogue. In addition to being oppressed by external forces such as exploitative labor conditions, of which Karabo and millions like her serve as a case study, Biko believed blacks were oppressed psychologically and were in a state of self-alienation (22).

Since Black Consciousness came into its own in South Africa in the early 1970s and "Mrs Plum" was published in the late 1960s, the novella is arguably on the cutting edge of Black Consciousness literature. It may accurately be viewed as an early pioneering expression of black pride and consciousness, one that exercises greater restraint, without necessarily sacrificing greater effect, than is seen, for example, in the raw wounds and gunshot expletives that characterize the early works of poet Mongane Wally Serote. Jane Watts states that the "evolution of black consciousness in South Africa" owes much to "the ideas broadcast long before by Ezekiel Mphahlele" and that Mphahlele's "exploration of the function of culture ran so closely parallel to the practical aspirations of the black consciousness writers that it is difficult not to assume that a number of them had read his critical writings, banned though they were" (Watts 1989, 86). But Mphahlele is never just an ideologue—the resistance of the alienated writer is balanced by the affirmation of the African humanist. In "Mrs Plum," the "ironic meeting between protest and acceptance," between Africa and the West, finds a meeting point in the person of Karabo and in her reclaiming of self (Mphahlele 1959, 217). The key that unlocks the process, Mphahlele seems to suggest, is self-transforming knowledge through education rather than Fanon's prescribed violent revolution. Like Gandhi and King, Mphahlele, the democratic author utilizing folk culture to flesh out his hidden polemic, also believes in building on the existing culture and in the need for elements of continuity in the process of political and social transformation.

In Karabo's case, self-knowledge is preceded by a disturbing identity crisis, lending support to Biko's idea that psychological oppression leads to fragmentation and self-alienation. Karabo is sickened by "the smell of madam" and the "dirt from Madam's body." Here Mphahlele uses "meiosis," or the "lowering of metaphors to their physical origins" and words such as "bodily filth" and "stain" related to excretory functions to suggest the rottenness and depravity of the system and to demystify Mrs. Plum's white-divine status as well as to symbolize Karabo's spiritual degradation. Karabo, disgusted, throws away all the cosmetics she owns that are the same as madam's (symbolically affirming her own self-worth, separate identity, and value system) and finally looks into the mirror and wonders "is this Karabo, this?" (247–48) Karabo's crisis is defined by a sense of "spiritual extinction," of metaphysical dread and pathological anxiety. Her crisis occurs because there is so little that confirms or acknowledges either a servant's or a black's identity, and so much that devalues it. Her crisis centers around the conflict and fear of loss of self in a relationship at once too intimate and too distant, based on artifice (cosmetics), distorted values (the mirror), and hypocrisy. Karabo's emerging independent self is jeopardized by her childlike status and Mrs. Plum's patronage. The artifice of the mask, of cosmetics, suggests a sense of dislocation, of inner versus outer reality, the danger of becoming the "other." Nevertheless, Karabo is saved because she continues to grow and learn. She is ultimately able through her new self-knowledge, based on past experience and the guidance of mentors like Ngoyi, to choose whom she wants to be, symbolized by her throwing out the cosmetics. She can draw strength, moreover, from her African support system—a circle of friends and extended family that stands out in dramatic contrast to Mrs. Plum's rather pathetic isolation.

Karabo's terrifying and diminishing sense of loss of personal identity is reinforced by frequent breakdowns in communication between black and white; employer and employee (of which there is either too much—and it is one-sided, didactic, and superior—or too little). Thus, there are failures in communication (linked to class, culture, or generation) between Mrs. Plum and Karabo, Dick and Mrs. Plum, Kate and Karabo, Karabo and other English-speaking blacks, and whites and blacks in general. Such failures lead to stereotypical thinking which, in turn, produces fear, conflict, and violence. Mrs. Plum frequently underestimates or fails to notice Karabo's wit and humor, and her grasp of issues. Although she readily defends Karabo's and black people's right to have a say in government, she patronizingly assumes a need to speak on their behalf. The respect articulated becomes an abstract principle, not an internalized reality. Mrs. Plum, as her daughter Kate tells Karabo, is a member of Black Sash, a white liberal women's organization. She writes books, holds English classes for servants, and attends many meetings on behalf of Karabo's people. Karabo wonders, in turn, why Kate's mother finds it necessary to speak for her people who "are in Phokeng far away. They have got mouths, I say. Why does she want to say something for them? Does she know what my mother and what my father want to say?" (221).

This tongue-in-cheek observation was echoed nearly two decades later ("Mrs Plum" was written in Paris in the early 1960s) by Biko who stated that liberal whites pressing blacks for dialogue "are the greatest racists because they refuse to credit us with intelligence to know what we want" (1979, 299). Mrs. Plum fits the description. She is exactly the sort of white liberal who, Nadine Gordimer says, sees but does not see. Although these liberals "don't want to be boss," they "have become used to being bossy" in their role as tutors, guardians, and spokesmen on behalf of the right of Africans as a group to enjoy free expression and the franchise (Gordimer 1988, 35).

Mrs. Plum is not only a typical "bossy" white liberal activist, but as the author of books and tracts she is, unlike her black counterparts, free to distribute these at her pleasure and without fear of reprisals. There may be a subliminal need at work here for Mphahlele to twit the white liberal writer who, as he points out in his essays *Voices in the Whirlwind* (1972), "can still get away with a lot in South Africa. A black man who wrote the same things . . . who represented the same liberal and egalitarian ideas, would most likely be banned" (Mphahlele 1972, 214).

Mphahlele, writing in the early 1970s, remarks that while it was true that travel restrictions were placed on Paton and Athol Fugard, their works were not banned. Nor was Gordimer restricted, although two of her books were banned. Gordimer, addressing the censorship issue in a talk presented in 1980, herself refers to the release from banning of her novel *Burger's Daughter* along with André Brink's *A Dry White Season* and a volume (just in time for Easter, she wryly notes) by Afrikaans writer Etienne le Roux. These releases were a part of a new "reform" strategy in censorship. Yet the Censorship Act remained in place, unaltered on the statute books. As Gordimer states, the release from banning of books by liberal whites carried the "sinister implication" that white liberals "can be bought off by special treatment" since books by blacks were not being accorded similar treatment (Gordimer 1988, 250–51). Such inequities feeding intellectual apartheid no doubt aggravated Mphahlele's own sense of disaffection, frustration and alienation. Thus, he has a certain amount of perverse pleasure poking fun at Mrs. Plum's writing endeavors. Karabo, for example, wants to know why her madam is "always writing on the machine," and Dick, the gardener, would sometimes do humorous imitations of Madam at the table writing, in effect using carnivalesque laughter and mimicry to break down formalities of hierarchy (221).

Mrs. Plum, as a symbol, takes the flak for Black Sash, members of the white liberal writing establishment and possibly even Mrs. Hoernle, a prominent liberal who played a part in Mphahlele's dismissal from Orlando High, and who in her "liberal arrogance" provided the smoke and mirrors to cover a witch hunt to get rid of Mphahlele after his protest against the Bantu Education Act (Manganyi 1983, 104). The theme of the alienated writer is but one of several significant examples of themes of alienation that serve as catalysts for subsequent intertextual themes of alienation. The boiling anger and frustration Mphahlele no doubt feels is vented like steam off a pressure valve in the story and person of Mrs. Plum, the white liberal book-writing, political activist invariably operating within the letter of the law. Ironically, Mrs. Plum as a character is just the sort of person in real life whom white readers are most inclined to admire—high-minded, hard-working, devoted to a cause. She is also reform-minded, highly ordered, and puritanical in her ostensibly strict and closely regulated habits of life. Unlike Dick, whose "large mouth is always making ready to laugh," Mrs. Plum is, in the Freudian sense, anal retentive and intrapunitive with an urge to dominate that is infantile in origin.

The glimpse through the keyhole reveals the shocking truth behind the public image—even though this view is a symbolically restricted one just as Karabo's own view of Mrs. Plum is limited by misunderstanding, unequal status, and a relationship of close proximity in which nonetheless Karabo is at best nothing more than what Karen Hansen in her book by the same title refers to as a "distant companion." The keyhole as a symbol of black/white alienation "is an extraordinarily rich metaphor with complex implications to do with spatial access and spatial control, containment and penetration, mysteries and insight, and of course the channeling of vision, partial vision and perspective" (Ruth 1986, 76). In reality, Karabo does not know the person behind the madam (although she has more insights on this score than her employer does about her) just as the madam does not know or understand the person behind the maid. But the glimpse into truth the reader eventually obtains through the keyhole suggests that behind superficial appearances of normalcy lies a sick reality.

Then come the shock tactics that galvanize the reader into a more prob-
ing assessment of the story and its meaning. Because Mphahlele is notably
restrained in the use of sex and violence throughout his writing, there is additional impact to the readers' riveting glimpse through the keyhole where
they make the voyeuristic and disturbing discovery that Mrs. Plum is masturbating with her dog Malan. Bestiality was the last thing the reader had
come to expect or was prepared for, especially from the exemplary Mrs.
Plum. After the high-voltage shock comes the belly laugh—at an author
who pulls off rather effectively what amounts to the literary equivalent of a
practical joke. Grotesque realism breaks down barriers, degrades, and in-
verts, in a carnivalesque fashion, "received social categories" (Gardiner 1992,
46–47).

Mphahlele rightly assesses the enormous built-in potential for irony inherent in the fact that such a raw, brutish, disgusting scene was apt to prove
more shocking to potential white readership and play greater havoc with
their Judeo-Christian sense of morality than the portrayal of brutality to
blacks, which had become almost a commonplace. Mphahlele has manipu-
lated symbols to allow "the repressed" as well as the oppressed "a measure of
representation" (Crews 1970, 13). This is the act of a lettered and humane
revolutionary with a down-to-earth sense of humor who does not throw
bombs, but who chooses to make his points in other ways. After laughter
comes the shuddering aftershock in the chilling realization that we have
reached what Ruth describes as

> a realm laced with the evidence of psychosis. The paranoia that whites
> show over their pets and which leads to Dick's dismissal is psycholog-
> ically consistent with psychosis. Mphahlele has structured the story in
> terms of recent psychoanalytic theory. From an era of neurosis we
> have been moved to a concern with the narcissistic phase marked by
> images of mirrors and cosmetics and ultimately masturbation, charac-
> terized by rapid reversals from one side of the keyhole to the other,
> which is followed by paranoia. (1986, 82)

According to psychiatry the cause of such bizarre ritualized, narcissistic,
compulsive-obsessive psychoneuroses may include not only deep-seated
anxiety, but also socioeconomic and cultural factors. Mrs. Plum is clearly
caught in the grip of an irreconcilable inner conflict between her strong
desire to have the competitive edge as "baas" and her equal but contradictory wish to gratify her desire for "belongingness," in this instance with the
black majority whose cause she champions. There is, moreover, a primal
conflict at work between Mrs. Plum's head and her heart—what she believes

and what she feels; what she professes in terms of egalitarian liberal values of "love," "brotherhood," and "justice" and what she actually does, which is made even more complex by the guilt she feels as a privileged white. Additional layers of tension are added by cross-cultural conflicts and lack of understanding between whites and blacks, in this instance as represented by Mrs. Plum and Karabo, due in part to class differences and geographic separation. Inner conflict and socioeconomic and cultural fault lines are further stressed by the ever-present potential for violence and political instability that infuses the social climate with an insistent low-grade tension.

Neo-Freudians such as Fromm and Horney aver there is a direct link between culture and personality disturbance. Therefore, ethnic groups, organizations, class position, urbanization, dramatic changes in social codes, and "prejudicial attitudes toward minority groups affect the development and content of neuroses." The very fact Mrs. Plum does not believe blacks should govern or be allowed an equal franchise suggests the presence of deep-seated bias that takes the form of white patronage and ultimately of narcissistic neurosis as Mrs. Plum turns her inner conflicts and her frustrated desire to belong and to care for someone inward.

In Mrs. Plum's efforts to resolve her conflict-induced anxiety, she falls prey to obsessive-compulsive responses that focus on "sexually perverse impulses," and which in turn induce fear (Trosman 1967, 296–98). To relieve this fear she engages in the aberrant ritualized act with Malan. To justify a preexisting sense of guilt, she masochistically commits an unspeakable act. The act carries self-pollution and contamination to a logical extreme, playing on post-Victorian anxieties centering on purity and loss of control. Like Freud, Mphahlele seems to be saying that mankind has no right to think it is so civilized it is no longer a member of the animal kingdom. The irony is profound, since white liberals define "civilization" exclusively in terms of Western values.

Of course, the not-so-coincidentally named dog Malan symbolizes apartheid, taking its name from D. F. Malan, one of its chief architects, who claimed that Afrikaners had been "divinely appointed to their task" of governance of South Africa and that they could lay "historical claim" to having founded "South African civilization" (De Villiers 1987, 247). In view of such a mindset, it is not surprising that Mphahlele feels inspired to resurrect national myths and African values in the form of African humanism. To counter the myth of Afrikaner nationalism and its claim to civilization, there was a need to assert a powerful and empowering myth that affirmed in equally unequivocal terms the civilization being denied to blacks. White liberals were inclined to be so entrenched in abstract ideals on behalf of the group that they tended to lose sight of individual blacks and their purely human needs. In the process liberal whites tended, moreover, to lose sight of their own essential humanity, as we see both literally and figuratively in the story of Mrs. Plum. The Afrikaner nationalists had forfeited their own claims to a humanistic culture—since to do violence to the other is to do violence to one's own humanity. In effect, Mphahlele steps into the void by affirming the values that blacks have been denied and that whites have lost. Accordingly, the emphasis is placed on caring, compassion, kinship, the valuing of people over things—whether material goods that fostered the greed of apartheid economics or abstractions of the sort to which liberals like Mrs. Plum are wedded, frequently at the cost of "heart."

It is also not surprising that Mphahlele was attracted to a cosmology that would establish his separate identity from the Christian church with which white liberalism as well as Afrikaner nationalism was associated. Finally, it is to Mphahlele's lasting credit as thinker and visionary that he recognized in the retrieval of African myths, values, and modes of behavior a means to reclaim history as well as alienated black youth and the rural masses. Beyond its cultural and historic appeal, Mphahlele sees African humanism as a powerful unifying tool serving "to critique" the barbarism of the West and "the new order" of state apartheid while reaffirming the ancient indigenous civilization and the rich culture of Africa (Bravo 1991, 60). In a very real, positive, and historically significant sense, Mphahlele himself becomes a cultural nationalist and liberator, well in the vanguard of such other notable political leaders and thinkers as Biko.

In "Mrs Plum," Mphahlele has made a strong, unforgettable political statement that is heavily underscored with Black Consciousness thought and aesthetics. Like all great literature it "typically invites us to undergo a symbolic process of self-confrontation" (Crew 1970, 19). The fact that Mrs. Plum, a white liberal, masturbates with Malan, metaphorically suggests that she and, by extension, the white liberal establishment are masturbating with the system—lending it credibility through their outspoken but measured criticism, their organized protest within the letter of the law, their advocacy of a qualified franchise, and their implicit endorsement of "universal" Eurocentric values, while never posing any serious threat to the system's continued existence. As Coetzee's magistrate suggests, "I was the lie that Empire tells itself when times are easy" (1980, 135).

Thus, in a conflicted atmosphere of ambivalence, contamination and fear, we glimpse the white liberal through the keyhole and are shocked and surprised to discover that behind the Christian asceticism and pride, there lurks a pervert and hypocrite. It is the jaundiced, unvarnished, restricted view as seen though the keyhole (for contact has always been limited between black and whites) by an alienated and angry but never totally humorless or uncaring author. There is a break between feeling and function—even the dogs are things to be possessed in a world that is solely object oriented. While poking fun at Judeo-Christian ethics, Mphahlele seizes control of his own image-making. The shock tactics work effectively to make the reader reflect on the warped perversity of the white liberal's stance as well as the brutish immorality of the system of state apartheid symbolized by Malan, not to mention the equally perverted coupling of the Afrikaner nationalist and the English-speaking liberal—or, in Freudian terms, the white liberals' "family romance" with the Boers.

Although critic Ursula Barnett dismisses the episode of bestiality with a fastidious shrug (perhaps of distaste or denial) as being "completely out of character," such dismissal is tantamount to endorsing as true the predictably stereotypical character of the do-gooder upright white liberal (Barnett 1976, 109). But the yardstick of consistency, predictability, and normalcy does not necessarily apply in the South African context. The author seems to be telling his reader that where the system is sick and dysfunctional, the people frequently are, too. Deviant or excessive behavior is a symptom of the alienation that afflicts the oppressor as much as if not more than the oppressed.

Mphahlele is intensely obsessed with dogs. Dogs are a lightning rod for his despair and his hatred of white oppression. The issue of dogs in Mphahlele's novella is critical to the understanding that the conflict and alienation that exists between blacks and whites affects not only questions of fundamental civil liberties, which are Mrs. Plum's chief concern, but the whole of the black person's humanity. It is the hurtful rejection and debasement that is felt when black men are called "boy," when there are "dogs with names and men without," and when dogs, with maddening perversity, enjoy greater luxury and privilege than people do (234). Indeed, white farmers have been known to kill farm laborers over the death of dogs and to receive light sentences while the uncompensated widow is left as the sole means of support of several small children (Tsedu 1991, 6).

Thus, in winter, when white suburbanites from Johannesburg travel to Durban for the holidays, dogs in effect become as Karabo wryly observes, "the masters and madams. You could see them walk like white people in the streets. Silent but with plenty of power" (Mphahlele 1987, 238). That kind of conduct by white liberals toward dogs followed to its logical conclusion leads to perversion. Mphahlele describes in realistic detail the rich, fat, beribboned comforts enjoyed by Mrs. Plum's Monty and Malan. "Mrs Plum," the bridge between Mphahlele's short stories and his first novel, *The*

Wanderers (1971), was in part inspired by watching the "French upper class ladies with their pets [who] could, in a way that Nigerians could not, remind me about the dehumanizing potential of class privilege" (Manganyi 1983, 218).

In this case, class and color are inextricably linked. Although unstated, it is clearly understood that the luxuries enjoyed by Mrs. Plum's dogs are not often enjoyed by the average black person, let alone by Dick, the gardener, whose job it is to look after Monty and Malan and the garden. Dick fears whites, but he is also "long hearted" and, recognizing the fundamental absurdity in the situation, he knows how to laugh (231). Dick says to Karabo that "one day those white people will put ear rings and toe rings and bangles on their dogs. That would be the day he would leave Mrs Plum. For, he said, he was sure she would want him to polish the rings and bangles with brasso" (232). A part of the perversion that occurs in the disproportionate distribution of wealth, privilege, and power is a corruption of values in all areas of life. There is no sense of proportion or of appropriate priorities. There is no common sense. There is no heart. There is instead a desperate yearning for genuine affection, which has been somewhere lost in the pursuit of material goods. Thus, dogs are lavished with the affection of children in a manner that is both funny and grotesque. The issue of how whites treat blacks as compared to how they treat their dogs is raised several times in *Down Second Avenue* and finally and definitively is dealt with in "Mrs Plum."

If the keyhole is a metaphor for alienation, the frequent mention of "heart" and use of such idiomatic phrases as "long-hearted" to describe Dick equally stands as a metaphor for African humanism—so that metaphoric language as well as style, characters, and themes, all reflect the tension and polarity between alienation and African humanism that are the warp and woof of the text and that are extant in society at large.

Norman Hodge suggests that "heart" is the "dominant image of the story." Although the reader only knows how Mrs. Plum and Kate think, we know how Karabo both thinks and how she feels about events as they transpire. Mrs. Plum and Kate are less than human because they only think; Karabo, on the other hand, is fully human because she has a heart as well as a mind. Apartheid itself is heartless, dehumanizing, and inhumane. The answer, the author seems to say, is to fight back affirming the very humanity being denied, which ironically exists in greater abundance with blacks than whites. Though I cannot agree with Hodge that the "heart" symbol serves as the only didactic function in the story, it is true that the story does center on the "heart" symbol more than any other, including the obverse symbol of the keyhole. As Hodge notes, those who have a "heart that can carry a long way," *pelo e telle,* show a basic humanism through their compassion for others; those who have a "short heart" or "no heart no sense" are dehumanized, more like machines than human beings. When Dick is unjustly sent away by Mrs Plum, who fears that he might poison her dogs, Karabo has an "open sore" in her heart; ironically, Dick is one of the innocents of the world, one who has a "long heart". One might say that for Mphahlele "heart" represents African humanism, the only alternative to violence (Hodge 1981, 42).

Thus, the pendulum swings back and forth between the "heart" of African humanism and the "keyhole" of alienation, each of which serves an important "didactic function" as well as an artistic one. It is characteristic of Mphahlele's humanism that the pendulum is consistently weighted in the direction of "heart," to which there are repeated references in the text.

In addition to racial, spiritual and psychological forms of alienation, blacks, as the story suggests, have long been treated as dispossessed, displaced aliens in their own country. They are caught in the limbo of being deprived of productive farm land in the country, while they are also unwelcome in the city unless they have verifiable jobs and carry one of the hated "daampasses" (damn passes). When the police come around to search servants' quarters, looking for men without passes, Mrs. Plum, in a rather humorous episode showing considerable pluck, turns the garden hose on them (241). She is then sentenced either to pay a fine or go to jail. The irony here is that Mrs. Plum decides to suffer out a jail term over so trivial a matter because a principle is involved while refusing to confront the larger issues altogether.

Furthermore, Mrs. Plum can afford her gesture of defiance because she is protected by the very system she challenges. When Mrs. Plum returns from jail, she is quiet and looks unhappy, suggesting that she is, at a deeper level, aware of the discrepancy between her act and her true feelings—an absence of ethical integration and personal authenticity.

Nevertheless, later she does not hesitate to fire Dick whom she mistrusts and fears will harm the dogs—this, on the basis of a rumor circulating that servants had plans to poison white people's dogs (and possibly even the dogs' owners as well)—indicative of the level of paranoia among Johannesburg whites. Although servants and slaves did occasionally poison their masters, Mrs. Plum fails realistically to assess the threat on the basis of any understanding of Dick's true character. So cruel and unfeeling does her firing of Dick appear in light of Dick's true nature and his generosity that

Mrs. Plum appears cast in the mold of the castrating white female, motivated by a sense of primal ambivalence—blacks are useful, but, also, threatening. Whites like Mrs. Plum ironically feel threatened by the very system designed to insure their feudal privilege and comfort. "The psychic valve of projecting one's abusing tendencies on others is obvious" (Horney 1937, 186). To add to the irony, the human and very real needs of the individual black person, on behalf of whose community Mrs. Plum spent time in jail, are ignored. To Mrs. Plum, principles count more than people. This time, however, not only humanitarian concerns, but also the liberal principle of "innocent until proven guilty" is sacrificed.

Karabo, under close questioning from her employer, reassures Mrs. Plum that Dick is, in fact, a "long-hearted" person, a genuinely good, bighearted man who is totally harmless. Karabo's assurances, however, carry no weight. Mrs. Plum is so caught up in causes and so unaware of people as individuals that she fails to notice that Dick is the sort who sends home all his pay in order to support a much beloved younger sister. Because she is so heartless and because principles concern her more than people, Mrs. Plum represents the very antithesis of the African humanist for whom people are paramount to places and things.

One of the most poignant episodes in the novella—an episode that is the very paradigm of themes of alienation and African humanism—reads like a case history of the devastating socioeconomic and cultural impact of apartheid, verifying the truth of Fanon's statement that "for a colonized people the most essential value" is "the land which will bring them bread, and above all, dignity" (1963, 44). Karabo's friend Chimane who works as a maid next door falls pregnant and resorts to an abortionist in the black township of Alexandra because she cannot afford both to support her aging parents—who are totally dependent on her earnings since they no longer own their own small plot of land—and keep the child. Thus, Chimane's parents have been denied their dignity and Chimane her own child. In the old days, the grandparents would have cared for such a child on their small plot. Karabo listens, supports, and cares. She also takes time out of her own limited leave to pay Chimane a visit at the abortionist in Alexandra, a harrowing experience.

Karabo exemplifies the compassion of the practicing African humanist; just as she did previously in gossip exchanged with Chimane over the back fence, providing news round-ups of people at home—mentioning father, mother, sisters, teachers, friends—that illustrate the inclusiveness of African society which is "implicit in all tenets of African humanist thought" along with "mutual aid, acceptance . . . co-operativism, egalitarianism, . . . respect for human dignity, respect for age and for authority and hospitality" (Mee-belo 1973, 11). Karabo demonstrates the tenet of mutual aid and cooperation when she collects money to help Chimane pay for the abortion. Karabo's humanism is juxtaposed to the selfishness displayed by Chimane's employer who forces her own mother-in-law to cook on separate facilities and gives the cat preference in the use of the only chair in one of the living areas.

Mphahlele is in the vanguard in addressing feminist issues of marriage rights in his novel *Chirundu* (1980) and abortion issues in "Mrs Plum." By blurring fact and fiction, the author/narrator holds himself and the reader responsible, fulfilling Bakhtin's axiom that: "Art and life are not one, but should become one in me, in the unity of my responsibility" (Danow 1991, 59).

He provides a grimly realistic description of Chimane's abortion as well as an explanation for its underlying causes, which is an indictment of both the system of apartheid as well as the skewed priorities of white liberals like Mrs. Plum. Prior to February 1997, abortion in South Africa was illegal with the result that, according to Margerie Sithole, a nurse at Baragwanath hospital, "Women come here with their uteruses in tatters after back-street abortions" (1997, A17). The painful and dangerous procedure involves the use of a long, sharp needle in order, as Chimane's aunt—the contrapuntal voice of the African past—puts it, for "a worm to cut the roots." Nor is any anesthetic provided, causing Karabo to swear in compassion on the "spirits of our forefathers" (250). Just as Chimane is a victim of the system, the township with its lawless *tsotsi* culture is another of its products and helps to set the stage. Karabo describes how she finds Chimane in bed "in that terrible township where night and day are full of knives and bicycle chains and guns and the barking of hungry dogs and of people in trouble. I held my heart in my hands. She was in pain and her face, even in the candlelight, was grey" (249). In the old days when Chimane's parents still owned a small plot of land, they would have been able to provide for Chimane's child, sparing Chimane both the pain and the indignity of her loss, but this is no longer the case.[1] Moreover, it is clear that Chimane is exploited and powerless as an underpaid worker. Thus, we see the far-reaching and devastating socioeconomic effects of apartheid, which, in turn, lead to a breakdown in personal values and family structure.

That evening Mrs. Plum and Kate discuss the prospect of a plan by whites to purchase a dog cemetery so dogs like "Monty and Malan could be sure of a nice burial" (250). In short, blacks must suffer economic deprivation, the loss of human dignity, even the loss of a child's life because the land was taken from them, but dogs will be buried on precious urban land in posh pet cemeteries—a situation surely as warped and perverse as Mrs. Plum's bestiality.

Karabo experiences both alienation and friendship in the course of her "growing up" as a domestic working for whites in the metropolis of Johannesburg. Initially, it appears that she and Mrs Plum's daughter, Kate, might become friends. They are the same age and there is a seeming rapport. But the employee/employer relationship and the unequal levels of education as well as the fact that Kate and Karabo are attracted to the same young black doctor which makes Kate seem like a thief to Karabo—like "a fox that falls upon a flock of sheep at night"—all prevent the realization of true friendship (237). For the foreseeable future, it would appear that the romantic conflict, not to mention class differences based on socioeconomic status and education, present too great a chasm to be easily and immediately bridged by age and mutual liking.

An unbridgeable distance also exists with the English-speaking blacks Mrs. Plum entertains who are better educated and from a different socioeconomic class than Karabo. Yet Mrs. Plum also objects to Kate's marrying a black, even from this class, an objection that leads to intergenerational conflict. Here are still more levels of alienation—one based on the generation gap; the other on black on black, stemming from social, economic, and educational origins rather than racial ones. Karabo, being sensitive and intelligent, is aware of the discrepancy and under a more equitable system she realizes she, too, might have enjoyed the benefits of an education and a better life and, perhaps, even the love she now longs for. As it is, she knows she is no match for the young black doctor she likes and admires. In this area, she can never compete with Kate. The pain of Karabo's alienation becomes almost palpable as she says:

> I shall never forget that night, as long as I live. He spoke kind words and I felt my heart grow big inside me. It caused me to tremble. There were several other visits. I knew that I loved him, I could never know what he thought of me, I mean as a woman and he as a man. But I loved him, and I still think of him with a sore heart. Slowly I came to know the pain of it. Because he was a doctor and so full of knowledge and English I could not reach him (236).

Sorrow, however, is balanced by laughter; pain and loss by affirmation and caring. Another key identifying feature of the African humanist way of life is hospitality, generosity, and sharing, whether in good fortune or bad. As Henry S. Meebelo notes: "Hospitality, by implication, is a negation of selfishness. It was part of the general communalist social code in the traditional society and the altruism which was manifest in African hospitality among other aspects, impressed the European observer" (1973, 7). There is irony, humor, and survivor strategy seen in the manner in which some of the aforementioned tenets of African humanism were adapted to the urban setting in the context of the grave economic disparities that existed as a result of apartheid. Despite everything, Africans found ways to express their *joie de vivre* and their humanistic beliefs, in short to practice *ubuntu*. To be inhospitable in the African humanist world view is to be selfish in the way that Chimane's employers were selfish toward their mother-in-law. Such selfishness, in the African humanist view, is tantamount to immorality and is contemptible, especially when directed at elders or relatives. Perversions of values, however, occurred on both sides of the racial barricades—some with serious consequences and some with humorous, understandable, and possibly even laudable ones.

One is amused, for example, when "home-girl" Naomi's boyfriend, who enjoys a winning streak at the races, decides to share his good fortune by entertaining his friends royally with sweets, soft drinks, and gramophone records featuring pennywhistle music and singing by the likes of Miriam Makeba at his employer's home while they are off on holiday. He welcomes his guests with a speech befitting an African humanist aware of old ways and new and in a purely African idiom: "Now my brothers and sisters enjoy yourselves. At home I should slaughter a goat for a feast and thank our ancestors. But this is town life and we must thank them with tea and cake and all those sweet things. I know some people think I must be so bold that I could be midwife to a lion that is giving birth, but enjoy yourselves and have no fear" (241). Here "laughing truth" and parody is directed against the monolithic world of apartheid. A mockery is made of officialdom as its "received social categories" are inverted. Material bodily functions, such as eating and drinking, reduce cliched ideals to the profane. Norms and rules of daily life are turned upside down and ridiculed. Marketplace speech is used to praise and to joke, while the atmosphere is one of collective unity (Gardiner 1991, 46–53). Time after time the reader is allowed to see the difference between "a society that reifies systems at the expense of humans" and that subsequently pays the price in loneliness, conflict, and alienation and a society that does just the opposite and enjoys the benefits of mutual support, love, fun, laughter, and caring—even and especially in the midst of great privation and great pain (Ruth 1986, 67). The narrator's internal polemic is to suggest that the conflict is no longer, in the Freudian sense, simply between instincts and institutions, but between values of competition and cooperation (Rieff 1959, 338–39).

"Mrs Plum" is nothing less than a fictive treatise on themes of alien-

ation and African humanism. The alienation experienced by whites is identified with the totality of their value systems and beliefs. It is internal as well
as external. Relatives, for example, are treated with selfish disregard. Dogs
are more important than people. Principles are glorified while individuals
are treated as expendable. We see the difference between white alienation
and black humanism in the interaction between generations and family
members as illustrated by Karabo's relationship with her parents. "There is
harmony between the two generations which does not exist between Kate
and Mrs Plum, nor between Chimane's employers and their mother-in-law.
Nor has Karabo been estranged from her family and rural background by
her years in Johannesburg. She goes to the city with certain fixed values of
right and wrong which act as a foundation for her growth in the story, regardless of environment" (Hodge 1981, 37). In *The African Image*, Mphahlele
differentiates between the Afrikaner who dislikes blacks as a group but tol-
erates the individual so long as he knows his place and the Englishman who
accepts the group but despises the individual (Mphahlele 1962, 42). Indeed,
the Afrikaner's attitude toward the group helps explains the "*laager* mentality" based on the fear of extinction and being under siege by the *swart
gevaar* (black peril), that is, of being swallowed up by the overwhelming
black majority. But being African himself the Afrikaner is better able to
maintain a certain easy rapport with individual blacks and, even in a pater-
nalistic fashion, to treat his servant with decency. The Englishman, on the
other hand, with his class consciousness and his cultural insularity, exhibits
a more conflicted and even hypocritical approach to blacks as seen in that
of Mrs. Plum.

The conflict between white liberal beliefs as ideals and their actualized
expression in human interactions is one of the central themes of alienation
in Mrs. Plum. It is also a manifestation of what is clearly Mphahlele's own
frustration at his inability to "dynamite his way in" when it comes to getting
to know the Englishman on a purely human and personal level. The conflict, moreover, may help explain the gulf between professions of liberal
sentiments and the relative failure, on the part of the white liberal establishment, to mobilize in any long-term, meaningful, and effective manner
against the regime during high apartheid. In short, "abhorrence of the individual seems perverse in those who espouse liberalism, which has as its cornerstone the rights and protection of the individual" (Ruth 1986, 80). Thus,
the story of Mrs. Plum concludes with this meaningful and supremely
ironic exchange between Karabo and Mrs. Plum: "Mrs Plum says to me she
says, you know, I like your people, Karabo, the Africans. And Dick and me I
wondered" (1987, 261).

White alienation because of such contradictions is cosmic, existential, and lonely. Whites may enjoy great luxury and privilege, but, suggests Mphahlele, they live under a social system that serves to pervert rather than promote morality. Their greed and materialism isolates whites and they have lost their ability to recognize another because they are out of touch with their own humanity. Blacks, on the other hand, are alienated largely because of external factors, but they have not lost touch with their quintessential human values, with their African humanism. By continually juxtaposing the two opposite and parallel themes of alienation and African humanism Mphahlele achieves balance, tension, and meaning as well as humor, writing memorable literature of protest without ever having to resort to polemic or self-pity. Mphahlele, in this manner, "sets up a certain rhythmic pattern" in the view through the keyhole "of the white world as impersonal, sterile, estranged, abstract, a world of economically independent individuals [which] is contrasted with the black world of communal support, birth and death, practical issues and individual economic dependence" (Ruth 1986, 82).

"Mrs Plum" stands as one of Mphahlele's most definitive statements on African humanism, as both a philosophy and as a way of life manifested in the characters of Lilian Ngoyi, Karabo, and Dick, among others. In the words of Fanon, Mphahlele has managed in his writing to "delve deeper down" and lay claim to and rehabilitate a part of a "national culture" (1963, 210). In the end, Karabo, as a symbol of that culture, has reclaimed her sense of personal identity, serving as role model and inspiration for thousands like her. According to Freud, "to become self-conscious about a prototype helps dissolve it" (Rieff 1959, 262). Karabo has become self-conscious, rejecting negative prototypes in favor of positive ones.

In *The African Image*, Mphahlele examines, among others, Cameroonian writer Ferdinand Oyono's novel *Une Vie de Boy*. The protagonist Taundi's "sad end reminds us that even though a servant is in a position to outwit the master . . . the white man has the ultimate power of dispensation" (254). With Mphahlele now at the controls, however, the power equation in the "uneasy relationship" between master and servant has been effectively reversed.

Although Karabo has successfully negotiated improved working conditions with madam, she continues to the end to "monitor" Mrs. Plum's motives. Perhaps, Karabo muses, Mrs. Plum has asked her back merely to fill the void left by the dogs, Monty and Malan. Karabo's concern bears out observations made by Karen Tranberg Hansen in *Distant Companions*, a study of servants and employers in Zambia through the mid 1980s. Hansen states that servants and employers bring "intentionality to the workplace. They monitor their behavior in an uneasy relationship of cooperation and conflict that masks the essential ambiguity: its personalized nature. These circumstances force persons with few means to make a living by working for those better situated, who in addition to getting housework done cheaply also get some one to be around the house in a role *almost akin to a watchdog* ([emphasis added] 1989, 247). In "Mrs Plum," with its realistic, multilingual "dialogized heteroglossia" and "character's expressed ideology," Mphahlele raises authenticity to the level of art. The author, himself, was pleased enough with his success that he wrote in a letter to Barnett that he regarded "Mrs Plum the best thing I ever pulled off" (1976, 111). As Norman Hodge notes, "Mrs Plum" probably comes as close as any fiction Mphahlele has written to providing an "index of the writer's tone and how he views human behavior" (Hodge 1981, 33).

Mphahlele's elation over "Mrs Plum" is well deserved. He wrote a finely crafted story, with strong narrative line, believable and interesting characters, and crackling dialogue that serves to advance plot and shed light on characters. He has also written a piece that is indelibly stamped with the history of its time. He has, in depicting interracial and class struggles between Mrs. Plum and Karabo and between Karabo and educated blacks, "link[ed] individual[s] to the social whole" and created "'representative'" characters that "incarnate(s) historical forces without thereby ceasing to be richly individualized" (Eagleton 1986, 550). In "Mrs Plum," Mphahlele has produced a story that both reflects and is a product of its "social and historical milieu," while in the Platonic sense creating a moral vision in which the aim is to teach. Moreover, he has accomplished these ends without sacrificing either artistry or his uniquely African humanist voice. This, indeed, is a major achievement.

Mphahlele—despite the extent of his own great suffering as a result of apartheid, dire poverty, unjust socioeconomic conditions, and racism—reveals himself to be surprisingly free from the "moral cynicism" that had, for example, pervaded much of the thinking of South African Marxists from the 1950s on (Gerhart 1979, 9). In its more pessimistic or perhaps realistic sociological vein Mphahlele tells a story that shows that "whites in Africa live in fat feudal comfort which the servant class affords them. And even although they do not pay the workers well, the whites lose heavily: their humanness. A kind of moral corrosion has set in this privileged society. And what is more they are never sure, by virtue of this master-servant relationship, what goes on in the mind of this seeming black automaton.

But it is a menacing automaton" (Mphahlele 1962, 145). At the same time, Mphahlele concludes "Mrs Plum" with a coda that is positive and upbeat—implicit in which is a belief in the possibility of change, based on reason, compassion, and a just universe. Thus, as a self-professed African humanist, Mphahlele shows his true colors. He reveals, in short, his own inclination toward the "liberals' optimistic faith in the triumph of generous impulses over the forces of economic determinism." (Gerhart 1979, 9)

Furthermore, Mphahlele becomes, to quote Serote, "two tongued" in that he both defines the problem of white exploitation and oppression and proposes solutions that will empower blacks and give them hope (Serote 1990, 8). He accomplishes this through the brilliant use in his narrative of multilingual heteroglossia and the development of complex characters who as ideologues convincingly express opposing world views. The internal polemic of Mphahlele's double-voiced, two-tongued speech is the need for a revolutionary new culture which "would incorporate, but transcend the corrupted European culture of humanism, which perpetuated racism at the same time that it advocated universal values" (King 1991, 210). Of Mphahlele's contemporaries, the writer who, perhaps, comes closest to sharing his visionary outlook is Bessie Head, with her love of African traditional life and "its slow courtesies" and her experience of "crippling alienation" (Head 1990, ix–xiii).

Mphahlele's "two-tongued," double-voiced approach stands in direct opposition to such works as Alex La Guma's *A Walk in the Night,* which, for example, "makes no social visionary claims but restricts itself to a near obsessive delineation of the physical, particularized reality of a South African ghetto existence" (Soyinka 1992, 65). Similarly such stories as Modisane's "The Beggar" tend to document, without presenting a transforming redemptive vision. Nathan, the beggar and central character in Modisane's story, has been co-opted by Western materialism of which a much coveted piano stands as symbol. Unlike Karabo, he is a rather debased figure, offering no model for self-empowerment. Even while stories such as Richard Rive's "African Song" reflect elements of African humanism, frequently the text does not incorporate those elements into its heteroglossia. Rive's story, for example, harks back to the biblical style of the mission presses.

In "Mrs Plum," Mphahlele moves beyond a literature of protest to a literature of black consciousness and resistance in which the old order is critiqued in a style that is at times both angry and bitter. Nevertheless, Mphahlele refuses to drown in his own bile, offering instead a social vision at once philosophic and pragmatic—a black ethos, which he chooses to call African humanism, in which the "I," in Bakhtin's words, can only realize itself on the basis of "we." In contrast to the white liberal's abstract idealism, Mphahlele presents a down-to-earth, working-class realist in the character of Karabo, who serves as admirable role model for ways in which blacks can seize responsibility for their own economic and political empowerment.

As a novella of education and initiation, "Mrs Plum" stands out as one of two or three in the South African literary canon, published between the late 1940s and 1970s, that features a black protagonist—let alone a black female protagonist. We are already well acquainted with Paton's Rev. Kumalo, who, believing he must suffer and endure, comforts himself with the idea that there is something inherently ennobling in the process. If there is truth in such a belief, then there should be no good reason to remove the causes of such tribulations. Rather, in order to continue producing saints, such tribulations should be fostered and encouraged.

A more recent *bildungsroman,* published in the late 1970s and written in the same vein as *Cry, the Beloved Country,* that is instructive to compare with "Mrs Plum" is Afrikaner writer Elsie Joubert's *Poppie*—the story of Poppie Nongena, a black domestic who undergoes terrible hardships as she battles heroically to hold her family together.

The double-voiced narrative, in this case, frequently proves misleading unless the reader happens to be reasonably well grounded in its historic context. In the first place, the author/narrator is a privileged white, assuming the voice of a black domestic. In the second, Poppie's message is identical to that of Rev. Kumalo. Indeed, she is a female variant of Kumalo. In "faction" of this sort, it is difficult to know where fact ends and fiction begins and whose voice is speaking.

The subtext of the narrator's insidious, if perhaps not fully intentional hidden polemic appears in various guises. For example, it is most often black (rather than white) police who "followed the people running down the lanes, hitting everybody with their kieries" and who otherwise engage in acts of violence (123). People in rural areas are often referred to with disdain as people who practice "bush business" and "bush rituals." Evidence of hardships and oppression are referred to as "grievances" (318). When the family is separated because Poppie cannot afford to keep her children with her, due largely to conditions brought on by apartheid economics, she faces up to her sorrow with a heavy heart, rationalizing her situation with words that precisely echo the *umfundisi* in Paton's *Cry, The Beloved Country.* Like Kumalo, in her passivity and resignation, Poppie falls back on the Lord's will to justify her fate, saying: "If it is the Lord's will that you stay, you will stay, and if it's the Lord's will that you go, you will go. . . . If this is what she was born for, then she too must carry her burden" (244). But in truth, the going and staying have everything to do with Poppie's struggle to get a pass and with the Group Areas Act, and her inadequate pay. It is cosmic buck-passing such as this that keeps people powerless, giving the "Lord" a bum rap to boot. The "Lord's will" is, in fact, the pitiless will of D. F. Malan and Hendrik F. Verwoerd. Although there is some fine and empathetic writing in Joubert's work—which was described by Brink "as an unforgettable vision"—centering on Poppie and her values, as for example, when Poppie says, "We are the help-each-other-people," there are even more times when the double-voiced narrative reveals an inner polemic misleadingly at odds with historic realities (264).

Violence is mentioned repeatedly throughout Poppie's narrative, always in terms of black youth, who upset Poppie when they tease the police by tossing stones at them, or by black police, but rarely, if ever, in terms of the apartheid system itself. Whites are most often cast in the role of rescuers, as in the case of the social worker who gives Poppie assistance. Poppie talks about voting in the Ciskei, an apartheid-sanctioned homeland, in a way that makes it sound as if she is exercising an important democratic right. Because the novel is based, according to its author, "on the actual life story of a black woman living in South Africa today," it does has its moments when Poppie seems to loom larger than life, Mother Africa, brave and believable.

Nonetheless, while Karabo talks about being inspired by ANC leader Lilian Ngoyi, Poppie mentions hearing prime ministers of the Ciskei and Transkei speak, thereby conferring, once again, a measure of legitimacy on the homelands. Poppie's struggle to secure a pass is ongoing, but she blames it on the faceless law as if the law, no matter how immoral or undemocratic, were sacrosanct and itself the cause: "The big boss . . . can't give the extension. . . . It's not him that wants the people to leave. It's the law" (170). At another point, Poppie sounds like a variant on Mrs. Plum who insists one must follow the law, even when it hurts. Poppie asks: "What can I do? . . . I can't break the law with my hands" (185).

Poppie sounds like the excuses heard at Nuremberg, Coetzee's Magistrate (who is the "lie the empire tells itself"), and the Rev. Kumalo (always explaining problems in terms of the "Lord's will" and "the broken tribe") rolled into one. Children are depicted as stoning their schools—because, as a result of the Bantu Education Act, their schooling is "different" from whites (305). But Poppie expects the matter will pass and believes it is only a matter of the "teachers [needing] to show themselves stronger than the pupils." Here the "word" penetrated with its ideology is loaded, with the narrative voice anticipating the objection of the other (in this case, perhaps the system, itself). Just as "oppression" is not the same as having a "grievance," an education that is "different" is not the same as an education being made deliberately "inferior" through the dismantling of excellent schools and the legislating of disastrous ones. As Bakhtin suggests, there are no "neutral" words since each word "tastes of its context" (Danow 1991, 24–25).

Furthermore, "all words are linked with a particular society, generation, historical period" (Bakhtin 1981, 293). In this light, one of the most fatuous observations in Poppie's narrative occurs when the students in Soweto hold a protest against the imposition of Afrikaans. The question Poppie raises is why, since students are willing to learn English and Xhosa. The students reportedly answer, because "We heard them saying that in the Soweto schools and now we say that too" (307). The clear implication is that the Soweto students have no valid objections of their own and are just mindlessly parroting political platitudes—as if Afrikaans, unlike English, were a world language and the fast track to progress; as if Afrikaans were not considered by blacks the "language of the oppressor"; as if Xhosa, unlike Afrikaans, were not their native tongue and therefore a waste of time to study. The polyphonic dissonance between authorial voice and that of narrator/protagonist is not just hard on the reader's figurative ear, it raises serious questions about the text's authenticity.

Poppie Nongena (a euphonious name with Freudian overtones hinting at oblivion and the philosophy of nothing chanced, nothing gained) when she frees herself from this double-voiced schizophrenia and manages to utter her own thoughts in her own words emerges, at times, as a strong, even a memorable character, but one who is not nearly so psychologically nuanced or self-aware as Karabo is. No one would ever mistake her for a model of the new woman or man rising up out of a new aesthetic and a new dispensation.

The Life and Times of Michael K (1985) by Coetzee is an example of a *bildungsroman* in which the protagonist, a male born with a hare lip (thus avoiding the issue of color altogether) is more a psychological construct than a three-dimensional reality. Michael K is so isolated from society, in a Western existential sense, that the humanistic quality of African life that balances the ruthlessness of the "system" by which he is driven like fate itself, does not figure in. The suffering of Michael K, as he struggles heroically to return his ailing mother to her rural roots before her death, in a South Africa torn apart by civil war, effectively becomes the reader's suffering. But historic time and community are sacrificed in the process. The allegory in which Michael K is defined by his hare lip rather than skin pigmentation allows whites to identify fully, while gazing into a crystal ball at a ghastly doomsday scenario of what South Africa could become if civic society does not change soon. Its internal polemic is to criticize rather than affirm or offer alternatives. It is a brilliant, affecting, and effective work that is ultimately antihumanistic in its brooding tones and existentialism.

This is why on the basis of an examination of the dialogics of existing works in the canon that are intended as novels of initiation and education and that feature black protagonists—or their symbolic equivalents in the case of Coetzee's novel—one can safely say that "Mrs Plum" stands out as one of the most authentic pictures of human behavior and of socioeconomic and political conditions prevailing in South Africa from the late 1940s to the late 1970s.

Chapter Seven

Back from the Wilderness

AFRIKA MY MUSIC

> *The African sage says you cannot compare pain.*

> *This quality of compassion has a lot to do with African humanism . . . I am attracted to an existence in which people treat each other as human beings and not simply as instruments or tools.*
> (Manganyi 1983, 49)

> *Your mind operates in a foreign language, even while you are actually talking in your mother tongue.*
> (Mphahlele 1972, 127)

> *The dialogue between two selves never ends. The pendulum swings between revulsion and attraction, between the dreams and the reality of a living past and the aspirations, the imperatives of modern living. Ambivalence.*
> (Mphahlele 1974, 41)

February 11, 1990, was the unforgettable day in South African history when ANC leader Nelson Mandela was set free after being held as a political prisoner for twenty-seven years (eighteen of which were spent on infamous Robben Island). As of this writing, South Africa is at a major crossroads, after a "forty-year detour against the tide of post-war history, when . . . many whites and blacks could not communicate properly, as equals, because of the years of apartheid" (Heard 1990, 228). Even as a new democratic constitution has been hammered out and elections based on a universal franchise have taken place, questions are being raised about multiculturalism in the arts and education, particularly in view of the alienating intellectual apartheid that has long existed among the three tribes of Afrikaner, English, and blacks in South Africa (Mphahlele 1960, 342). At such a historic juncture any study that undertakes to examine the works of Mphahlele in terms of the literary and philosophical synthesis based on a black aesthetic and a nationalist vision is timely.

In order to overcome the cultural and intellectual apartheid that bred fear and ignorance and leads to conflict and alienation among ethnic groups, it is important to climb out of the "closed circuit" of studying and reading only about one's own culture where preconceptions have a way of confirming themselves while lending themselves to the appearance of "universality" (Bates 1993, 226). Wise and imaginative leadership is needed in the cross-cultural endeavor to decolonize the arts and education as well as to promote better understanding and to heal the ancient wounds of racial strife and antagonism. In this regard, Mphahlele, with his strongly integrationist approach—regardless of his post-Sharpeville shift in emphasis away from nonracism to black identity—stands out as an eminently qualified thinker, role model, and mentor (Mphahlele 1984, 255).

In the course of his lifelong search for a synthesis in the dialogue of two selves, Mphahlele has dealt in richly paradoxical dichotomies, such as West versus Africa, and individual versus communal self, and the equally thorny dualities in themes of alienation counterpointed against African humanism. There has always been a spiritual struggle involved in the search—at once nuanced, complex, and contradictory—and arising out of the progressive alienation of the teacher, writer, and scholar as political exile.

Affirmative though it is, Mphahlele's human-centered unitarian African philosophy is not the easily arrived at, oversimplified, absolutist answer of a Pollyanna. Mphahlele does not, to quote Soyinka, revel in a "dangerous hara-kiri humanism" (Soyinka 1992, 75). Mphahlele steers clear of the romanticism of negritude. Balance and realism are his hallmarks. While professing African values and espousing an African humanistic metaphysics and way of life, he never overlooks the potential for violence in the black character, as may be seen in both the "Lesane" stories and *Down Second Avenue*. Like many West African thinkers and writers, Mphahlele has "thought through [his] culture deeply and [is] able to take new root in it" (Kesteloot 1991, 325). Thus he is able to explore opposite poles of north and south without tumbling into the yawning crevasse of polemics. Eventually, in the movement back to Africa, Mphahlele arrives at the "ironic meeting point" between total acceptance of the West and outright rejection. From a position of negritude, "as a quality of revolt which derives from the political and cultural oppression the negro has known," Mphahlele moves to a position of Black Consciousness, a movement he anticipated by at least two decades in his criticism and in his novella "Mrs Plum," a story forged on the "white-hot anvil" of anger that galvanizes readers into political awareness (Wallerstein 1961, 132–33).

Mphahlele's African humanism is a broad-gauged concept that he was the first on the continent to articulate, embracing elements of both politics and culture, a South African equivalent to Senghor's negritude, Nyerere's *Ujamaa* socialism (minus the strong economic component), and Kaunda's Zambian socialism. *The African Image* represents African humanist aesthetics applied to literary criticism. *Down Second Avenue* illustrates African humanism as it is lived. The unforgettable "Mrs Plum" is the most definitive socioeconomic and psychological expression of Mphahlele's African humanist stance and the one most strongly informed with Black Consciousness thought.

Mphahlele's writings both define the problems created by intellectual and racial alienation and propose a solution, which is why, in a postcolonial South Africa, they are especially relevant to the process of conflict resolution and healing. Without exception, all of Mphahlele's works of prose and fiction document myriad themes of alienation. Although Western alienation stems from internal causes and is often marked by existential despair, the alienation described by Mphahlele in all his works stems from largely external causes. Political alienation caused by his banning as a teacher and writer wins out with Mphahlele's decision to go into exile. African humanism, strongly motivated by a desire to serve his community, triumphs when Mphahlele returns to South Africa "from the wilderness," despite the cries of "sell out" from certain intellectuals, once more to cast his shadow on ancestral soil (Mphahlele 1991, 144).[1] This decision, at age 57, to give up a full professorship at the University of Pennsylvania, "to return to a depressed Bantustan" in Lebowa "surprised his friends" and "amazed his five children" (Lelyveld 1980, 3). Moreover, it was still a criminal act to quote or publish any of Mphahlele's works in South Africa since he remained a "listed person."

Of the multiple themes of alienation in the works of Mphahlele, including professional alienation and censorship, three are paramount. These begin with those of the political exile (both internal and external) who as a writer, teacher, scholar, and visionary discovers in his pan-African, transcontinental wanderings that placelessness itself is a form of exile. Mphahlele's desire to recover a self-identifying sense of place where he could "cast his shadow" drove him back to South Africa in 1977. Inextricably bound up with political exile is the theme of racial oppression and alienation, as expressed in its worldwide context by the words "race" and "color." These two words, Mphahlele states, are "the most emotive . . . in the dictionary of human relationships" (Mphahlele 1984, 154). The third strand in the rope of steel is the continuing dialogue of a divided self—one that is Western-educated and colonized and the other African.

Mphahlele's writings, in detailing these recurrent themes of alienation, at times reflect deep bitterness and anger, but they also demonstrate an open-ended desire to synthesize, to preserve the best, to continue the "dialogue" of what Mphahlele referred to in an interview with the author of this study held at the Funda Center in Soweto as two streams of consciousness: the African and the Western (Obee 1992, 5–6). Indeed, Mphahlele is the living prototype of what he defines the writer and artist as being: that is, "a rebel who has the gift of language," an activist, and one "who is engaged in a revolution of mind and feeling . . . he is a teacher, an interpreter" (Mphahlele 1990, 17–18).

Two of Mphahlele's more recent works, one the novel *Chirundu* (1979) and the other his memoir *Afrika My Music* (1984), both of which were published after his return to South Africa in 1977, are sufficiently forward looking, visionary, and experimental that they constitute important literary and philosophical road maps to the future in a new South Africa. Both in terms of pointing the way to the building of a postapartheid body of South African literature and in the practical application of Mphahlele's African humanist vision, the two volumes are virtual gold mines. These and other works are testimony to Mphahlele's considerable output after his controversial return to South Africa at the end of a twenty-year period of exile in West and East Africa, Europe, and the United States.

Moreover, Mphahlele's creative output affords substantial proof of his personal triumph over the intellectual, spiritual, and political alienation of the internal exile that continued to be imposed on him after his return, vindicating the perennial optimism of an African humanist. Pursuing his longtime interest in African traditional culture and community history, Mphahlele conducted research into oral poetry in the North Sotho, Tsonga, and Venda languages in 1979 and served as a founding member of the African Writers' Association in Johannesburg. He subsequently accepted the offer of a professorship at the University of the Witwatersrand at its Center for African Studies, becoming, in 1983, the chairman of the Division of African Literature. With the unbanning of *Down Second Avenue* and *The African Image* (first edition); and the publication of *Chirundu* (1979), *The Unbroken Song* (1981), and *Afrika My Music* (1984), Mphahlele was able at least partially to begin to realize two of his most cherished cultural goals—those of teaching and writing. Indeed, Mphahlele considers that the teaching of African literature in itself "should be the starting point . . . [for] a culture striving towards a synthesis that will be truly *African*" and that will "promote the black man's aspirations" (Mphahlele 1984, 7).

With the publication of his memoir *Afrika My Music* and of *Chirundu,* Mphahlele provided the answer to Berth Lindfors' question, raised nearly two decades after Mphahlele's own return: "When black South African writers currently living in exile begin to return home in the next few years, what kind of literature are they likely to produce?" (1993, 70). Once again, Mphahlele served as trailblazer. His answer to Lindfors's question, before Lindfors thought to ask it, was to write one of the first South African memoirs of a returning political exile—an exploration of themes of loss, bitterness, and reconciliation. In doing so, Mphahlele turns to forms and conventions rooted both in African and Western traditions. *Afrika My Music* is African insofar as it examines self-in-community and draws on oral forms such as the *isibongo* or praise poems of naming as well as on the eastern and southern Bantu traditional hero tales—epic narratives, interspersed with songs, in which the hero returns home at the end of an epic journey to far-off places. In such epics the hero's trials are sometimes precipitated by a king or father's rejection of son (father and son conflicts are a recurring, painful theme in nearly all of Mphahlele's works and are brought to a resolution in *Father Come Home*). The hero then having triumphed over forces of nature and magic returns to his rightful home and to his people.

Mphahlele's memoir, unlike some of its Western counterparts, does not declare the primacy of subjective consciousness. Mphahlele discovers who he is in part through others. Self-examination serves to reintegrate, but never becomes obsessional. It is a literature of self in which the narrator delivers the news, yet never stoops to "autopathography." *Afrika My Music* chronicles, instead, lived experience and memory, a mature life in progress—one about an exile who still has some time left in harness and for whom, as Mphahlele puts it in his inimitable and, at times, earthy style, "It is not yet time to fart like a horse or dangle on an elongated burp" (1984, 162). Neither self-indulgent nor confessional in tone, Mphahlele's memoir engages in self-examination without navel-gazing. He deplores what he sees as the confessional streak in American society, at the root of which he perceives a deep, underlying loneliness. Mphahlele's memoir, like southern and eastern Bantu hero-epics, reflects "values and aspirations, the search for equity and justice and the ever-present need to deal with evil forces" (Courlander 1975, 400). Although Mphahlele did not consciously set out to become a quest hero or a political martyr, his journey became the life experience from which, as suggested by critic and philosopher John Dewey, all "art springs." Dewey's critical approach is one Mphahlele finds both apposite and persuasive (Mphahlele 1990, 5).

Along the way, the African epic hero of old may encounter monsters that take (appropriately enough) the form "of a range of hills" and he returns "to receive recognition and achieve his proper place . . . among the people" (Courlander 1975, 400). Mountains indeed haunt Mphahlele's dreams. The Rockies loom over him "like giant apes marooned on a patch of Time" (Mphahlele 1984, 131). When Mphahlele drives through Zion in Utah, the skeletal, stark mountains leaning over him cause him to feel so claustrophobic that by the end of the drive he is shaking. So disturbing is Mphahlele's experience (a psychic alienation of place) that his colleague Robert Pawlowski later makes it the subject of an eloquent poem that is one of the many special gifts assembled in the form of a book with stories, poems, interviews, and articles, under the title *Footprints along the Way*—a magnificent tribute paid Mphahlele on the occasion of his 70th birthday in 1989.

Both *Footprints along the Way* and Mphahlele's welcome back at Jan Smuts International Airport on July 3, 1976, to deliver a keynote address at the Institute of Black Studies in Johannesburg are in keeping with the recognition accorded a returning African quest hero. The crowds who turned out to welcome Mphahlele included some one hundred "screaming and jostling" Africans. "Such was the overwhelming ecstasy of that reunion. The police had to come disperse the crowd, as they had by now taken over the concourse" (Manganyi 1983, 17). Without question, the lot of the exile is painful, depressing, and lonely. Nonetheless, I believe Barnett misses the point in her assessment that "Mphahlele remains, as he has always been, a lonely man, destined to think in isolation" (1976, 173).

Mphahlele introduces *Afrika My Music* with a poetic fragment that is one of his most lyric and celebratory, and that is a mini-manifesto of the guiding precepts of an African humanist:

> We carried the song across countries
> over oceans
> over snow-topped mountains
> Afrika my music.
>
> You carried us across countries
> over oceans
> over desert and savannah
> Song of Afrika.

> How could we not return
> when this is where
> the afterbirth was buried for rebirth?—
> Afrika my music.

In this panegyric to Africa, a praise poem, with its encomiastic verse and nationalist flavor, the African humanist has come in from the cold. When he reflects on Africa, the land, his teacher, on whose breast sleep his ancestors, there is no sense of fractured identity or disinherited psyche. In an organic gathering up in which the all is now, he is reconnected to land, to past and future, by the buried umbilical cord. Mphahlele brings to the fore in his memoir both the novelist's tools of setting, dialogue, flashbacks, and the poet's.

Like the "immense paradox" of exile itself, re-entry, however, is also fraught. There is a gulf between the promise and the hope, and the grim daily realities of a return to a racist society. For the entire Mphahlele family, it is difficult to unlearn the freedoms they became used to as international citizens. It was also a shock to be plunked down in the midst of ghetto culture again with the lack of basic amenities, privacy, and decent schools for the Mphahlele children. In a sense the Mphahlele children are the true professional exiles, partly at home everywhere, totally at home nowhere. (Boarding schools proved to be the answer for Tony and Puso.) Mphahlele compares Soweto, with its violence, garbage heaps, and rows of tiny box houses, to a "grinning skull." Yet it did offer community: "We sought community, we found it. We sought an identifiable culture, we found it. We sought relevance, we found it. We sought a return to ancestral ground, this is it, and it cuts across all man-made boundaries. We tasted liberty—freedom of association, expression, mobility. We came back to none of these" (250). Initially, Mphahlele suffers through a continual turning of the screw—once again, subjected to a daily barrage of hurtful insults by white petty bureaucrats—this, after being courted and honored on the international circuit. One evening as he and Rebecca are driving home to Lebowa, they are overtaken by a truck driven by a pair of Afrikaans-speaking thugs, who continue to follow and harass them. This chilling experience reminds Mphahlele of Fromm's observation that the paranoid is victim of his own power—power with which he both tyrannizes others and himself (200–203). Next, Mphahlele badly mangles a finger while using a power lawn mower. At hospital he is delivered a smug lecture by the white doctor, to the effect that that will teach him for mowing his lawn on Sunday instead of being in church. Mphahlele, enraged, shoots back: "It's the white man's

Sunday and church, *yours*. You people brought the church to Africa and fouled up the continent" (204). At a lecture to students in Lesotho, Mphahlele is attacked by exiled South African students as being intellectually dishonest.

Then, he witnesses "what twenty-five years of Bantu Education has done to the standard of English. Just flattened it." (5) Finally, this award-winning novelist and Nobel Prize nominee, who just left a position on the faculty of one of America's most prestigious universities, fails to secure the chair of English at the University of the North in 1978 after undergoing a bizarre, Orwellian interview, and five years of negotiation filled with raised hopes and endless paper work. Mphahlele's newfound serenity based on his African humanism, his belief in a Supreme Soul, and his determination to "keep his eyes on the prize" is sorely tested. Nevertheless, he continues to live and articulate positive (at times even heroic) attitudes, precisely of the sort needed to help a dysfunctional society heal. Mphahlele is never just an ideologue, however; he is also a pragmatist. His decision to move ahead with the process of peace and reconciliation at a personal level is doubtless based to some extent on enlightened self-interest and the old truth enshrined in the Sotho proverb: "A bitter heart eats its owner" (Courlander 1975, 440).

On his return to ancestral ground, Mphahlele is constantly reminded of the numberless lives lost in the struggle for liberation. An entire section of *Afrika My Music* is devoted to a lyric lamentation, an *isibongo* of naming lost lives that reads like a veritable Who's Who of Black South African literature. Death itself becomes the ultimate adjudicator of alienation. This recurrent theme of futility, of death-dealing loss and alienation, is elaborated on in greater specificity in *Afrika My Music* than it is anywhere else in Mphahlele's works. Mphahlele laments in *Afrika My Music* that

> one felt diminished every time another exile or refugee was diminished. Oftentimes it was diminution by death. Like Todd Matshikiza .... His mound stands in a Lusaka graveyard. Short little man. Unpredictable temper. A coil of barbed wire beneath the cultured, jovial, even-tempered exterior. Don't take it ill, Toddy-boy. I'm telling my fellow-mortals—aren't we all inscrutable mortals, even the most predictable fool? ... And Can Themba. He lies in Swaziland. Canadocea—what a name for an unclassical fellow like you. When I say this to you in the Fordsburg shebeen, you turn round and say, how come a barefoot boy wallowing in the dust of Marabastad with two large holes in the seat of his pants found himself saddled with a Hebrew name like Ezekiel? (119–23)

The African praise poet presents a brilliantly profiled gallery in three dimensions. Sketches range from brilliant and troubled Arthur Nortje, studying at Oxford, to Gerard Sekoto, the noted South African artist living in Paris. Pain swaddled in laughter, in the best tradition of the African humanist narrator, lends depth of feeling to elegiac passages in their shadings of light and shadow. Mphahlele's epithetic roll call and lamentation of the demise of so many of South Africa's most talented black writers in the prime of their lives is moving precisely because of his admirable self-restraint, the absence of self-pity, the abundant presence of compassion and the writerly skill with which it is handled. As with all of Mphahlele's works, African humanism leavens the need for social reportage. The natural concern "with what [is] happening to [his] people" combines with that special quality of aesthetic pleasure and elusive truth one hopes to discover in great literature. Although liberal whites might write polished satires, they have no mythic countersystem with which to fill the guilt-plagued void left by apartheid. Mphahlele came up with a countersystem that could balance the many self-obliterating negations with hope, love, courage, humor, optimism, and artistry. African humanism, as counterbalance, serves thus effectively to heighten the dramatic intensity of themes of alienation that under state apartheid affected every realm of human experience.

In Mphahlele's African humanist aesthetic there is no separation between art and function. Although content may dictate form and, when apartheid is the enemy, plot often supersedes character, this is rarely the case in Mphahlele's works. Mphahlele showcases people and characters over places and things. Just as often in his works, theme transcends and supersedes plot in importance. Thus, the dual themes of alienation and African humanism frequently become the single most important unifying elements in any given plot, narrative, poem, or criticism. Not only do these contrapuntal themes provide cohesion, they are vital to Mphahlele's social vision, unifying the twin aims of artistry and education.

For a brief moment in *Afrika My Music,* Mphahlele brings the vanished black writers, one by one, back to life in his portraits of them. The reader shares the pain of the loss in a way that makes a more effective protest than volumes of bitter propagandistic satire. We learn as much about the writer and his humanity as about his notable works and often also about his violent or debased demise from alcoholism or suicide, the tragic finale for a disproportionately large number of exiles. This approach enhances the pain of loss while not requiring a single drop of poison in the palette to get the word across, serving to exemplify ways in which African humanism balances and yet adds depth and meaning to the themes of alienation in Mphahlele's writing.

As is true in Mphahlele's earlier works, his later works such as *Chirundu*
and *Afrika My Music* exemplify ways in which themes of alienation and
African humanism function as strong unifying counterweights. Furthermore, they reflect the creative synthesis between Africa and the West
Mphahlele actively seeks and promotes. *Afrika My Music* in its lyric prose
documents Mphahlele's years as a pan-African and trans-American writer
and teacher. It also presents a series of fascinating miniatures of some of the
best-known African writers of English on the continent between the late
1950s and the present. These include Soyinka, Gabriel Okara, Amos Tutuola,
Christopher Okigbo, Kofi Awoonor, James Ngugi (Ngugi wa Thiong'o), as
well as Lenrie Peters, "another second-rounder, landing on African soil like
a parachutist . . . coming through condensed time, hitting the ground with
a jolt, then lugging his paraphernalia across the field—his new cultural
equipment" (40). This sketch of Peters could equally well serve as portrait of
the artist Mphahlele on his return to South Africa.

Since Mphahlele knew, encouraged, worked with, and inspired most, if
not all, the writers he describes, these portraits are also highly personal.
Straight from the heart and in the best African humanist tradition, they
highlight the writers as much as their literary achievements. Aside from
Mphahlele, there are few, if any, living African authors who could have
penned these portraits, both from the point of view of style and of firsthand
intimacy. As a document of African literary history, the memoir itself would
serve to enhance and enrich any college syllabus on African literature. The
roll call is also proof that while Mphahlele left South Africa as an exile and
alien, he continually found ways to overcome that alienation as a writer,
teacher, and scholar. In this instance Mphahlele reveals himself as an insider
among the true greats in African literature—not only an insider, but, indeed, a pioneer, leader, role model, and friend.

Afrika My Music is the most recent chapter of a life in process that recapitulates "themes of alienation and African humanism in a dialogue of two
selves." Reading on a philosophical level, the critic is able to see how the
concept of African humanism when integrated into a philosophy of and
used as a tool for living promotes the author's personal growth, his will to
survive, and his self-healing at the end of a long, difficult journey full of tra-
vail and loss that had already claimed far too many casualties. As a teacher,
Mphahlele leads the way. In this sense, he is not only a cultural carrier but
an exemplar and messenger. Thus Mphahlele places reliance on African
humanistic compassion, the "superior spirit" and love as opposed to self-
destructive forces of hate and fear to overcome alienation in all of its manifestations—be it personal insult, political banning, fatherlessness, commu-

nal breakdown, tyranny of place and placelessness, intergenerational alienation within the family structure, censorship, meaninglessness, and a long litany of bereavements through state-sponsored violence, suicides, and drunkenness. Mphahlele's African humanist philosophy is key in two vital decisions: his decision to return to South Africa, and his decision on how to respond to continued insults and white oppression experienced after his return.

Perhaps the first step toward synthesis in the dialogue of two selves and between countervailing themes of alienation and African humanism must involve healing. Thus, Mphahlele observes, "Rightly or wrongly, anger becomes a compulsive way of asserting our ethnic or racial or political identity. . . . I feel enriched by love and impoverished by obsessive hate" (156, 221). Finally, he says that "we have come back and are involved in the creation of something bigger and more splendid than the wretched creatures who spend some part of their waking hours debasing and humiliating black people" (237).

Mphahlele's decision to return to South Africa in 1977 was in part determined by his growing conviction as a self-professed African humanist that it was irrelevant to try to teach people, in this case Americans, whose cultural goals were so different from his own. Moreover, as he grew older he preferred to be among his own people, for whom age is still venerated in an African humanist sense, and for whom growing older could be a much "gentler" process. Ultimately, however, Mphahlele as a visionary, thinker, educator, and writer, came back to participate in the building of a "new South Africa" that encompasses Mphahlele's vision of an education system "based on this philosophy of African humanism," which will "truly express our independence of mind, a decolonized mind" (209). Mphahlele's concludes his African humanist odyssey with the statement that:

> I was an agnostic when I left [South Africa] in 1957. Now I am a confirmed African humanist. I have said that West Africa gave Africa back to me. The difference between me and western humanists is that I cherish the African's belief in the Supreme Being as a vital force, a dynamic presence in all organic matter and in the elements, in Man, where those of the western world feel uneasy with belief in the supernatural and dismiss African religion as magic. My God is not a product of Hebraic-Christian culture but of African culture. Like Rabindranath Tagore's, my religion is a poet's religion. (248–49)

Thus it is possible on the basis of the critic's understanding of African humanism, as Mphahlele defines it expressly or implicitly in all of his works, to suggest that African literature like African art is representational insofar as it deals with the communal rather than the particular, the Platonic ideal rather than the Aristotelian real. It posits "its ultimate reality in pre-existent and transcendent ideas rather than in the appearances and the categories of the created world" (Olney 1973, 180). Yet at the same time African humanism, besides encompassing a metaphysical philosophy, a nationalist vision, and a black aesthetic, is a concrete way of life. This is amply illustrated, for example, in Mphahlele's autobiography *Down Second Avenue*.

By briefly comparing Mphahlele's memoir with ones written by two of South Africa's best-known contemporary women writers, it is possible to gain a clearer understanding of ways in which Mphahlele's stylistic aesthetic is uniquely informed with a nationalist vision and philosophy. Although all three writers make skillful use of multilingual heteroglossia, when it comes to marketplace speech, Jabavu and Mphahlele show the most finely attuned ears. When it comes to capturing the humanistic spirit and *ubuntu* of an African landscape, whether rural or urban, Bessie Head is one of the few southern African writers who can hold a candle to Mphahlele, and who shines out, not only as his contemporary but as his peer. A brief comparative analysis will help further to illuminate Mphahlele's own distinctive vision and voice.

Both Head, born in Pietermaritzburg in 1937 of racially mixed parentage and one of Africa's most notable women writers, and Noni Jabavu, born in 1920 and the daughter of Professor D. D. T. Jabavu, president of the 1936 All African Convention, wrote autobiographical sketches or memoirs. They, like Mphahlele, explore and celebrate African traditions and culture. Head left South Africa because of a failed marriage and her abhorrence of South African politics, and settled in Botswana. Jabavu returned to Cape Town from England for a visit with family and friends after having married into the wealthy British Cadbury family. She was regarded with suspicion as being "unAfrican" and as too sympathetic to the white man with whose "fear of the unknown" she professed sympathy, since she had experienced that fear herself when visiting the Ghanda in the north. To some extent, all three African writers are outsiders looking in who re-examine their African and South African roots from the perspective of travel and Western education. A mission-school trained teacher like Mphahlele, Head taught school for four years and also worked as a journalist for *Drum* magazine. Unlike Mphahlele, Head did not, despite her refugee status, think of herself as an exile, but considered that she had put down deep roots in Botswana despite her initial refugee status.

A Woman Alone is a collection of autobiographic, multi-genre writings, in which there is a marked blurring of fiction and fact, covering Head's entire creative life up until her premature death at age forty-nine. Although Head found peace and security in Botswana, whose "old tribal way of life and its slow courtesies" she admired, she nonetheless felt as rootless and alienated at times as Mphahlele, the perennial wanderer (MacKenzie 1990, xiii). In "Preface to 'Witchcraft'" she says, "nothing can take away the fact that I have never had a country; not in South Africa or in Botswana where I now live as a stateless person" (28).

Head also shares with Mphahlele a deep appreciation for the humanistic values of African traditional life. In both cases there is realism and balance. Head, for example, is well aware of the patriarchal element in African life that often keeps women powerless. In her sketch "The Woman from America," she notes that the American woman's husband "effortlessly and naturally keeps his eyes on his wife alone. In this achievement he is seventy years ahead of all the men here" (31). Yet she deeply admires the way the Batswana people, despite their hardships and extreme privation, care for and support one other, the presence of "soul." Some of these humanistic values are described and documented by Head, the author; others are internalized by her and echo Mphahlele's beliefs. For example, in "Notes from a Quiet Backwater I," Head says: "If I had to write one day I would just like to say people is people and not damn white, damn black. . . . Make you love them, not because of the colour of their skin but because they are important as human beings" (6). Head and Mphahlele are in complete agreement on this fundamental precept of African humanism and its primacy in human relations. In "A Gentle People," Head makes another observation bearing close similarity to ones made by Mphahlele, that it is "another fallacy of the whites . . . that they are the preservers of White Western Christian culture in Africa. Culture is not limited to the West, or Europe or a white skin or Christianity" (10).

On the one hand Head celebrates community, but on the other her narrative voice is more isolated, lonely than Mphahlele's. Community, for Head, is often on the outside and her loneliness is, at times, haunting. Botswana, however, gives her back a sense of being a part of, rather than apart from. Thus, she writes about her life in Botswana: "I have lived all my life in shattered little bits. Somehow, here, the shattered little bits began to come together. There is a sense of wovenness; of wholeness in life here. There were things I loved that began to grow on me like patches of cloth" (30). Although Mphahlele underwent periods of situational depression, unlike Head he did not have to combat the self-alienating disease of mental illness, a battle Head fought with courage throughout her relatively short life span. In addition, with Head's mixed race background she had to deal with some insidious forms of racism on both sides of the color bar, another manifestation of a divided self not experienced by Mphahlele. Most South Africans of mixed race backgrounds chose to ally themselves with the white Afrikaners, which is one reason why the "in between people" are becoming the new target for ugly manifestations of racism in postcolonial South Africa. Head, however, chose Africa.

Head writes of her deep reverence for ordinary people in the same lyric vein as Mphahlele:

> There isn't anything in this village that an historian might care to write about. Dr. Livingstone passed this way, they might say. Historians do not write about people and how strange and beautiful they are—just living. There is so much necessity living they do and in this village there is so much mud living. . . . Poverty has a home in Africa—like a quiet second skin. It may be the only place on earth where it is worn with an unconscious dignity. People do not look down at your shoes . . . . They look deeply into your eyes. . . . This eye-looking, this intense human awareness, is a reflection of the earth all about. (30, 39–40)

With regard to mission-school Christianity, Head is perhaps more strongly antagonistic than even Mphahlele. Although Mphahlele's aversion is, in part, based on political and cultural objections, Bessie Head's are profoundly personal. When she was thirteen, a missionary informed her in the cruelest possible fashion that her mother was white and insane, and had to be locked up because she had conceived a child by the African stable boy. That child, of course, was Head. For good measure the missionary added, "If you're not careful you'll get insane just like your mother." For years after, Head "harboured a terrible and blind hatred for missionaries" (4). Although Mphahlele was fatherless, Head was motherless. Both experienced and wrote memorably about cruelty at the hands of whites. Mphahlele saw such cruelty as a manifestation of a mindset that was "authoritarian rather than humanitarian."

Of all the southern African writers who were shaped by the style and politics of the 1960s, Head comes closest to sharing Mphahlele's breadth of vision, informed as it is by African humanistic thought. There are, however, two pronounced differences. Head is almost entirely apolitical. She despises racism yet is optimistic enough to believe the time will come when that blight will be removed from the world. Nevertheless, she rarely probes the ideology and politics of apartheid. Unlike Mphahlele, she does not address such questions as how to salvage African culture in order to build on its values, both in terms of black education and nation building. Head examines African culture almost exclusively from the point of view of what we can learn from it. Mphahlele is looking at not only what we can learn, but how it can be taken beyond a "survivor's culture." Although Head makes no conscious effort to formulate a nationalist vision, she raises our consciousness in ways that are poignant, moving, and unforgettable. Through her writing she demonstrates how an African aesthetic has both profound beauty and long-term meaning.

Another key difference between the works of Head and Mphahlele is the extent to which the former dwells on nature description. Mphahlele is not a landscape artist, in part because he is largely concerned with an urban setting. Head, on the other hand, lives in a rural area. She by disposition is more inclined to describe it in lyric detail, while not forsaking realism in the name of the romantic. An example is her description of rainfall in Serowe: "Sometimes all the horizon rain sweeps across the village in glistening streams. Then the grass roofs of the mud huts shine like polished gold. The barren earth, grazed to a shred by the goats, becomes clothed by a thin fine carpet of green. Under the trees there is a sudden, lush wild growth of long green grass. Everything is alive in this short dazzling summer. Forgotten are the long months of bleaching scorching sun and intense blue skies" (29).

Like Mphahlele, Noni Jabavu is a memoirist utilizing the novelist's tools of dialogue, portrayal of major and minor characters, and descriptions of place. Her book *The Ochre People* (1963), with its theme of the returning exile, is a heartwarming celebration of extended family and kinship, the support among age groups and the respect shown elders. Yet in her narrative she does not overlook the great suffering of the people from apartheid dislocation and economics. Unlike Mphahlele, Jabavu had not been officially banned. She was not a political exile. Moreover, Jabavu comes from a far more privileged background than either Head or Mphahlele. Perhaps this is why she does not probe human motive or racial issues with the same depth of understanding that either Head or Mphahlele brings to bear on the subject. There is less emphasis in her text on human suffering, political oppression, and related themes of alienation. Nevertheless, Jabavu, like Mphahlele, rejoices in utilizing African metaphoric speech (often she is warmly greeted as "the calf of here-at-home") as well as proverbs to describe local customs (4). Like Mphahlele and Head, Jabavu is struck by the fortitude and grace with which ordinary people—including the Xhosa-speaking Mrs. R., who made a comfortable if cramped home for her family in an abandoned rain-water tank—manage to live with dignity amidst squalor. Jabavu sums up an African ethos and way of being, underscored by a fighting spirit, in the following passage:

> "Yes, hark, Ntando," my aunt teased me, smiling, "For what is it we hear but that *amaAfrika* love life? We are conservatives, we; and cling to custom; but at the same time learn and adapt. No longer do *we cling like a grasshopper to the barbed wire fence on which it is impaled in flight, and remaining static only because dead!*" She looked around for the ironic applause that would greet this ... figurative chestnut that illustrates the difference between constructive tenacity ... and sterile ossification.... The party broke up to comfortable elderly laughter. (236)

Jabavu describes what Mphahlele both documents and states, that "family allegiances ... informed a morality we associate with African humanism": an essentially spiritual humanism, defined by the "the unfolding of the collective imagination through folklore, proverbs, and allegory" (Mphahlele 1993, 180–81).

Jabavu, Head, and Mphahlele have all written exilic memoirs that describe and document, while being informed to some degree by an African aesthetic. Jabavu's memoir is the work of a facile writer who knows, cares, and was once a part of that aesthetic, and whose use of language reflects that identification.

The suggested nature/culture divide between Head, as a landscape artist, and Mphahlele, as a nationalist visionary, is not intended to be understood in a Freudian sense. Head, too, is a thinker, but her vision tended, especially toward the end of her life and in her harrowing account, *A Question of Power*, to be directed more toward issues of gender, personal identity, and cosmology, rather than literary criticism and politics.

Of the three, Mphahlele is the only memoirist who writes about the experience of return from the perspective of someone who is not a visitor (in the case of Jabavu) or who wants desperately to belong (in the case of Head). Of the three narrators, he is the only one who consciously set out to develop a working aesthetic and a nationalist vision that served effectively as a weapon in the era of resistance, that can serve in nation-building in the new South Africa, and that helped sustain him during a difficult transition when changes in South Africa were in the making, but when Soweto was still a tragic place, a "grinning skull," and when his people were still in a state of collective, spiritual exile.

Shava quotes Mphahlele as saying that the frustration of twenty years of exile drove him back:

> I am an African humanist and an empiricist, as well as an idealist. I can function here in South Africa. . . . Compromise? Life for an oppressed person is one long protracted, agonizing compromise. . . . I [realized] the longer I was away from here, the angrier, the more outraged, I felt against the suffering of people here. Out of sheer impotence. In a sense, my homecoming was another way of dealing with the impotent anger. It was also a way of extricating myself from twenty years of compromise, for exile is compromise. Indeed, exile had become for me a ghetto of the mind. My return to Africa was a way of dealing with the phantoms and echoes that attend exile. (1989, 45)

In the end, Mphahlele felt no regret about his decision to return. For one thing, there was much work to be done. There was also a need to reconnect not only with South Africa, but also with the African continent itself. With this in mind, Mphahlele extends an invitation to all his fellow exiles to join him, "to come back from the wilderness" (1991, 144).

Chapter Eight

Colonials in Black Skins

CHIRUNDU

Mphahlele's novel *Chirundu* (1979) is based on a true story of bigamy. While living in Zambia from 1968 to 1970, Mphahlele read in the newspaper about a cabinet minister who was being prosecuted for bigamy. From this event the seed of his story grew. Barnett suggests that on first reading *Chirundu* seems trivial. I disagree. In pan-African literature, novels that address women's issues of marriage and inheritance and related rights are a rarity. Equally rare are ones that feature a black female protagonist who is as rounded and believable, and active, as Tirenje in *Chirundu*. As a South African novelist writing about black abuse of power, Mphahlele raises timely historical questions about the need in postcolonial Africa to find "viable structures of self-government from the lessons of Africa's own historical experience" while simultaneously addressing vital women's issues within the framework of the dominant discourses of patriarchal societies (Davidson 1991, 363).

Chirundu is highly experimental in its use of narrative form, incorporating three heteroglot, socio-ideological voices, representing diverse professions, classes, generations, and speech types, and permeated, to paraphrase Bakhtin, with present and future intentions. These voices are Chirundu, minister of Transport and Public Works in an independent central African country recognizable as Zambia; Moyo, his nephew who leads a transport strike; and Tirenje, Chirundu's legal wife who eventually presses a charge of bigamy against him. Mphahlele's allusion to trade unionism and the invaluable role it has played in empowering black resistance movements is an important underlying theme. So is the portrayal of the mistreatment of South African refugees by neighboring African countries who have been bullied into acquiescence by the threat of South African closure of trade routes and ports backed up by bombing raids.

In addition to the three-part narrative, Mphahlele utilizes a chorus of commentators (the people's voices, as opposed to that of the authoritarian,

omniscient narrator) in the form of southern African exiles Chieza from
Zimbabwe and Pitso Mokae from South Africa. Through this choral device,
Mphahlele effectively creates a polyphonic resonance, a story line that
constitutes more than a single melody. Among the novel's ironic historical
footnotes is that South African refugees are discriminated against in part
because they come from an industrialized country and are educated. In the
case of Pitso and Chieza, who lack official passports, they have also been de-
tained without trial. Thus they have escaped white oppression only to fall
into black.

Confirming Bakhtin's core belief that "word" is determined by context,
it is often possible to trace in Mphahlele's works of nonfiction the contextual inspiration for his fiction. For example, in *Afrika My Music,* Mphahlele
observes that while white South Africans live "off the fat of the land in the
copperbelt . . . coming and going as they please," capable, educated blacks
like Bernard Magubane, socialist at the University (and one possible model
besides Mphahlele himself for Studs Letanka in *Chirundu*) and Livie Mquotsi,
also a teacher, receive notices to leave the country because they have no
"valid travel documents" (1984, 99).

Through *Chirundu*'s multi-voiced narrative, Mphahlele as both "real"
and "implied" author makes the most of the opportunity to examine the
issue of bigamy from every conceivable angle—legal, personal, religious,
cultural, and historical. In order to elaborate on his theme and further develop Chirundu's character, he also draws on African cultural symbolism.

As in African praise poems where characters take on the attributes of
creatures, Chirundu's character acquires an added dimension through his
being associated, totem-like, with *nsato,* the mythic python. A powerful objective correlative exists between *nsato* and Chirundu's drive to power. According to Mphahlele, pastoral people living south of the equator regard the
python as a symbol of fear (1986, 28). In addition to *nsato,* another richly as-
sociative, culturally derived African symbol Mphahlele effectively utilizes is
that of the building or burning down of the house to symbolize the forming
and dissolution of marriage alliances. Chimba's ultimate failure to establish
two houses symbolizes his failure on the marital front as well as the political, and at the socio-ideological level, is "symptomatic of his failure to operate between two levels of society, the rural masses and urban elite" (Johnson
1984, 114).

In the postcolonial, socio-ideological discourse, Chirundu serves as
what Bakhtin refers to as an "ideologeme," expressing a certain point of
view on the world, giving voice to certain codes and values that have, in
turn, been affected by the discourses of the past. Chirundu, for example,

disdains Christian morality because he has seen his own father become
tyrannical and disown his own wives under its sway "and something in him
... laid to rest forever" (51). Yet, at the same time, Chirundu is manipulative
and self-serving. Wanting to have it both ways, he decides to play Bemba
tribal law against Western law to facilitate his keeping both a town and a
country wife, both of whom he professes to love.

Wishing to avoid his father's mistakes, Chirundu ironically carries nationalism and his own personal ambitions to the same extreme his father
carried his zeal as a Christian convert, driven not by a "humanistic conscious," but a "superimposed kind of thing" (Mphahlele 1986, 30). Like
many politicians, Chirundu—fueled by motives of greed, the prestige of a
trophy wife, and a power-tripping ego—is a complex, contradictory figure,
who openly challenges the system. The reader, in turn, is not unsympathetic
to Chirundu's rationalizing and self-justification based on objections to the
imposition of Western morality and law on African traditions and culture.
The claims, in themselves, do not lack validity.

Nonetheless, it is when we hear the story from Tirenje's point of view
that our emotions are engaged. She, unlike Chirundu, is compassionate,
loyal, and authentic. Tirenje embodies African values deriving from the
rural past as opposed to Chirundu's mistress, the superficial and sophisticated Monde, who symbolizes the urban, Westernized upwardly mobile
elite. Tirenje comes to life as an African woman who "stands on strong legs,"
with breasts "you want to put your head between and listen to an ancient
story." With "no make up," and "just commonplace good looks handed
down by the gods . . . [she] braids her hair and puts on a headcloth when she
goes out" (99). Because of the courage and integrity with which Tirenje
adapts to modern ways while not losing her fundamental values and dignity, we are outraged by the crass manner in which she is wronged and exploited by the power-hungry Chirundu.

In 1996, a trial took place in South Africa—a country that has a new
constitution, one of the few in Africa to explicitly address women's rights.
The trial concerns the very themes and issues *Chirundu* prophetically raises.
According to a story in *The Economist,*

> A Zulu woman, Mildred Mthembu, lives with her daughter in a Jo-
> hannesburg township. Three years ago, her husband was shot dead.
> Because she was married according to African traditional law, under
> which property passes to the nearest male relative, her father-in-law
> then claimed ownership of her house. South Africa's bill of rights
> guarantees freedom from discrimination on the grounds of sex, but in

Mrs Mthembu's case the country's Supreme Court has just ruled that African custom should prevail over the modern concept of women's rights. (South 1996, 79)

On the basis of this case, it is clear Tirenje had reason, besides her clear pref-erence for monogamy, for insisting on marriage by civil law. When she presses bigamy charges against Chirundu, however, her motive is not re-venge or even to claim property rights. Rather she hopes to force him to give up politics and his town wife altogether.

When Chirundu, instead, receives a prison sentence, Tirenje is discon-solate. She attempts to explain to the judge, who will not listen. Tirenje be-haves according to an African code. Traditionally when there are marital problems, the concerned parties confront their problem, meeting with fam-ily members and elders to talk it out. Talk therapy "which cleanses and heals the heart .... [and] helps the boil to burst" is not new in the African context (24). Accordingly, Tirenje brings the problem into a public forum where el-ders sit. But the eyes of justice are blind to such human needs and concerns. In desperation, Tirenje burns down the city house Chirundu built for him-self and Monde to occupy. Her act symbolizes her starting over anew. She recalls the words of Elena Mwansa, her admired teacher, who tells her stu-dents that a "man who wants a woman for a thing to kick about is himself very weak" (84). Tirenje, having begged for a chance to join Chirundu in town, to support him in his work and also to engage in some work herself laments her loss. Both metaphorically and literally she also overcomes her fear of *nsato*. With these acts, "Tirenje is now a symbol of a new woman, who is not going to be in a polygamous situation" (Mphahlele 1986, 29)

Another novel in the African repertoire that deals memorably with the theme of bigamy is by Senegalese writer Mariama Ba, published in 1980, just a year after *Chirundu*. While *Chirundu* explores the issue of bigamy from the point of view of tribal and Western law, conflicting cultural values, and down-to-earth human concerns, Ba's *So Long a Letter* examines the im-pact of polygamy as sanctioned under Islamic law on the life of the novel's narrator, Ramatoulaye, an independent, well-educated mother, wife, and teacher. In a sensitive, deeply moving exploration of the issue, Ba, like Mphahlele, brings vividly to life a purely African setting while appealing to both African and universal human concerns.

Bessie Head's *Maru* (1971) does not focus quite so extensively on gender issues, but like *Chirundu* and *So Long a Letter*, it is concerned about forms of black oppression and prejudice practiced by blacks against blacks, a dra-matic change from the theme of white on black oppression which, in the past, formed the basis of so much of South Africa's literature. In the case of Head's novel, the discrimination is painfully experienced by a Masarwa (bushman) teacher, Margaret Cadmore, at the hands of Batswana villagers, who historically had kept Masarwa people as slaves. Like Tirenje and Ramatoulaye, Head's Margaret Cadmore is an interesting, believable, fully realized modern African woman—a woman who must do battle against at least one virulent form of oppression, either racism or sexism, and not infrequently both.

Unlike Mphahlele's strongman, Chirundu, Head's protagonist Maru shows signs of genuine enlightenment. As hereditary chief, he is in a position to challenge his people's prejudices, and he fearlessly does so. Acting on his liberal beliefs, he not only flies in the face of long-entrenched prejudices but hopes to be an entirely new kind of leader. He exhibits both compassion and a concern about change, about the need for a new dispensation. None of these traits, by contrast, are modeled by the power-driven, opportunistic Chirundu. Like Mphahlele, Head is adept at drawing on idiomatic, proverbial speech to illustrate a point. For example, the Batswana, shocked at the idea that a Masarwa will be teaching their children, take comfort in proverbial wisdom, reminding themselves that "Prejudice is like the old skin of a snake. It has to be removed bit by bit" (48). Head, like Mphahlele, continues to explore and redefine levels and kinds of colonial and imperialist discourse, whether through dialogizing voices, historicity, or presentation of character. Thus, another colonial in black skin in Head's novel puts in a brief cameo appearance in the person of the education supervisor who "was an exact replica of a colonial officer, down to the Bermuda shorts" (36).

The romance between Margaret and Maru as depicted by Head is both mythic and with a pronounced element of Western romantic love, characteristics far less in evidence in Tirenje's relationship with Chirundu, for whom sex, power, and self-interest are primary motivators. Like Mphahlele in *Chirundu*, Head's *Maru*—with its clear focus on women's issues of work, marriage, relationships, racism, and the conflict between traditional and new ways—is successful in presenting a new African aesthetic, a new person.

It is also illuminating to compare *Chirundu* with Gordimer's novel *None to Accompany Me* (1994), written in postapartheid South Africa. Gordimer's novel portrays both white and black characters who have played active roles in the freedom movement. All are coming to terms with change and with the new South Africa as it affects their professional and personal lives and those of their family. Vera, the main protagonist, a white, English-speaking liberal, is the very antithesis of Tirenje. Unlike Tirenje, Vera is unfaithful in marriage. She is also an indifferent parent and grandparent who never gives her grandson advice or, when he visits, bothers to "sew on his buttons or supervise his activities."

Vera and her grandson eat at different times and simply share "a convenient roof" (293). While Tirenje fights to keep her family together, Vera is bent on individuating. Vera's belief is that politics like art transcend personal life and that: "Everyone ends up moving alone towards the self" (306). "Love," "tenderness," and "loyalty" are not words in Vera's lexicon. Causes for Vera, as for Chirundu, count for more than people. Vera's loneliness is palpable as she dances solo to some vintage rock, a stiff vodka in her hand, her house the only thing she has left—with her daughter, Annick, now cohabiting with a lesbian lover, a son in London, and her husband, Ben, an "ex." Ultimately, Vera's house, too, is sold, symbolizing, as with Tirenje, the end of the old life. Vera's future, however, seems less sanguine than Tirenje's. Tirenje's conflict had been that of the individual "in relation to his/her human environment" (Mphahlele 1986, 24). In Vera's case, Western-style individualism appears to be a synonym for alienation. One wonders, "Is it worth it?"

Chirundu himself is caught between social systems and conflicting values. Like all colonized people Chirundu also has two selves—"the indigenous self and the one that's superimposed by the new culture" (Mphahlele 1986, 24). Although it is clear that the "implied" author is "more ruthless" with Chirundu and in greater sympathy with Tirenje, there may also be a hidden polemic at work in the narrative. Mphahlele does not endorse polygamy. Yet, like many black feminists, he "objects even more strongly to the way it was condemned by white missionaries as a barbaric African custom" (South 1996, 80).

Throughout the text, Mphahlele poses, by implication and parable, timely questions about how postcolonial Africa will handle new political and economic systems. He causes the reader, whether African or Western, to reflect on the awareness that there remains an unfinished revolution—one in which displacement, dispossession, and alienation is sexual and gender-based in origins. This revolution is based on the perception that black women are "triply oppressed by virtue of belonging to a devalued race, class and gender" (Byrne 1994, 23–24).

In one other important respect, Chirundu is anything but "trivial." By creating a composite historic figure in the "big man" mold of a Kaunda-Banda-Mobutu, who learned well from Europe's example of power politics and plunder, Mphahlele is serving notice that in the colonial struggle, to quote Fanon, not "every Negro or Moslem is issued automatically a hallmark of genuineness" (Fanon 1963, 146). In Wole Soyinka's words:

The consideration that brings me, personally, hard to earth is the thought of the Angolan or South African writer either in exile or stretching out his last feeble twitches before the inexorable maul of a desperate regime ends him. . . . And he sees, and he understands for the first time that, given equal opportunity, the black tin-god a few thousand miles north of him would degrade and dehumanize his victim as capably as Vorster or Governor Wallace. (1967, 31:13)

At the end of the day, Chirundu is not demoralized by his prison term. He continues to plot his return, to believe he is destined for great things. Chirundu, the ultimate politician, will make a comeback, Mphahlele leaves no doubt about that, raising, in the process, some timely and prescient questions about the specter of "black tin-gods" making their presence felt in independent Africa states. This is hardly a "trivial" or meaningless concern. Barnett misses the point when she questions whether Mphahlele has anything "important to communicate" in *Chirundu* (1976, 163).

Chirundu, viewed from the dialogic frame of themes of alienation and African humanism as they affect the formulation of a new South Africa, is as much a literary and political ground-breaker as *Afrika My Music* is a philosophic and educational one. In addition, *Chirundu* is an interesting novel to read. It comes as a welcome relief that the otherwise ever-present, ominous, spectacular stage set of apartheid is rendered a mere shadowy prop by the presence of two minor characters, Pitso and Dr. Studs Letanko, who are South African exiles.

Published in 1979 after Mphahlele's return to Johannesburg, *Chirundu* marks a shift in his thinking from the progressive alienation that found its lowest ebb in the days after Sharpeville in March of 1960. Structurally *Chirundu* is of interest not only because of its tri-part narrative, but also because it combines dramatic forms with the genre of a novel. Some chapters, for example the court and prison scenes, read like plays. *Chirundu* succeeds in its counterpointing of the theatrical and lyric, as it does in its postmodern use of multigeneric forms and pastiche. Moreover, it abounds in conflicts and ironies of the sort that have become recognizable as Mphahlele's trademark.

Mphahlele's fictive universe, as re-created in *Chirundu* with its crosscultural clashes and its conflicts between tribal practices and Western laws, avoids Manichean dichotomies. Mphahlele was both fearless and realistic in his satiric portrait of Chirundu as a corrupt, tin-pot dictator—a genuine "bad guy." Chirundu's profile bears uncanny resemblance to several real-life models, so much so that initially Mphahlele encountered problems getting the novel published in England for fear of libel charges (Manganyi 1984, 173).

Mphahlele is not driven to "correct a negative, derogatory image of Africa" promoted by colonialist literature by going to the opposite extreme (JanMohamed 1983, 8). Chirundu—the black cabinet minister and corrupt politician, riding the twin horses of modernism and tradition, and espousing views based on class and entitlement that reflect a colonial education—exhibits the same authoritarian pigheadedness and greed that whites have displayed in the racist regime of South Africa.

Chirundu may be read as a parable on how a modern postcolonial African state should and should not govern itself. In the heteroglot discourse, another ideologeme helping to play out that parable is cast in the character of Moyo (in Kiswahili, "heart"). Moyo is light to Chirundu's dark. Making nepotism into a virtue in the African way, Chirundu initially hires his nephew without a second thought then discovers that the approach—given Westernized institutions and a modernized nephew—in the end works against the ambitious minister.

Similarly Chirundu, just as he has discovered what James Olney refers to as "pleasurable polygamy," finds Western law, government, and modern politicians looking askance at a cabinet minister who openly insists on keeping a town wife and a country wife. Moyo, on the other hand, rather than exploiting, combines the best of two worlds. A political activist who gets involved in trade unions, Moyo is African enough not to want to criticize his uncle and modern enough to see the need to do so. Realistic and modern, he is engaged in building a new order. He also adheres to the best African humanistic values without experiencing conflict. He reveres his grandfather and his wise counsel, respects his aunt, and shows compassion for his peers.

Moyo's relationship with his grandfather bridges present with past. Old Mutiso, unlike others in the narrative, enjoys an almost mystic relationship with *nsato.* As an African symbol, the python also represents strength and power at its best. Age and its collective wisdom is part of that strength to which even Chirundu pays eloquent tribute.

> Old age draws me to itself. You look at old age and you seem to be in the presence of an awful mystery. One that commands reverence and at the same time seems indifferent. . . . He is an ancestor now. Time has poured into this life all it could ever invest. This man, this woman you see in front of you in their seventies, eighties, nineties, has earned that status. In Europe and America, I've been told, they would be tucked

away . . . out of the concourse of general humanity. Moyo would be
seen as having towed behind him a wreckage for the scrapyard. To us,
he would be walking behind a god. (53)

Moyo, closely bonded with Old Mutiso, combining respect for the
African past and a modern outlook, serves as a positive role model for how
the new generation can assert black values while also becoming thoroughly
modern. "Moyo," says Mphahlele, "is a young man who is going on into the
future to create something new" (Mphahlele 1986, 23).

Just as Chirundu is Moyo's opposite, Monde (meaning "world" in
French) is Tirenje's foil. She is materialistic and shallow, having absorbed
some of the worst of Western ways. Tirenje by contrast is less educated in
the ways of the world, but in her rural African roots, she does not lack culture. She, like Karabo in "Mrs Plum," never loses track of her values or her
sense of personal worth. Ironically, she, a village girl, grows from strength to
strength, becoming more liberated and self-aware than the book-read
Chirundu with his colonial education.

Like Moyo, Tirenje symbolizes the coming together of two streams of
consciousness—African and Western. She is a working prototype of a new
African aesthetic, of what the new woman can become. The clash of wills
between Tirenje and Chirundu on such issues as the sanctity of marriage as
it reflects on tribal versus modern customs and law raises highly relevant
questions revolving around women's liberation and equality. Yet, Tirenje, at
her most eloquent, comments on one of the gravest risks posed to indigenous culture by Western industrialized society, saying: "Something strange
has touched us in the white man's school and church, in the white man's
town and we make loneliness in our selves as the factory makes clothes"
(Mphahlele 1973, 89). Thus, she gives voice to the self-alienating sense of
loneliness Africans feel when caught between old communal ways and new
ways in an industrialized urban setting.

In the parable and cautionary tale of *Chirundu,* the dialogizing voices
continues to probe such questions as: What is of value? What should one try
to preserve of the old and traditional and how much of the new to assimi-
late? How can a society modernize without losing those ancient values that
are worth preserving or without the risk of being culturally colonized by the
West? African humanism, the author/narrator seems to suggest, can continue to provide a useful tool with which to approach synthesis and assimi-
lation, operating from a psychological position of strength, after the pain of
colonial domination while also contributing to a movement of cultural nationalism and unity (Wallerstein 1961, 122–35).

In *Chirundu,* Mphahlele as African humanist narrator demonstrates the continued usefulness of such a tool. Just as he did in his early stories, Mphahlele draws imaginatively on symbols and myths from the deep African past to criticize the existing order, in turn, reflecting his own successful decolonization as an African humanist author. In *Chirundu,* the classic pan-African myth of the python appears repeatedly throughout the text as a powerful metaphor to symbolize the strength of old values, as well as sexual virility and the abuse of raw power (Davidson 1991, 16). In the act of having Tirenje burn down the house Chirundu has built, Mphahlele again resurrects a culturally derived myth from Bantu societies which believe that an established house should never be allowed to die out (Johnson 1984, 6). The message is clear: Chirundu and all such dictators will ultimately destroy themselves. Decadence, oppression, and exploitation contain the seeds of their own conflagration.

Several critics, not least among them Lindfors, have raised the question of what black South Africans returning from exile will begin to produce in the way of a new postapartheid body of literature. Lindfors notes that "nearly all of these long-term expatriates—Dennis Brutus, Mazisi Kunene, Lewis Nkosi, Keorapetse Kgositsile, to name only the most prolific—have focused almost exclusively on one subject: South Africa" (1994, 63). Just as Mphahlele led the return to South Africa, he leads in this area as well. In *Chirundu* he has planted a literary landmark, writing a novel refreshingly free from the cliché apartheid had long been as a literary subject.

Because state apartheid had for so long provided a made-to-order modular plot and dictated the themes in South African literature, a related question of whether authors would be able to fill the postapartheid vacuum with their own inventiveness is also frequently raised. Gordimer once said that a good author can make even the death of a canary affecting. This Mphahlele has more than achieved in his portrait of the suffering Tirenje endures as a result of her bigamous betrayal. In so doing Mphahlele has updated and redefined the terms of conflict. If Mphahlele's *Chirundu* can be considered a harbinger, the new thematic arena of alienation and conflict may not be racial at all. Instead, it may be gender-based and dear to the hearts of feminists concerned with such issues as equal rights and opportunities for women like Tirenje.

In *Chirundu,* Mphahlele makes clear that between Western ideals of love and that of a communal ideal based on procreation and the continuation of the ancestral line, there may be a built-in clash between Africa and the West, one lending itself to exploitation by the unscrupulous. Such themes demonstrate that in any body of postapartheid South African literature the possibilities in terms of subjects to be explored are ripe for the picking. Moreover, there are no easy dichotomies. Not all Western values are bad. Not all traditional ones arising out of vanished agrarian societies and related economic constraints are necessarily practical. There can be no Manichean absolutes, but there is the realistic and hopeful possibility, as demonstrated by Moyo in *Chirundu,* of a positive working synthesis being achieved between Africa and the West in the continuing dialogue.

In the past, African humanism, by calling attention to an indigenous culture of great richness, diversity, and value, and by demanding its just preservation for no other reason than its intrinsic worth, served as a useful cultural weapon with which to confront the brutality and daily humiliations of state apartheid. Apartheid denied the black man's humanity, but African humanism affirmed it. Today, African humanism, Mphahlele suggests in his double-voiced discourse, can continue to play an important role by criticizing the existing order, while simultaneously reintegrating the intellectual with his African past and bringing the undereducated rural masses into the dialogue.

Chapter Nine

The Unbroken Song

STORIES AND POETRY

> *We keep on talking across the wall, singing our*
> *different songs, beating our different drums*
> —Es'kia Mphahlele

Stories

The Unbroken Song, published in 1981, is a collection of a dozen and a half stories, several poems, and a letter to the father of negritude, Leopold Senghor. Many of the stories in this collection appeared in earlier anthologies or were published elsewhere. The volume begins with an introduction from the African humanist narrator who invites his readers to "come on over" and "let us talk" about the "unbroken music" African communal culture and history can produce, despite the cruel efforts by others to silence it. To listen to this "unbroken music" is to experience renewal. Through the "spear point" of his sensitivity and his "strong beautiful words," Mphahlele, the storyteller/*griot*/praise poet, hopes to contribute to the unbroken song. Combining, as it does, African idioms, philosophic thought, and poetry, Mphahlele's introduction is not the standard one the reader expects to encounter in such an anthology—but it is unmistakably vintage Mphahlele.

In *Afrika My Music,* Mphahlele talks about the ballad and how he finds in its "leaping" and "lingering" effect, its sad ironies and silences, a good model for the short story form and one that bears close kinship to African oral tales. Some of the stories appearing in *The Unbroken Song* do bear close similarity to the ballad, particularly the Nigerian tales. Others, such as "The Living and the Dead" and "He and the Cat," are more structurally and psychologically complex.

Interestingly, these two stories have evoked diametrically opposed reactions from two critics. Gerald Moore, in *Seven African Writers,* states that in these two stories Mphahlele moves "on to an altogether richer level of awareness" (1962, 100). Barnett feels, however, that in the former, "plot and character have little chance to develop, either spontaneously toward a pleasing work of art, or according to the laws of probability and the principles of psychology." Barnett takes on a shrill tone as if a raw nerve had been touched, pronouncing the events and characters in "The Living and the Dead" "impossible" in the South African context (1976, 71).

"The Living and the Dead" begins when Lebona, a railway sweeper, sees a man trampled to death by the rush-hour crowd. He also picks up a letter which he finds lying on the track. He mulls over the brutality of the man's sudden death (a metaphor for human life for blacks in apartheid South Africa and one of the motifs related to the title itself). Lebona decides to return the letter to the addressee. Meanwhile, Stoffel Visser, a government official, is completing a report on "kaffir" servants, recommending that they should be moved out of the suburbs. His report is late and he is upset, for he has been taught from his university days that things must be right. The report itself is a satiric profile of Visser and other whites in their programmed racist thinking. Words such as "breeding," "swarming," "wooden-headed" are freely used by Visser to suggest that blacks are nothing more than animals—that their numbers are taking over. Underlying the racist labeling is fear of the *swart gevaar.*

Internal monologue is used effectively both to develop and to parody Stoffel's character. When Lebona arrives at Stoffel's door, bearing a letter, a duo of internal monologues is dramatically juxtaposed to underscore the mutual mistrust and hostility between the white "baas" and the black railway sweeper (and by extension all black workers and white officials). The letter is addressed to Jackson, Stoffel's servant, who had not returned since he left work to take his children to the zoo. Jackson's wife, who works in another part of town, was not free to accompany the children. Irony builds on irony. When Jackson inexplicably fails to return to work on time, Stoffel, who depends on Jackson to wake him up in the morning and serve him his breakfast, is late with his official report. Yet the proposal Stoffel is drafting will insure that servants no longer live in the suburbs.

As Stoffel expresses anxiety over the lateness of his report, his internal monologue is strewn with words such as "must," "detail," "right." In his dialogue with his subordinate "Doppie," a drunk, who is more concerned with drinking whiskey than with the report ("dop" means "tot" in Afrikaans), Stoffel trots out all the ideological clichés of the apartheid state, including the need to protect "white civilization" (104). Doppie, a carnivalesque figure who gives us insight into Stoffel's character, is also a prototype of whites who, like sheep, go along with the double-think of apartheid, never questioning. Stoffel, who does think and feel, bears many of the hallmarks of the obsessive-compulsive, paranoid, neurotic authoritarian personality, the Afrikaner equivalent of Mrs. Plum. But he also defies easy labels.

In the dialogue between Lebona and Stoffel, Stoffel questions Lebona's motives, suggesting that perhaps the black railway sweeper opened the letter first before delivering it to see if there was any cash inside. Lebona ironically enjoys the lie he tells when he denies any such motives while thinking, these whites: "They're not even decent enough to suspect one's telling the truth!" Stoffel at the same time is thinking, "They always lie to you when you're white . . . just for cheek" (111).

First Jackson's wife, Virginia, shows up in a desperate state, worried about how she will manage to bring up her two small sons if something has happened to Jackson. Then Stoffel reads the letter delivered by Lebona. It is from Jackson's father who is dying somewhere in Vendaland. He implores Jackson to come soon, for not only does he expect to die soon, but the government has told him to get rid of some of his cattle. He returns the pictures of Jackson and his grandchildren for safekeeping. From these details, not only does the narrative progress, but a picture emerges of how the state works under apartheid economics. Art and function are united, springing from lived experience.

At this point, a chink begins to appear in Stoffel's "crocodile-hide" armor. In so many ways Stoffel is the nonpareil Afrikaner government servant. Still, there is a part of him that rebels against the work he does. His entire past begins to feel like a dead weight, the "brutal" history of his people, the overwhelming demands of the present, all bearing down on him. He realizes he lacks the strength to stand up to the "brutal" weight of this dead past—giving it up would be tantamount to his "losing his identity" (109). Yet suddenly, Jackson, Virginia, their two sons, and Jackson's dying father take on human faces.

Stoffel returns from the office to find Jackson back at the residence, but in a bad state, having been insulted and beaten up by white police. For the first time, Stoffel calls a personal physician to come to the house to look after Jackson:

> For four years he had lived with a servant and had never known more
> about him than that he had two children living with his mother-in-law
> and a wife. Even then, they were such distant abstractions—just names

representing some persons, not human flesh and blood and heart and mind.

And anger came up in him to muffle the cry of shame, to shut out the memory of recent events that was battering on the iron bars he had built up in himself as a means or protection. There were things he would rather not think about. And the heat of his anger crowded them out. What next? He didn't know. Time, time, time, that's what he needed to clear . . . the fog that rose thicker and thicker with the clash of currents from the past and the present. Time, time. . . . And then Stoffel Visser realized he did not want to think, to feel. He wanted to do something. Jackson would want a day off to go visit his father . . . sack Jackson? No. Better continue treating him as a name, not as another human being. Let Jackson continue as a machine to work for him. Meanwhile he must do his duty—dispatch the commission's report. That was definite, if nothing else. He was a white man, and he must be responsible. To be white and to be responsible were one and the same thing. (117)

Gerald Moore suggests that "it would have been easy to make this story the preparation for a reformation in Stoffel Visser, the breaking of a new light upon his bleak corridor of bigotry" (1962, 101). But Mphahlele is much too clear-sighted and realistic for this easy option. Barnett on the other hand suggests that Mphahlele is too compassionate. Such compassion, suggests Barnett, leads Mphahlele to erroneous perception. "He cannot envisage others not sharing his deep feeling for his fellowmen" (1976, 71). According to this view, the author endows Stoffel with the capacity for too much humanitarian feeling and thought. I believe the truth lies somewhere between. "The Living and the Dead" is a good example of how Mphahlele effectively strikes a balance between themes of alienation and African humanism. The fact that Stoffel had a moment of self- and other-awareness, in which he comes alive, not only suggests hope and the possibility of change, it gives Stoffel psychological depth that makes him both rounded and plausible as a character. Moreover, such humanistic optimism on the part of the narrator in presenting Stoffel as human, rather than as a mere machine, appears to have been redeemed in light of recent historic changes that have occurred in South Africa. Although Stoffel is recognizable as the quintessential Africaner government servant, as a human being he is far more complex than any label could encompass, and that, too, suggests Mphahlele, is reason to hope.

"He and the Cat" is one of Mphahlele's most widely reprinted stories. The story has no plot sequence. It takes place in a lawyer's office where the narrator has gone to seek help in the resolution of a undisclosed problem. The narrative involves impressionistic but concrete details of the setting—from a fly on the window, to the cat picture that sits observing, keeping its secrets, almost like fate. We know that the narrator is African and unaccustomed to seeking the help of a lawyer. As he observes the scene, he rehearses, nervously in his mind, how he will present his case. The narrative shifts from first to second person, helping to universalize the waiting-room experience in which a person is in the "no-time of feeling and thought" (120).

Although Barnett suggests the story has a Kafkaesque feel to it, such an analysis overlooks its African humanist canvas in which marketplace proverbs and speech—the interconnected organic whole of ghetto life, with its sense of the carnivalesque sacred and profane, laughter, ridicule, rejoicing, the presence of the stupid and the wise, the sense of the "relatively of history"—are all summoned up by the narrator in the course of a few paragraphs, bristling with proverbs. We hear talk of bride prices, of death in which the dying is oppressed by Christian-induced thoughts of original sin, African views on child-rearing and the respect owed elders, and even a description of the rural Magaba, whose women sell fruit and where the people are as "red as the ground on which they stand" (121). The proverb, "our sages say that the only thing you have that's surely your own is what you've already eaten" is an implied commentary on apartheid economics and the hardships people experience simply trying to meet their basic needs (120). Here is the entire panorama of African life, urban and rural, sketched out, and highlighted by several polyphonic voices. The narrator, then, is not marooned in Kafkaesque isolation, existentially isolated in a western sense. He hears the collective voices, albeit he initially responds to them with a "carnivalesque" ambivalence.

Not only is life sketched out, but death and the changes brought by urbanization are woven into the canvas—for, "death is in the leg; we walk with it." Still another voice expresses dismay over the change in young people, citing the example of a daughter-in-law who beats her mother-in-law, suggesting, in turn, the fragmentation of indigenous culture and family life, resulting from dire poverty, state apartheid, and urbanization.

Across the room, with the picture of the cat behind him, sits a man sealing envelopes. He is the source of most of the proverbs that are "old as the language of man" (123). He comes more sharply into focus as the story progresses. Eventually, he takes center stage as:

> An envelope fell to the floor. He bent down to take it up. I watched his large hands feel about for it, fumbling. Then the hand came upon the object, but with much more weight than a piece of paper warranted.

Even before he came up straight on his chair I saw it clearly. The man at the table was blind, stone blind. As my eyes were getting used to the details, after my mind had thus been jolted into confused activity, I understood. Here was a man sealing envelopes, looking like a drawing on a flat surface. Perhaps he was flat and without depth, like a gramophone disc; too flat even to be hindered by the heat, the boredom of sitting for hours doing the same work; by too many or too few people coming. An invincible pair, he and the cat glowering at him, scorning our shames and hurts and the heart, seeming to hold the key to the immediate imperceptible and the remote unforeseeable. (124)

The question that arises at this point in the narrative is what are we to make of this surprise revelation—what is the significance of the blind man? In Barnett's judgment, the blind man is a "meaningless" figure. This assessment totally disregards Mphahlele's fundamental African humanist aesthetic. The final lines of the story provide the clue to a more meaningful interpretation: "I went in to see Mr B., a small man (as I had imagined) with tired eyes but an undaunted face. I told him everything from beginning to end" (124). Although the blind man is as flat as a gramophone disc, this lack of sharp edges has enabled him to survive. In Mphahlele's early stories the themes of survival and "man must live" are paramount. But in this story, the main character is jolted out of his complacency and the social Darwinist code to which ghetto life so easily reduces people. He sees that he, too, is in danger of becoming flat, of losing his humanity in the daily struggle to keep his head above water. His moment of awareness, empathy, and compassion for the blind man, which puts his own problems in perspective, reminds him of and reconfirms his own humanity. His own personal problem then takes on manageable proportions, enabling him to confront the lawyer with renewed confidence. As Bakhtin suggests, self is realized through other, in mutual compassion and mutual acceptance or as Mphahlele would say, "I am because you are because we are."

Gerald Moore sees these two stories, "The Living and the Dead" and "He and the Cat," as "an expression of life by one who has lived it with rare intensity and compassion" (1962, 102). South African critic Mbulelo Vizikhungo Mzamane points out that Mphahlele's Nigerian stories are frequently ignored by Mphahlele scholars (Thuynsma 1989, 43–53). Mzamane, however, considers that they have merit and represent pioneering work. In the Nigerian stories, for example, Mphahlele utilizes pidgin English in dialogue to evoke local atmosphere and color and brings it off successfully, again revealing his remarkable ear for marketplace speech, figuratively and literally.

Mzamane, who himself has lived and taught in Nigeria, believes the Nigerian stories are "amenable to more sympathetic treatment" than critics such as Barnett and O. R. Dathorne have shown (43). Barnett expresses her relief when in her analysis it is time to turn back to the South African stories. The conflicting views expressed by critics concerning Mphahlele's Nigerian stories might be puzzling were one to overlook Bakhtin's literary dictum that "word" is inseparable from context.

In the "Barber of Bariga," for example, critics may question, as Mzamane himself does, whether the elaborate scene between Anofi, the protagonist, and his father in the barbershop in Bariga township serves to advance the narrative or slow it down. Likewise, the seemingly unrelated episode of the auto accident involving a white couple that draws an instant crowd. If one examines only the structural demands of the plot, one might make an argument for the case that the two episodes do slow the narrative pace. Contextually, however, the two episodes are important to the story. The barbershop serves as a set that allows for the development of two contrasting characters with differing world views. From his barbershop, Anofi is well positioned to watch the world pass by, a world filled with activity and vignette, not unlike the world as seen in Mphahlele's earlier works. Anofi's disposition, however, is to detach from it all—an impulse running counter to the cultural imperative of communal involvement that runs throughout African cultures. Anafi's father, by contrast, likes to entertain waiting customers with funny stories, while chewing on a kola nut, "his jaws moving like a goat's." The old man is an engaged participant in the "I am because you are because we are" ethos that binds African cultures regardless of locale or ethnicity.

Anofi's father, as an exemplar of community involvement, serves as an ideological counterpoint to Anofi. Similarly, the car accident between a Yoruba cyclist and a white couple serves to elaborate on context, both historically and culturally. The fender-bender draws an instant crowd, which in turn becomes a communal experience with a certain built-in entertainment value in the same way it would in any similar setting all over Africa. Such events are proof that life is not predetermined by neat and tidy formulae, with events happening predictably according to some abstract ideal of a perfectly symmetrical beginning, middle, and end. In Mphahlele's aesthetic, art springs from life, with all its bustling chaos and color. Anofi's father's lively exchanges with customers and the car accident are part of the unfolding tapestry of experiences witnessed from the barbershop. "Always people gathered around some place where something was happening that was not daily routine: a man changing a tyre; a petrol attendant checking tyres; a motorist stopping to drink tea out of a flask, and so on. Whenever there had been an accident, the crowd had many observations and opinions to air, far more of the latter than the former" (131). When the white couple feel overwhelmed by their experience of the instant crowd, the wife behaves in an ugly, overbearing manner. Her husband then pays off the Yoruba cyclist, who may have staged the accident, in the first place, for the express purpose of extracting payment. The entire scene is "carnivalesque" in its ridicule of all participants, including the whites, behaving like neo-colonialists. Wringing their hands and tut-tutting, they wonder how nation-building can proceed with people behaving in such fashion. In a not-so-hidden polemic in the narrative that comments on Nigeria's colonial past and more recent cultural conflicts between the West and Africa, the woman and cyclist exchange insults:

> "I think you're just being silly," the woman insisted.
> "Joo can't abuse me like dat, a-ah! It's un insolt. I say joo can't abuse me. Um not your stewart."
> "No, you're too silly to be anybody's stewart." (132)

Although Bariga, as a particularized setting, differs from South African Nadia Street in its local color and traditions, there are certain commonalities. Both South Africa and Nigeria have experienced forms of exploitative, self-alienating colonization. Both share elements of an indigenous, self-unifying humanism, purely African in spirit. Once again Mphahlele presents life in all its complexity.

Mphahlele's Nigerian story, "The Barber of Bariga," has as its central theme the abuse of the working class by the nouveau riche, in this case personified by Bashiru, who uses wealth to seduce other people's wives, though he has several of his own. Male domination and the exploitation of women are important subtexts. Black on black class and gender discrimination are thoroughly examined in the text. Okeke, an aggrieved husband, recounts to Anofi the modus operandi of Bashiru. "'Look um. His grand-dad don' eat his chief's title. His dad don' try to force it out to be made chief un he don' fail. Bot his dad was clever un he don' take oder people's houses un moni. Don't'ief t'ief everyt'ing un now his son Bahsiru take his blod of t'ief from his dad un ti'ief t'ief wife un moni un houses all over now he be fat un rich'" (135). Bashiru's ancestors knew the reasonable use of power. But the capitalist Bashiru, like Chirundu in the novel by that title, in his greed, understands only its misuse. There are no longer any strong traditional or cultural brakes to temper the use and abuse of wealth and power as there had been in the past.

Mphahlele's description of Bashiru's head and the cut Anofi gives him is masterful. It is, as Barnett suggests, a case of one craftsman, the writer, paying tribute to another.

> Anofi knew Bashiru's head very well; round with an eternal pimple or blackhead on the side near the ear and an old scar in the form of a slight dent in the flesh of the skull. It was an easy head to handle for a cut. . . . The barber seemed to own the head, as if there were a point of identity with it, as if he would be hurt if someone else gave it a haircut. As his clippers nibbled down the slopes, he seemed conscious of his physical ease and the good job being done of his cut. (126)

The head, as disembodied symbol, becomes the point of identity when Anofi receives the news that Bashiru "had died by accident at a wedding." Anofi is called to perform the ritual shaving of the head required by tradition before burial. As he performs the task, he is shocked suddenly to discover that Bashiru had been murdered, a nail driven into his skull. Anofi can no longer remain detached, and the final shock to his lethargy is administered when the culprit, Akeke, reveals that Bashiru had also seduced Anofi's beautiful wife.

The "Ballad of Oyo" is the most lyric of Mphahlele's Nigerian tales, utilizing as it does such devices as repetition of phrases, an abrupt beginning, simple language, and "the leaping and lingering technique," to suggest a tragic folk tale or ballad. Ishola, the main character, is "slender," with dark, smooth skin and "piercing eyes" (141). Except for class differences, Ishola and Ba's Ramatoulaye share a common cause based on their feminist, postcolonial discourses concerned with sexual and socioeconomic identities.

While Ishola sells fruit at the market, struggling to support the family and, at the same time, tending to three small children, her useless husband, Balogun, spends their meager earnings on palm wine and enjoys the pleasures of polygamy up north where he keeps other wives, for whose favors he periodically abandons Ishola. Ishola's sister, with a babe on her breast of her own and no husband in sight to lend a hand, nonetheless scolds Ishola for letting Balogun kick her around. "'You are everybody's fool, are you not? Lie still like that and let him come and sit and play drums on you and go off and get drunk on palm wine, come back and beat you, scatter the children, children of his palm-wine-stained blood (spitting), like a hawk landing among chicks'" (141). Barnett finds the presence of Ishola's sister in the story of little purpose, but the sister plays an indispensable role, as catalyst and in offering extensive commentary on Ishola's situation.

Barnett also claims that Ishola, as a character, is someone "we never learn to know" and who "fails to arouse our sympathy" (1976, 89). Yet what we do know is a surprising amount considering the shortness of the tale. Ishola, from the start, is presented as spirited and resourceful, and later emerges as brave and enduring. She is a product of her culture and, to some extent, a victim of it as well. Yet, when Ishola finds a tramp asleep on her stall, early one morning, she furiously "poked the grimy bundle with a broom to tell him a few things he had better hear: there are several other places where he could sleep; she sells food off this counter, not fire-wood" (140). From this scene, we gain the impression that whatever choices Ishola may make, they are made actively, not because she is a passive victim.

Mphahlele then pans the marketplace setting and creates a three-dimensional scene as timeless as an African *makonde* carving. In a lyric, ballad-like refrain that pays tribute to the courage and endurance of market women everywhere, to their resourcefulness and capacity for nurturing, Mphahlele memorializes the burdens they carry both figuratively and literally, while evoking the folk culture of the region.

> Day and night the women of Oyo walk the black road, the road of tarmac, to and from the market. They can be seen walking, riding the dawn, walking into sunrise; figures can be seen, slender as twilight; their feet feel every inch of the tarmac, but their wares press down on the head and the neck takes the strain, while the hip and legs propel the body forward. A woman here, a woman there in the drove has her arm raised in a loop, a loop of endurance, to support the load, while the other arm holds a suckling child in a loop, a loop of love. (141)

On the way to market one day, a cloudburst foreshadows the miscarriage that causes Ishola to collapse by the roadside. Balogun is meanwhile in the north. Ishola, having to suffer through this loss alone, decides she has had enough and that she will press for a divorce and accept the love proffered by her lover, Lijadu, who is willing to pay the necessary bride price. Once she has secured her divorce, Ishola leaves town with the children and meets Lijadu. But he brings word that her elderly father-in-law, Mushin, has died and that with his last words he prayed for the return of Ishola and his grandchildren. Hearing this, Ishola decides to return.

Western readers, in particular, may find the story's resolution a disappointment. As Mzamane in his critique of the story observes: "One would have wished to see more resolve in the central character of a story that appears to champion the rights of women in a male-dominated society. . . . [But] in the Yoruba traditional world view, the curse of a dying parent is as potent and devastating as it is nearly always irrevocable" (52, 152). Clearly, some contextual knowledge of the story's Yoruba roots is needed in order for the reader to more fully understand and appreciate its ironic complexity and true meaning.

Critics O. R. Dathorne and Willifred Feuser raise the question of whether or not it was appropriate for Mphahlele in his Nigerian stories to make use of pidgin dialect, with its mix of English and vernacular words, in the discourse between the women in the marketplace. Mzamane, however, assures the reader that this is entirely as it should be—that pidgin is the lingua franca of marketplace speech in Yoruba markets in West Africa and that Mphahlele has accurately transliterated this marketplace speech into the stories themselves.

The Nigerian stories are a good example of how far Mphahlele, the master storyteller, inventively using the speech of the marketplace and a worldview informed with the symbols, folklore, myth, and imagery of a black aesthetic, has come from his early efforts in *Man Must Live* in which Victorian pastoral settings, contrived romantic endings, and mission-press English figured heavily.

Poems

If Mphahlele's monumental work of criticism, *The African Image,* is his most dynamic political and aesthetic expression of his African humanist voice, and *Down Second Avenue* its most communal expression as lived experience, then poetry is among its most definitive spiritual expressions. As the mother tongue of all languages, poetry has been the most closely connected of all literary forms to community. Since poetry, with its oral roots, is readily transmitted without the necessity of a press, it also provided a good tool during the post-Sharpeville era to strike a note of protest. The communal voice of poetry is expressed, as Mphahlele observes in his essay collection *Voices in the Whirlwind*, through a need to resolve tension between the artist's "private instinct and his social environment." While the novel "represents change and diversity; poetry [stands for] changelessness and unity" (Mphahlele 1972, 7).

Mphahlele's poetry has been perhaps even more often overlooked than his Nigerian tales. Fortunately, several poems by Mphahlele are collected in the anthology *The Unbroken Song.* They represent a period in the 1970s in which Mphahlele was concentrating more heavily on poetry. His interest in poetry and its oral roots, which he has researched in the field, going back to sources in the manner of Renaissance humanists, provided the impetus for an outstanding lecture and monograph presented as one of the Raymond Dart series of lectures at the University of Witwatersrand in 1984, titled "Poetry and Humanism: Oral Beginnings." Although African humanism is not a doctrinaire ideology, or myth or belief system, or aesthetic, it does incorporate certain overarching precepts that Mphahlele outlines in his monograph. With erudition and eloquence, Mphahlele begins with the inception of Western humanism during the Renaissance and works his way up to the present, establishing historic links between African oral poetry and African humanism. He argues that poetry is the voice of African humanism in which reverberate the "dialogue between two streams of consciousness: the present and the living past"; between an ancient humanism and the alienation of a stateless, dispossessed exile (1974, 70).

As Mphahlele suggests, in poetry the "I" becomes the collective "we," which in turn is communal, manifesting the spirit expressed in the Xhosa proverb that "people are people because of other people." The cooperative spirit of *ubuntu*, or participatory humanism, is a vital part of this communalism. Elders are respected and families are sacrosanct. Social relations within the framework of the nuclear family and community constitute "a formidable network in Africa" and at the center of life is the person, including ancestors, who knew "the joys and pains of living" (1986, 9–10). African humanist metaphysics embraces a pantheistic view of the universe in which "the living and dead belong to the same category of beings . . . in an interplay that enables them to communicate the particles of a vital force" (Wauthier 1979, 171–72). "The Supreme Being is the Vital Force that is present in all forms of life, so that the plant, animal and human kingdoms form a sacred organic unity. Among human beings we say, 'I am because you are, you are because we are'" (Mphahlele 1986, 9).

Black Consciousness, African humanism, and its Western counterpart hold in common a belief in man's ability to realize his potential through his own efforts. Mphahlele shares with Julian Huxley the belief that "humanism is unitary"; it affirms the unity of mind and spirit, natural and supernatural and of mankind (23). Blacks are more concerned, states Mphahlele, about "maintaining that delicate balance between individual aspiration and communal will" than about past transgressions and rewards in an afterlife. This places the African squarely in the present in which the now is all or, as James Olney expresses it, "the African sense of the present as [it exists as] the spiritual nexus between revered ancestors and reincarnate children" (1973, 75).

African humanism, says Mphahlele, is a way of life as much as a philosophy. Peter Thuynsma further notes that this humanism is manifest in the way blacks interact—open in self-expression, unafraid of their bodies, "not all bottled up. They dance, laugh, sing, touch" (1991). Mphahlele adds that, "Our people are very frank in telling you what's going on inside them"; there is always "a free expression of grief and of joy" (1986, 25).

African humanism, says Mphahlele, as a way of life has been "challenged, fragmented . . . devastated in such places as South Africa" (1986, 8). It has often been misunderstood as well. Reverence for ancestors, explains Mphahlele, is different from ancestor worship. Respect for ancestors reflects man's place in history and in his group. The awe felt for ancestors was a source of moral support, a means of transmitting social and spiritual values and mores. African humanism is "deeply embedded in our proverbs and aphorisms and oral poetry, and in the way our elders spoke to us, and their children passed on the wisdom" (9–10). For Mphahlele an African humanist aesthetic and its expression in art begins by finding its inspiration in the community while at the same time serving that community. This principle can be seen as much or more in Mphahlele's poetry as in his prose.

The extent to which an African humanist aesthetic figures into black poetry of protest written in the 1950s through the 1980s may best be appreciated by making a brief comparative study of poems by Mphahlele and two of South Africa's best-known living poets, Mongane Wally Serote and Dennis Brutus. Such a comparison, in turn, will help illuminate the forgoing exegesis on African humanism.

Serote is well known for what Mbulelo Vizikhungo Mzamane calls his "making-by-naming" poems, which draw on the traditional oral form of the *isibongo*. These include his panegyrics on Johannesburg, the township of Alexandra, and on black women. From 1969 on, Serote began to write poetry of liberation in which the focus was on "the problems of squalor, violence, death, destitution, exploitation and the Black people's quest for identity and a sense of community." After Sharpeville, Serote turned to a style sometimes referred to as "the mother-fucker school" of screaming poetry. It was blunt, violent, sensationalist, agonized and effective. Expletives were used as bullets. Anger and bitterness transformed words such as "fuck" and "shit," as Serote notes, into "poetical terms" (1990, 9). Serote says that while the style served its purpose during the post-Sharpeville era of despair and activism, it is now time to move on to something new. Black Power poetry, he says, was like soap that "has washed away the shame of those who were black. . . . [And] like soap, that poetry is finished, it has done its job" (10). A good example of Serote's most screaming, as well as effective, Black

Consciousness poetry is the poem, "No Baby Must Weep." It is an extended dirge and praise poem, utilizing simple language and repetition, intended for a black audience. It is "carnivalesque" in its juxtaposing of the sacred and profane.

> *No Baby Must Weep*
> let me hold your hand
> black mother let me hold your hand and walk with you
> . . . .
> mama
> you know you never let me become a caddie
> or a garden-boy
> let's stop here a little mama
> . . . .
> alexandra is full of shit i know
> . . . .
> i am fucking tired
> shitlessly tired of talking, writing hoping people can hear
> a song
> from a child whose heart was broken
> . . . .
> i am the man you will never defeat
> i will be the one to plague you
> your children are cursed
> . . . .
>   (Serote 1982, 73–82)

"No Baby Must Weep" is a consciousness-raising poem, an affirmation of blackness and a declaration of black power. Its polemic is overt. In its simple, powerful language, and conversational style, making use of oral devices such as repetition, it is accessible to a black audience whose English standards may have dropped under the onslaught of Bantu education, while, at the same time, maintaining its appeal to a more literate audience. As in oral tradition, it is a poem meant to be heard as well as read on the page. In it, Serote celebrates the township of Alexandra which, despite its filth, is still a township with a soul. He celebrates the strength and dignity of black women, questions the cultural colonization of mission-school education, and calls our attention to the psychological, economic, cultural, and spiritual oppression of the apartheid state. The lower-case "i" is the collective "I" of self-in-community, for whose strength and resilience "mama" is also the symbol. In all of these thematic concerns, Serote is kin to Mphahlele, partaking in the same African humanist spirit.

Serote has a gift for capturing the immediate in words both simple and sublimely lyric and, in turn, which evoke the pain of the moment so intensely that it becomes almost physical, bridging the gap between temporal and spiritual. One well-known example is his memorable poem "For Don M.—Banned," from which André Brink took the title for his book, *A Dry White Season.*

> it is a dry white season
> dark leaves don't last, their brief lives dry out
> and with a broken heart they dive down gently headed
> for the earth,
> not even bleeding.
> it is a dry white season brother,
> only the trees know the pain as they still stand erect
> dry like steel, their branches dry like wire,
> indeed, it is a dry white season
> but seasons come to pass. (1982, 52)

This is a poem about collective pain, exquisitely but powerfully evoked by words and phrases such as "broken heart," "bleeding," "dry white season," and, equally, about resilience, suggested by words such as "erect," "steel," "wire." The symbol of trees and the intrinsic music and rhythms in the language itself work beautifully in the hands of a master poet to convey a profound sense of suffering and loss, and at the same time, a sustaining hope, for "seasons come to pass." Despite its gentle introspection, there is no sense in this poem of Western existential despair. The alienation is externally imposed. The use of the word "brother," makes the collective "other" more immediate. The use of the lower-case and of sparse punctuation makes the poem seem more down-to-earth, accessible. One can accurately say of this poem that it is suffused in the spirit of African humanism.

Dennis Brutus, another South African poet, is well known for his collections *Sirens Knuckles Boots* and *Letters to Martha* written while he was in prison. Much of Brutus's poetry bears closer resemblance to Western traditions of poetry writing than African oral traditions. Community may be implied, but the "I" is uppercase and paramount, somewhat isolated and removed from that community. African idioms are not frequently employed. The diction is more formal and in the English literary tradition as seen in the following stanza from "At a Funeral."

> Black, green and gold at sunset: pageantry
> And stubbled graves: expectant, of eternity,
> In bride's-white, nun's-white veils the nurses gush
>   their bounty
> Of red-wine cloaks, frothing the bugled dirging
>   slopes
> Salute! Then ponder all this hollow panoply
> For one whose gifts the mud devours, with our
>   hopes.
>   . . . . (1973, 17)

Such images as "bride's-white, nun's-white" derive from Western conventions. The poem itself is written roughly in the sonnet form. The "other" whose funeral is taking place is not present in the poem, except in the abstract. The name of the honored deceased appears in a footnote in parentheses at the bottom of the page. There we discover that he is "Velencia Majombozi, who died shortly after qualifying as a doctor." Brutus, however, shares with Mphahlele a deep compassion and concern for others.

Both Brutus and Serote spent time in South African prisons or jails and both eventually fled into political exile like Mphahlele. Brutus was shot in the back while attempting to escape arrest and later was sentenced to eighteen months hard labor. Serote spent nine months in solitary confinement and then was released without being charged. These are the life experiences that inform the work of these two poets.

Other poems by Brutus are much more informed by Black Consciousness. In "Waiting (South African Style)," the language, similarly, is less literary, more accessible. Written after the publication of *Down Second Avenue*, the poem describes white clerks and typists who sound identical to ones described by Mphahlele in his autobiography, who "jimed and johned" him "to death" when he was employed as a clerk in Pretoria:

> *Waiting*
> *(South African Style):*
> *'Non-Whites Only'*
>   I
> At the counter an ordinary girl
> with unemphatic features and
> a surreptitious novelette
> surveys with Stanislav disdain
> my verminous existence and consents
> with langorous reluctance—

the dumpling nose acquiring chiselled charm
through puckering distaste—
to sell me postage stamps:
. . . . (1973, 11)

Brutus makes effective use of satire to criticize the system. African meta-phoric speech, however, is not in evidence.

We have already seen evidence of Mphahlele's most lyric African hu-manist voice at work in the poetic fragment cited earlier in the study that also provided the title for his memoir, *Afrika My Music.* Another poem that memorably serves to exemplify Mphahlele's Black Consciousness thought and his African humanist stance is "Fathers and Sons," anthologized both in *The Unbroken Song* and *Voices from Within: Black Poetry from Southern Africa* (Chapman and Dangor 1982, 172).

> *Fathers and Sons*
> Fifteen years ago
> they dragged me out at dawn
> blindfolded me and shot me,
> then—
> eternity wrapped me up
> in my dazzling blackness.
>
> Now you see I have returned with others—
> not like Lazarus
> jolted from his grave,
> maybe even grousing
> that they yanked him out of sleep
> that he so badly needed.
> . . . . . . (1987, 309)

In the opening stanza and in the beautiful phrase "eternity wrapped me up/in my dazzling blackness," Mphahlele echoes the negritude poets whom he took to task in *The African Image.* But what saves the poem from veering off into the romantic sentiment of negritude is its otherwise down-to-earth language and use of realistic, concrete detail.

Ever the storyteller and humanist, Mphahlele immediately places people in the foreground and his poetic form is narrative. The poem begins with the personal first person, then switches to the second. Mphahlele is angered by the way African culture was, at times, savaged by Christian missionaries, but he is inclusive in spirit. He apparently has no qualms about bringing

Lazarus into the poem and even injecting a note of humor, of carnivaleque laughter into an otherwise serious subject. He even manages uniquely and humorously to humanize Lazarus, who is sorry to have his sleep disturbed. Within the space of nine lines, Mphahlele has already internalized the "I-you-he" that becomes a circle and a community.

Then comes the anger, the irony, and the Black Consciousness spear hurtled in the night:

> I come with fury
> raising cyclones with my feet
> and I have come to stay
> come another dawn of firing squads.
> Tell me not of second comings
> or love of your god:
> . . . .
> all I know
> is that I'm 15 years of age
> is that I feel the prison's cold and vermin
> . . . .
> is that I'm scared
> because last night they buried many bodies
> in a big-big hole.
> Tell my Mamma that I'm scared
> . . . .
> Tell her that they asked me who's my father
> And I said to them he's dead
> and one of them had bluestone eyes
> . . . .
> and now my heart is telling me—
> that man with bluestone eyes
> has *got* to have been there at dawn. (1987, 310)

Here is a poem that works as a poem, as a narrative, social criticism, and an expression of the African humanist's sense of the communal. By the end of the poem, five individuals have been brought into it as well as the self-in-community, including the man with the bluestone eyes who killed the youth's father. We are utterly appalled by the coming together of a brutal past, present, and future, by the chilling bluestone eyes, by the big-big hole with its bodies, and by our realization that the youth who has not yet lived his life is now about to lose it. In the poem, a human presence emerges through internal monologue; through the expression of feeling. The youth says "I'm scared/ I'm scared." We share his fear.

There is a gathering drama and intensity, a sense of historic causes and immediate events evoked through the use of the carefully selected, telling detail that censures even as it provokes outrage. The poem is revolutionary in its subject and language, humanistic in its highly peopled narrative line. Line for line, neither Serote nor Brutus can match the presence of the "communal other" in Mphahlele's poems. The power of such lines as "I come with fury/raising cyclones with my feet" work to affirm black pride and, at the same time, are "beautiful, strong words" contributing to the unbroken song.

Chapter Ten

Father Come Home

The poem "Fathers and Sons" points naturally in the direction of a discussion of Mphahlele's work of juvenile fiction, *Father Come Home*. Although *Afrika My Music* is a book any returning exile, a decade or more later, could read and identify with, *Father Come Home* is a book that sounds an all too familiar and painful chord to too many black South African families. Yet, even as the story deals with the theme of the breakdown of the family structure as a result of segregation and apartheid, it also ends on a note of hope in which reconciliation and reintegration are modeled by the main characters. As is so often the case, Mphahlele has his finger on the pulse of the black community and on human needs that extend far into the future. Like Serote, Mphahlele recognizes that: "whether we like it or not . . . there is a very sharp and deep change taking place in how we are going to look at the family unit in our society. Lots of painful changes have to be made because of the process of struggle—there are lots of uncertainties. As a result, lots of families are breaking up—because of apartheid, because of the struggle, because of human frailty" (Serote 1990, 103).

Father Come Home is the story of the boy Maredi's search for his long-absent father, who left the family to seek employment in the city. The narrative deals directly with conditions set in motion by the Natives Land Act. The story is set in the 1920s, when "the mines, especially the gold mines, clamoured for more labour," and, at the same time, the 1913 Land Act meant that "thousands of black people had been driven off the land" (Mphahlele 1984, 15–16). The twin themes of alienation—of "fatherlessness" (with its strong autobiographic elements) and of disruption of families and community—are linked with the pervasive, harsh socioeconomic realities of the era.

As historian Charles van Onselen sums it up: "First, black sharecroppers . . . had been forced into overcrowded 'black spots' and then they were pushed out into the political oblivion of ethnically defined Bantustans, relegated to the national trash heap. . . . Poverty picked away at the remaining social fabric, and conflicts about money, liquor or labor turned father against sons" (Bernstein 1997, B4).

In Mphahlele's life as well as his fiction, father-son alienation is a paramount theme. The first chapter of *Father Come Home* opens with the introduction of Maredi's beloved aunt and describes customs in anthropological detail that are interwoven into the rural setting. Maredi teasingly calls his aunt by her praise name, Hunadi, which is ordinarily used only among adults. Maredi has had a bad dream which is related to his question about when his father will come back. We also learn that Maredi, at twelve and on the threshold of manhood, will soon be going to the mountain for *koma*, circumcision. Maredi comes to life psychologically through the convention of the dream sequence, and in the circle of family, through lively dialogue. Snatches of dialect and indigenous speech patterns evoke the rural setting in the village of Sedibeng. When Hunadi attempts to comfort Maredi, an owl hoots, provoking Hunadi to shout at the owl: " 'Waaiii—what have *you* to complain about, *tshikanosi*—you wicked loner!' " (4). Thus, Hanadi expresses a preeminent African humanist value—the desirability of being a part of rather than apart from.

The author sounds an autobiographical note when Maredi is taken out of school to herd goats, like Mphahlele in his youth, and is hired out by his wily and unsympathetic uncle (6–7). At age 14, Maredi is described as being physically compact, bow-legged, and frank. He is not given to flattery. Two African proverbs serve to underscore this description: "They say a baboon cannot see its own ugly forehead, that is why it is so loud about the ugliness in another's face" (9). Because Maredi is not given to flattery, he is unpopular with many of the girls who think of him "as a crocodile among river bathers" (9). Even though a mischief-maker, Maredi is serious about his schoolwork. Carnivalesque laughter is effectively used to raise philosophic questions about human values and the right way of being. Mphahlele's canvas is crowded with people and sociohistorical details. Like Bakhtin, Mphalele sees the novel's "crucial role as social document" (Danow 1991, 55).

At Christmas Maredi's favorite uncle, Namedi, who is the African humanist ideal of family loyalty and compassion, and the counterpoint to tyrannical Eliyase, brings gifts of white bread, mealie meal, sugar, tea, coffee, jams, rice, and vegetables as well as new clothes for the family. The fact that such staples as "white bread," "mealie meal," and "sugar" are counted luxury items speaks volumes about the minimal standards of living experienced by blacks, particularly in the rural areas.

We also learn that Maredi's favorite aunt, Hunadi, has a husband and son who went to Johannesburg and from whom no word has been heard. It is rumored that Hunadi's son has become a "hole digger," the ultimate in debasement. Hole diggers are housed and fed by *shebeen* queens "in return for digging holes in the yard to conceal tins of beer against police raids" (18).

Among the themes of alienation besides fatherlessness, dislocation, and poverty is the break experienced by many blacks between early rural background and the chaos of urban slums. Related to this break is the perception that tribalism is dangerous (a perception fostered by Christian mission teaching and Verwoerdian ethnicity). Mphahlele is well aware that blacks have been made ashamed of their rural roots because apartheid social engineers went to great trouble to link it with barbarism and backwardness. Ever the teacher and preserver, Mphahlele both documents that past and attempts to restore it to disinherited black youth without resorting to nostalgia or romanticism. He contrasts the African epic past with both the rural and urban present and thereby brings each into sharp historic focus.

Similar conditions described by Mphahlele in *Father Come Home* are documented by Ellen Kuzwayo in *Call Me Woman* (1985). Head writes in the introduction to the autobiography by Kuzwayo: "The abrupt break Ellen Kuzwayo experiences from an early rural background to the broken disjointed chaos of the slums and shacks of the townships of Johannesburg follows a pattern experienced by many black people. The men are forced off the land to earn money in the mines to pay poll tax. Starving women of the rural areas follow the men to the city and survive precariously, brewing beer or working in domestic service" (Kuzwayo 1985, xiv). Of Johannesburg, Soweto, Kuzwayo herself writes, "it is not easy to live and bring up children in a community robbed of its traditional moral code and values." This is a theme Mphahlele probes throughout his narrative, in which he asks, "What can be done to restore these values?"

In *Father Comes Home,* Mashabela, musician, poet, and doctor, serves as the voice of oral poetry and African tradition—the voice of the epic precolonial past and the people's history. Like Old Mutiso in *Chirundu,* he articulates African humanist precepts. Utilizing such a spokesman is one of Mphahlele's favorite devices. Like *Chirundu, Father Comes Home* employs mixed genres and conventions, some drawn from African oral traditions, others from Western traditions. Thus Mashabela sings an epic song (of the sort Mphahlele himself collected in the field when he studied African oral poetry) that serves to affirm black pride, harking back to a fast-disappearing past, thereby re-creating that past for a generation who has never experienced it:

> People of the nation!
> Hear me say this to you
> that the armies of Matome
> fought the whole of God's day
> against the armies of Mashao.
> Spears had eyes that day
> and blood came down like rain. (20)

Mphahlele's double-voiced narrative suggests that there was a time when blacks fought with valor, were not passive victims, and that that time promises to come again.

Mashabela continues for three entire pages in his recital:

> I sing today of
> the fearful cloud
> that has fallen over us,
> of suns that have been blinded by
> the book that came to us which they say
> was written by the hand of God,
> blinded by those among us
> who would laugh at our belief
> and trust in the God of Afrika. (21)

In poetic language evocative of the *isibongo*, Mphahlele is, in a not-so-hidden polemic, commenting on spiritual and cultural colonialism that Biko, writing in the early 1970s, also notes in *I Write What I Like*.

> Where they could, they [the Anglo-Boer culture] conquered by persuasion, using a highly exclusive religion that denounced all other Gods and demanded a strict code of behaviour with respect to clothing, education ritual and custom. Where it was impossible to convert, fire-arms were readily available and used to advantage. Hence the Anglo-Boer culture was the more powerful culture in almost all facets. This is where the African began to lose a grip on himself and his surroundings. (1986, 41)

Similarly, Mashabela sings of a time when Africans bravely defended "the land of their ancestors," and the silos were bursting with grain, before the arrival of men with "gray faces" and "green eyes." These were days of plenty and pride, "in which the conquered were not downtrodden for they and the conqueror shared an ancient faith" (23). The precolonial past he evokes precedes the 1913 Land Act, rural poverty, and urban slums. The epic sweep of the narrative into the past reflects a history that "crosses rivers and mountains and valleys" (23). He continues:

> Our women have been left
> alone to scratch the earth for food
> like chickens;
> our ancient songs of praise
> have now become a bowl of jackals;
> lead us back to ancient ways
> when your soil was here for anyone to plough . . .
> when we were one. (22)

Maleka, in the polyphonic historic discourse, becomes the voice of the more immediate present. Maleka, known later as Tintina, suffered from a blow on the head in a mining accident. Everything he has learned at school, on the job, or in the mines is all mixed up in his head. His favorite phrase is "tin-tin-na-bu-layshun!" Tintina serves as wise fool, who comments on the brutal life, violence, and ethnic strife in the mines and male hostels in Johannesburg. Maleka owns a battered old concertina that he brought back with him when he returned from the mines. In a story within a story, we learn of Maleka's life in Johannesburg and that: "Both man and thing were mine-casualties." Tintina would take out the battered concertina and attempt to play it. But "the lung-sick sigh of an old man was all that ever issued from the concertina" (33). We are reminded that men in the mines got black lung disease. If they were lucky enough to survive hard labor in the mines, they often suffered permanent ill health as a result of the unhealthy and dangerous work conditions.

But Tintina is compassionate. He offers to watch the cattle or goats so that Maredi can go to school. "'You must learn, man,'" Tintina would say. Despite the fact "Tintina was a difficult person to nail down to a proper exchange of thoughts and feelings . . . [and] made Maredi think of a butterfly," he shares the same deep respect for the importance of an education that prompted Mphahlele's mother to work her way into an early grave so that Mphahlele could enjoy the benefits of a higher education.

In view of this attitude, the Bantu Education Act, which closed down the few good schools that at one time offered decent education to those blacks who could qualify, seems not just wantonly destructive, but downright criminal. The emphasis in *Father Comes Home* on Maredi's desire to get an education is an important part of the subtext of the story and is consistent with Mphahlele's concern about rebuilding schools and curricula and encouraging an entire lost generation to follow Maredi's example. Again, Mphahlele, the engaged African humanist and educator, is mindful of the desires and the needs of the community. The immediacy and timeliness of Mphahlele's concern is verified by two young, American-trained academics, Maanda and Amy Bell Mulaudzi, who in 1994, lived in and conducted research in Venda, the very setting for Mphahlele's story *Father Come Home*. When Mulaudzi asked the question, "What is the most important change that needs to come to South Africa," nearly all respondees said "education."

> Even people living in rural areas that badly need basic services like electricity, a paved road, telephones, and a better water supply, say that education is the first thing that must change. And it will take a lot of money to upgrade the African schools—from rebuilding the classroom facilities and wiring them with electricity, to hiring more (and better qualified) teachers to reduce class sizes, to revamping the curriculum and re-writing text books so that students don't learn falsities like "homelands" are "natural" tribal areas, and that the poverty in these homelands is rife, not because of massive overcrowding so that whites can own 70% of South Africa, but because of "wasteful farming methods" that destroy the fertility of the land. (Mulaudzi 1994)

The narrative of *Father Come Home* then goes on to explore the issue of how Christian-mission teaching contributed to mistrust and prejudice between the Christians of Sedibeng and the "heathens" of Mashite. So fearful were the Sedibeng Christians of the Mashite "who followed the ancient ways" that the forest where they lived was "forbidden." The more tolerant Mashite "had no lingering dislike for the Christians" (35). At harvest time, the Mashite practiced cooperative labor, helping each other to plow and build houses. Although the Mashite wore skins, they had learned to cover the skins with long dresses.

Mphahlele's discourse on conflict between Christians and "heathens" gives him the opportunity to outline African humanist precepts such as the belief in a Supreme Being, "whose presence they felt where human relations were harmonious" and the belief in ancestors who "were always living and present to guide them into the paths of decency, of goodness, of harmony among people." He notes that people of Mashite "prayed to the Supreme Being through the ancestors, without assembling for the express purpose of praying" (36).

The novel's ideology, its abstract ideas on philosophy, education, and historic cause and effect, and its entire discourse, operates in what Bakhtin refers to as a chronotope, or cultural time and space, both taking on nuances of the past and anticipating the addressee in the future. The African humanist concept of "I am because you are because we are" or "people are people through other people" that is either stated or implied in all of Mphahlele's recent works is the collective equivalent of Bakhtin's theories on self and other—"I must find myself in another, by finding another in myself" (Danow 1991, 59). In the refracted speech of another, Mphahlele is Mashabela and Tintina, who in the heteroglossia of the text represent socio-ideological speech. The use of oral forms and Western conventions by the author and the counterpointing of lyric refrains with dramatic episodes set up a dynamic tension between centripetal literary language and centrifugal nonconforming devices and genres that are outside the accepted canon (51–52).

In a literary and metaphoric sense, Mphahlele, in the process of decolonizing himself, dares to venture into the forbidden forest of the people of Mashite, which is where Maredi later also dares to venture, provoking the wrath of his uncle and creating a major conflict in the process. But Maredi discovers that the people of Mashite are just people after all. They give him nice porridge and beans. His decision to take the risk prepares the way for Maredi's subsequent departure from Sedibeng to search for his father. It is at this major turning point that Maredi decides he will no longer tend other people's animals, but will devote himself to his education.

Mashabela, the African humanist voice of inclusion and tolerance, reminds us that "the people of Mashite, and all of us are children on the small finger of God" (39). In counterpoint is the lay preacher who preaches a fire and brimstone sermon, comparing "those poor souls of Mashite over there" to the city of Gomorrah, ironically praising the white man who "brought the light" (41). Thus we see the effect of colonialism, first from the spiritual and cultural colonization of missionaries, then from the social, political, and economic colonialism imposed by segregation policies, and finally by state apartheid, which included the setting up of chieftanships, paving the way for one more form of black-on-black, postcolonial conflict.

Maredi begins his journey in search of his father in picaresque fashion. He experiences a number of adventures, eventually passing out along the road from fatigue and hunger. He is rescued by a ginger-bearded, Afrikaans-speaking farmer who is kind to him. In this respect, the text does not unrelentingly show up the white ogre to himself, allowing for the possibility of the inclusion of a white readership who, in view of a shared history of brutal oppression, may already feel badly enough about themselves. Maredi also encounters a lion, which is his totem. Eventually, a dairy farmer named Du Plessis hires him. Again Maredi experiences kindness. On the basis of his experience, Maredi concludes that it is the system more than individuals that was at fault. Du Plessis himself "was not cruel: he was simply in charge of their [black workers'] fate" (69). The real issue is that no man should have that kind of power over another. If power corrupts Du Plessis, it corrupts absolutely the next generation. It is Du Plessis's twelve-year-old son who administers a cruel blow, both physically and psychologically, when he strikes Maredi with a stick and calls him "kaffir," saying to him: "Stop talking like a clever white man, you hear!" Maredi, however, does not take this sitting down. He fights the son and stands up to Du Plessis as well, earning the respect of the other workers, and regaining his own self-respect.

After two months away, Maredi returns home to great celebration and feasting. Before his departure, Du Plessis pays Maredi his earnings and kindly councils him not to run away from home again because "'you don't pick parents from trees, hear?'" (72). There is irony in this kindly advice because it suggests that Du Plessis has no conception of what the system of codified, state-sponsored racism has done to the family life of black people. Maredi's return, with its celebration and feasting, symbolizes his coming of age, the return of the exile, and the reaffirmation of self-in-community. Mashabela speaks his poetry saying: "People of the nation! / here is our son come back, / sons shall seek their fathers, / fathers shall seek their sons. / The mother of this son is the daughter / of the people" (76).

Sadly, in Maredi's absence, Hunadi has died. Neither her husband nor son returned for the funeral. Mphahlele, using the voice of another, in this case, Dineo, Maredi's mother, takes this opportunity to express to his reader another important value. Dineo warns Maredi that if he marries and then leaves his wife at home or otherwise "'throw[s] her away like a used garment,'" she, Dineo, "'will come out of the grave and breathe maggots into your life,'" (78).

In the end Dineo's husband and Maredi's father, Lemeko, does come home at last. Mphahlele uses psychological realism to good effect in making the reunion come to life. Maredi after all his questing and hope, feels let down, even angry about the suffering Lemeko has caused. Lemeko is sensitive to his son's unease and understands the reasons for it. The boil bursts, and the reconciliation between father and son takes place when the two talk and Lemeko attempts to explain why he did what he did. In a sense, both

Maredi and the family are made whole again by the reunion. Maredi decides to return to school and asks his father's help, a support his father gladly provides. Maredi goes on to live a productive and meaningful life, becoming, among other things, a teacher. Reconciliation, by extension, takes many forms—family, community, nation. Mphahlele seems to be saying, it will not be an easy journey. It will involve struggle and pain. It is best to keep expectations at a realistic level on this long, hard road of reconciliation and recovery. He concludes with the proverb: "When there is famine, be thankful that you are not driven to eat cow dung" (97).

In his psychological realism, Mphahlele has some of the farsightedness of a seer. A young researcher working in Venda describes the euphoria that people felt after a new nonracial, democratic government was voted into office with Mandela at its helm. People had great hope about their newfound freedom and their choices in life. Nevertheless, "the excitement that swept the country right after the elections is wearing thin, and many people don't quite know how to go about channeling their hopes for a new South Africa" (Mulaudzi 1994).

Father Come Home is a parable of how families can reunite and society can rebuild and it is written by someone who experienced three generations of father-son alienation caused by poverty, alcoholism, and dislocation. It affirms black pride, African humanist precepts and values, sociocultural history, family unity, and a nationalist as opposed to a tribal vision. It is also a story youth of all colors can read in postcolonial Africa, since not all whites are presented as ogres. It models ways in which wounds of anger, alienation, and abandonment linked to harsh socioeconomic conditions can be mended and healed in a society emerging from a long period of dysfunction. It reminds people to keep expectations realistic.

In *Anatomy of a Miracle: The End of Apartheid and the Birth of the New South Africa* (1997), Patti Waldmeir describes a South Africa beset with economic and social problems of enormous magnitude, but also a country that has set an example in conflict resolution for the rest of the world to follow. Waldmeir attributes the willingness of blacks to forgive the white tribe for a system of institutionalized bigotry and cruelty unequaled in history in part to the African spirit of *ubuntu*, which she defines as seeking out the humanity in others.

Ubuntu is one aspect of the African humanism Mphahlele first began to articulate in his thesis. From small seeds, such as this early piece of scholarship by Mphahlele, do mighty baobabs grow. One branch of that tree, *Down Second Avenue*, documents how the Mphahlele family survived ghetto life in the eras of segregation and state apartheid, in part because of the communal spirit of *ubuntu*. In another branch, Mphahlele's novella "Mrs Plum," it is Karabo's *ubuntu* as well as her newfound self-confidence that makes possible a negotiated settlement with her employer, Mrs. Plum, paving the way for Karabo's return to Johannesburg. The spirit of *ubuntu* makes reconciliation possible on a personal level in *Father Come Home*. By examining Mphahlele's early stories and his dissertation, by tracing the evolution of his ideas through his critical works, we see how a mighty baobab first took root in the culture, politics, and history of the time, growing into a black aesthetic and nationalist vision. By studying this particular baobab in its unfolding from tiny seed to mighty tree, it also becomes possible to better understand and appreciate the growth and maturation of its peers, whose historic and literary development parallels Mphahlele's own.

Conclusion

No words can better summarize Mphahlele's life than his own. As he writes in an article for *College English,* "It has been my fate to be a teacher and writer. . . . I come from a country where for virtually two centuries the people of color have, as a deliberate policy, been denied the freedom of association, assembly, thought, inquiry, and self-expression. For this reason I have treasured and savored every moment when I could snatch any one of the freedoms" (Mphahlele 1993a, 179).

Yet some of the freedoms Mphahlele was able to snatch in America were far from unmixed blessings. For example, he confesses to his psychobiographer, N. Chabani Manganyi, that his years in Denver were the most difficult in his life. His academic successes "masked a deep sense of grief." The losses he suffered included those of his children who were "failing themselves through various acts of rebellion" (274–75).

Mphahlele was unable to attend the funeral of his brother, and he felt the loss of "a native audience" for his writing. Denver lacked the throb of life, the color and smells of "home." He felt, as he expressed it, that his choices were either to die a slow death in Denver or return home and become a martyr. Despite the collegiality and warm friendship he experienced at Denver University and the down-to-earth friendliness of most western Americans, Mphahlele had also experienced racism in his search for housing in the Denver suburbs.

In Wayne, Pennsylvania, the Mphahleles encountered attitude problems of a different sort. Mphahlele and Dr. Houston Baker, Jr., concurred in the judgment that the University of Pennsylvania, for example, was not "equipped to perceive" the energy and brilliance of people like Wole Soyinka, Kofi Awoonor, and others descending on the place, with Mphahlele acting as magnet. Even one of America's finest universities reflected a certain cultural and academic insularity. Mphahlele, moreover, found the university "one cold place." Nonetheless, in 1984 he returned to the University of Pennsylvania as visiting professor of African Literature.

This was America's post-Watergate, post-Vietnam era when economic recession echoed America's own political self-doubts, a time when some Ph.D.s were driving taxi cabs. Mphahlele had been appointed to a full professorship on the faculty at University of Pennsylvania at the same time as novelist Philip Roth, and when Houston Baker, Jr., was director of Afro-American Studies. Despite this stimulating environment and the security and prestige afforded by his new position, Mphahlele believed his death as a novelist had already transpired, resulting from his perennial exile from self and self-in-community, and his condition of being a stateless wanderer. Rebecca, meanwhile, was strongly urging a return to South Africa.

Mphahlele's ambivalence on the question of whether or not to return is reflected in his continual agonizing over the decision. He was constantly aware of the need he felt for "self-renewal, self-creation in communion with people of my own kind" (Manganyi 1983, 290). Later, he says with ironic self-recrimination, tipped with a bit of poison aimed at critics such as Dennis Brutus, that

> I made the decision to end my self-imposed exile out of nothing nobler than self-interest. If such self-interest should result in a contribution to the well-being of my people surely this is good fortune. I never believed when I lived in exile that I was supporting the people's cause merely by being a writer and teacher of middle-class American students. Surely one must not confuse a healthy concern and opposition to fascism with a dramatic contribution in real terms in a situation in which one is removed from the heat. (Manganyi 1983, 294)

In the meantime, while in Pennsylvania, Mphahlele completed work on *Chirundu*. His agent sent the book off to Harper and Row, whose response spoke volumes about the need to understand Mphahlele's work within the framework of its African humanist context, which includes the African oral tradition. Frances McCullough of Harper and Row found the book "impenetrable," and "off the wall." No doubt the publisher's representative in this case would have also preferred, given a choice, a trip to Paris where the cultural signposts and maps are more transparent (even when in French) than to travel to Soweto or rural Venda, an undertaking that requires far greater risk and much more preparation and effort. At the same time, Mphahlele's agent said she liked the book, but found the "leisurely approach" and structure difficult. She wondered if this might not have something to do with the influence of the oral tradition. She suggested that the reason the British press reacted unfavorably to *Chirundu* was because of the book's implied criticisms of Zambia's Kenneth Kaunda.

Mphahlele left South Africa at age 37. By the time he returned, he was

57, and still in a sense a stateless exile, but no longer a wanderer uprooted from community. After Mphahlele's return to South Africa, *Chirundu* was published by major publishers in Britain, the U.S.A., and South Africa. As a teacher and writer, he was beginning, once again, to fulfill his cultural goals. He was granted a Research Fellowship at Rhodes University and awarded a Ford Foundation research grant to record oral poetry and to translate it from North Sotho, Tsonga, and Venda into English. He was a founding member of the African Writers' Association. He published *The Unbroken Song* and *Let's Write a Novel: A Guide* in 1981, and followed these in 1984 with *Afrika My Music* and *Father Come Home.* In 1983, he inaugurated the Division of African Literature at the University of the Witwatersrand, and was appointed to its chair. Over the years, Mphahlele received numerous awards and honorary degrees. After retiring from the University of the Witwatersrand in 1987, he was awarded a Fulbright professorship to the University of South Carolina for the 1988/89 academic year. In addition, he has continued to deliver dozens of addresses and to publish articles, short stories, and poems. He co-edited the ambitious and long-overdue anthology, *Perspective on South African English Literature,* published in 1992.

The acrimonious, at times unruly, dialogue of two selves, has quieted down as the writer, thinker, and critic increasingly has managed to "harmonize the two . . . through their organic vision of life," that is, through the myth and reality of an African humanist ethos and philosophy with its roots in community. Now in his late 70s, Mphahlele has returned to ancestral roots, living comfortably in Lebowakgomo, southeast of Pietersburg, not far from the Tudumo River and the Mogodumo mountain range, and only a short distance from Maupaneng in Mphahlele District, where as a child he herded goats and cattle. Here he enjoys amongst family members and books an active "retirement," as professor emeritus, grand *griot*, and African elder.

Mphahlele's experiences with racism in a Denver suburb, of parochialism at the university level, and of outright rejection by the publishing establishment on both sides of the Atlantic remind one of Du Bois's observation that racism is the issue of the century and of Bakhtin's that "I must find myself in another by finding another in myself (in mutual reflection and mutual acceptance)" (Danow 1991, 59). This is why an understanding of Mphahlele's African humanist aesthetics is important. First, it can advance the understanding and appreciation of both African literature and culture. Secondly, by virtue of that understanding, it can help overcome the ignorance and fear that leads to insularity and racism. Such ignorance and fear, added to economic greed, caused the pernicious system of apartheid to take root and flourish in the first place.

In the 1960s, close to two decades before Mphahlele's return to South Africa, the detentions, arrests, political exile, and imprisonment of many black leaders resulted in a temporary silencing. Then, by the 1970s, Black Consciousness leaders such as Biko had begun to speak out. The silence was further broken by successful trade union strikes in the manufacturing industry, leading to a period of sustained and active resistance.

In other parts of southern Africa, colonial rule in Mozambique and Angola, under the Portuguese, was collapsing, lending hope to the black South African resistance movement. In 1976, a year before Mphahlele's return, black school students in Soweto went on strike. In the first instance, the strike was to protest the imposition of Afrikaans (regarded as the language of the oppressor) in the schools. On June 16, 1976, two students were shot dead and several others were injured when police fired into the crowd of 15,000 protesting students. This event proved to be a political watershed in black resistance politics. Apartheid economics, in the meantime, were proving costly and inefficient. The white regime had become increasingly militarized. There were vast reservoirs of unemployed, undereducated blacks with no skills and a need in an increasingly competitive global marketplace to upgrade industry through a more highly productive, skilled labor force. White South Africans chafed under their global image of "international polecat." Economic sanctions, the sports boycotts, the collapse of communism in eastern Europe, the Soviet Union's increasing reluctance to underwrite neighboring client states, the sharp fall in gold prices, and rising oil prices all made their impact felt, signaling change in the *realpolitik* of South Africa.

By the 1980s, the white regime was beginning to show signs of its first death throes. Prime Minister P. W. Botha began reforms. He repealed the Group Areas and Mixed Marriages Acts and started work on a policy for releasing political prisoners. In the meantime, however, the police and military were given free reign. Repression grew even more ruthless; defiance more militant. In addition to school boycotts, there were "community battles over rent, housing and transport, and the explosion of industrial unrest" (Lodge 1990, 356). In 1986, a state of emergency was declared and in a three-month period "some 40,000 arrests or detentions were made" and what had formerly been a police state became "a shoot-to-kill state" (Davidson 1991, 347). Yet behind the scenes, Nationalist party leaders were conducting preliminary talks with Nelson Mandela, still a prisoner on Robben Island.

In 1989, after suffering a stroke, Botha was replaced by F. W. de Klerk, who began to work openly toward a peaceful transition to a nonracial democracy and decided in 1990 to free Mandela—developments even hard-headed reporters were quick to call nothing short of a miracle. It is virtually unprecedented for an entrenched regime, backed by a powerful military, to negotiate away its own power and position. Since 1993, when Nelson Mandela and F.W. de Klerk shared the Nobel Peace Prize, a democratic constitution has been hammered out in South Africa and free all-race elections have been held. On May 4, 1994, Nelson Mandela was inaugurated as de Klerk's successor as state president.

In *Footprints along the Way*, Guy Butler, retired head of the Department of English at Rhodes University, Grahamstown, who studied at Rhodes University and won the Queen Victoria Scholarship to Oxford, says of Mphahlele, "As a pioneer among the writers of Southern Africa, Es'kia Mphahlele's position is secure. He is more than a major figure in the intellectual resistance to apartheid; he is an eloquent exponent of African awareness and values: of *ubuntu*, of generosity, of "plain heroic magnitude of mind" (1989, 5). The sociopolitical application of *ubuntu*, one of the precepts Mphahlele has identified as key to African humanism, is an example of ways in which culture has supported reconstruction and healing in the new postapartheid South Africa. It also bears out the fact that Mphahlele's endeavor over the decades to identify, reclaim, and advocate an African humanist approach in education, nation building, and the arts was not mere ideological wool-gathering or whistling in the wind.

By way of illustration, one remarkable development in the process of rebuilding has been the establishment by the ANC–led government of a Truth and Reconciliation Commission, a panel headed by retired Anglican Archbishop Desmond Tutu and charged with investigating apartheid-era crimes. Part of the commission's impetus derives from the spirit of *ubuntu* and the belief healing cannot take place until the oppressor has acknowledged his deeds. *Ubuntu*, as earlier noted, is a cardinal precept of African humanism. Archbishop Tutu most recently explained that

> We say that a human being is a human being because he belongs to a community, and harmony is the essence of that community. So *ubuntu* actually demands that you forgive, because resentment and anger and desire for revenge undermine harmony. In our understanding, when someone doesn't forgive, we say that person does not have *ubuntu*. That is to say, he is not really human. (Waldmeir 1997, 268)

Patti Waldmeir, author of *Anatomy of a Miracle* (1997), argues that after his election, "Mandela made non-racialism the new civil religion of South Africa . . . . The politics of reconciliation reigned supreme" (286). The politics of reconciliation is not always an easy pill to swallow, however; there is sometimes a sense that the oppressor is benefiting from reconciliation more that the oppressed.

The legacy of the apartheid state includes internecine ethnic rivalry between the Zulu Inkatha party and the ANC, an enormous deficit, a serious housing shortage, high unemployment, an undereducated and underskilled populace, and entrenched racism. Aggressive pursuit of affirmative action has met with mixed results—from the point of view of both whites and blacks. Although the legal barriers have fallen, blacks still feel unwelcome in some formerly white-held enclaves. Black are still learning to deal with a new way of life that seems almost foreign to them—negotiating a mortgage, ordering at an upscale restaurant, dealing with "neighbors who assume they are the maid—or should be" (Daley 1997, 1). In *Afrika My Music,* Mphahlele noted a certain dysfunctional element in Soweto culture itself—a tendency for people to rejoice in others' disasters, for the urban to reject the rural, the absence of a black middle class, and a growing culture of violence. In addition to the needs for management of the society and economy, there is also a need to build a new sense of nationalism and unity.

Gail Gerhart describes the ideology of Black Consciousness as being "primarily a transitional philosophy" and suggests that in the future "the onus will fall on black leaders" to be "ideologically innovative" in order "to achieve a new social order worthy of everything sacrificed and suffered" a new black ideology will need to be "closely attuned to popular needs and the exigencies of a changing situation" (1979, 311). Although Gerhart's observations were recorded before the momentous changes of the 1990s, they continue to have relevance today.

In the 1970s and early 1980s, after Mphahlele's return from political exile to South Africa, literary output by black writers was largely devoted to poetry and theater, both forms well suited to reaching a large number of people in a short time. Piniel Viriri Shava underscores this point in his book *A People's Voice,* stating that since the Black Consciousness Movement "poetry and drama have been deemed more effective media for politicization than prose." Shava further argues that since Soweto, "no new significant novel by a black author has appeared" except Serote's *To Every Birth Its Blood* (1989, 57). To Shava's list should be added *Chirundu,* with its timely examination of controversial feminist and postcolonial issues and the political question of the sometimes abusive treatment of South African refugees by neighboring African countries.

Mphahlele is an African writer with a pan-African vision who has made major contributions to South African writing that have been influenced by an American perspective. His *The African Image* was the first major work of literary criticism to deal with questions of a black aesthetic. It was also the first comprehensive work of literary criticism written by any South African writer, black or white. *The African Image* and *Voices in the Whirlwind* in turn, "helped to launch a self-propagating cultural theory," prefiguring and nurturing the Black Consciousness movement (Watts 1989, 58). These works evolved, in turn, out of Mphahlele's pioneering endeavors to analyze and portray black characters in Western fiction. Two rivers came together at the confluence of his writing: Mphahlele's understanding of West African negritude and the writing of American blacks.

As elsewhere noted, Mphahlele published the first collection of short stories by a black in South Africa. He helped promote short-story writing as an art form by his fellow black writers, and, in *Down Second Avenue,* wrote one of the best-known township autobiographies, a uniquely South African form. He was a source of inspiration and encouragement to writers in English throughout Africa. These achievements deserve to be repeated because for too long they have been deliberately ignored. It is ironic that the "panopticism" of apartheid, the "alert gaze" that saw everything, resulted in so blinding and total a literary blackout on writers who lacked the correct political views and pigmentation.

Some of the fermentation and excitement of Mphahlele's early years as an exilic wanderer and father figure in the emergent tradition of African literature in English is brought to life in his description of the 1962 Makerere African writers' conference held in Kampala, Uganda—the first of its kind —which he helped organize. This, as Mphahlele states, was "before the fascist Idi Amin came in with his bloodthirsty soldiers to vulgarise the Makerere campus."

> The Makerere African writers' conference was the first to be held on African soil and I still cherish the memory of having been there when it happened..... The late Langston Hughes was there as well as Saunders Redding. The international atmosphere at the conference became pronounced as a result of the colourful array of dress as well as accents. It was a confluence of Africa, west, east and south. The Nigerians were unmistakable in the splendour of their robes and headgear .... Bloke Modisane, Lewis Nkosi, Alex La Guma, Bob Leshoai and I formed the South African contingent. The Nigerians with their boisterous and exuberant style introduced moments of dramatic seriousness. Wole Soyinka raised a question that not everybody wanted to talk about when he inquired just how African African literature really was? ... The witty and forthright Christopher Okigbo, also of Nigeria,

stunned the participants with his declaration that his mission was to
write poetry for poets. He spoke with a heavy Nigerian accent and he
did not know, as I now know, that in his posthumously published poetry he would show that he cared about non-poets reading his poetry.
(Manganyi 1983, 213)

Mphahlele's opportunity to meet writers and politicians on an international stage provided him, he says, "with an opportunity to continue my
quest for literary images. If there is any glory in having met, in one's life-
time, most of Africa's most prominent politicians, then I should claim that
glory" (213).

Hastings Banda of Malawi "arrogantly refused to give me an ear" says
Mphahlele, although a good friend had attempted to set up a meeting. It is
more than idle speculation to suggest that Banda was later accorded the distinction, along with Kenneth Kaunda of Zambia, of serving as one of the
models for Mphahlele's colonial in a black skin, that is, for the politician
Chirundu in the novel of the same name.

In postapartheid South Africa, postcolonial discourse with culture at
the core of literary analysis is becoming *au courant,* as is evident from the
September 1993 conference held at University of Cape Town, focusing on
the theme of "new directions in cultural studies in South Africa." The essential point underlying the contributions from the conference is the recognition that "what is at stake is cultural politics . . . [is] the wish to understand,
in order to challenge, oppression" (Cooper and Steyn 1996, 9). Ironically,
Mphahlele has been engaged in such a discourse for close to half a century.

Given Mphahlele's academic and literary stature and his lived experience of African political and cultural history, it is often surprising to find
that he or any similar-ranking South Africa literary scholar and thinker, for
that matter, is so frequently overlooked or ignored in the global and local
discourses on postcolonial literature.

In their study *Postmodernism and Society,* Roy Boyne and Ali Rattansi
note that there are a growing number of writers today who combine "Third
World origins with Western education and positions in Western universities
and cultural establishments—who have begun to challenge . . . the varieties
of colonial and imperialist discourse that have been so crucial in the intellectual formation of modernity" (1990, 35). Boyne and Rattansi offer as
names on an illustrious if incomplete list those of Edward Said, Gayatri
Chakravorty Spivak, Homi Bhabha, and Abdul JanMohamed.

Mphahlele, with his rural youth herding goats and his upbringing in a black South African ghetto, his positions on the faculties at University of Pennsylvania, University of Denver, and University of the Witwatersrand, his numerous academic honors, not to mention his sizable body of criticism that deals precisely with issues of colonialism and imperialism in all of its manifestations, is a worthy candidate for Boyne and Rattansi's profile. Yet any act of negation or destruction, the demolition of an historic building, for example, is far easier to accomplish, requires far less time in its execution, and is frequently farther reaching in its impact than the hard, disciplined, lifelong work of creating a respected body of criticism and literature or erecting a building of architectural splendor. The dynamite charge in this case was lit by the Banning and Censorship acts during the darkest days of state apartheid.

Mphahlele's time in America as a professor of English introduced him to a number of black American writers. He had already met Langston Hughes and exchanged writings with him. He and poet Sonia Sanchez, among others, became personal friends. His essay collection *Voices in the Whirlwind* was the first and only major critique by a South African writer of the Black Power poets in the U.S., starting with the Harlem Renaissance through to the late 1960s. His inside knowledge of American writers and academe, in addition to his exposure to American politics and culture in the West and on the East Coast, means that Mphahlele can bring a uniquely American perspective to bear on his understanding of South African literature.

As previously noted, black consciousness in America provided the political element Mphahlele found missing in West African negritude and, in turn, measurably affected his own writing and thinking. Whether in America or elsewhere, however, the dialogizing voices, in which present affects and alters past as much as past enters into and shapes present, allows for Mphahlele to change his mind, shift his position, revise his opinions on questions ranging from politics to black aesthetics. In *Voices in the Whirlwind,* for example, Mphahlele dismisses Langston Hughes as a "lightweight." In his memoir, *Afrika My Music,* Mphahlele, having reconsidered, now says he recognizes his own need for both in his writing: Langston Hughes and Richard Wright, emblematic of the fruitful marriage of black aesthetics and ideology as represented by two of America's foremost writers.

Occasionally, as an artist, Mphahlele in the continuing dialogue of two selves—African and Western, communal and individual, alien and humanist—must reach down inside his individual as opposed to communal self to process, recollect, and synthesize. In a previously unpublished poem titled "Silences," Mphahlele makes a lyric recapitulation of this truth when he writes:

> I cherish the silences in my life
> when I can think
> and feel the texture and content
> of my being
>
> . . . .
>
> When I can silence this chatterbox
> I call my mind
>
> . . . .
>
> Silence is the workshop of my mind
> where I'm making this poem. (1994a)

In the same poem Mphahlele refers to all the world's major religions, as well as to the African belief in a Vital Force, showing a multicultural approach to spirituality that is xenophilic. This approach, one of acceptance and inclusion, is typical of African humanism. It is an approach that carried equally over into Mphahlele's politics as one-time Secretary of the ANC, an organization that always repudiated racism and that was never anti-white (Benson 1986, 26).

In a symposium on black literature in South Africa held at the University of Texas in 1975, Mphahlele made a number of statements that sum up his position as a writer, educator, and scholar defined by African humanism. He began by commenting on one of the principal themes of alienation in his work as well as one of the burning political issues of this century. He states: "There is a big barrier between us and whites. We are looking at each other through the keyhole all the time." He then counterpoints this against the following statement of a self-professed African humanist: "I would like to be recognized in any literature as a person with a distinctive way of life, a distinctive way of dying, a distinctive way of being born. . . . Those are the particulars that lend color and meaning and authenticity to any work of fiction" (Lindfors 1985, 53). The emphasis on the "I" in this statement as separate from the "ego center" suggests an individuated self at odds with the communal. Yet it is the "distinctive way of life" that defines the meaning of that "I" which in turn finds meaning and self-validation in the communal, the source of renewal from which the "I" has been cut off. The statement gains added poignancy and power from its dramatic juxtaposition to the poetic fragment that follows.

Mphahlele's poetic fragment, "I Live in a Glasshouse," is a cleverly rendered take-off on Samuel Taylor Coleridge's "Kubla Khan." Reflecting Mphahlele's profound sense of isolation in exile, the "stately pleasure dome" is a contemporary glass house and the "cavern" a suburban basement

The "ego center" is at the controls and narrates. Glass, which is frequently cold, sterile, and anonymous and with all the sense of a suburban shopping mall, is a good choice of textural mediums. What is striking about this poetic-prose fragment is that Mphahlele's previously expressed desire for an African identity in his works and the immediate expression of self in this piece are in opposition. It is difficult, at first, to locate the African humanist anywhere in his glass house. Only after a careful search, do we eventually catch a glimpse of him:

> I live in a glasshouse, the one I ran into 17 years ago. It's roomy but borrowed. I can live in it as long as I pay the rent and as long as I don't start kicking things about scratching or staining the walls, I'm told. I can see the change of seasons light tints patterns of shade clearly when the rain is gone. In a way I could never have done in the painful south. I go down in the cellar often to sharpen . . . generally train the panzer division of my mind. I'm here not because I'm invisible. Sometimes it's cold in here sometimes warm sometimes full of light sometimes shadows come down upon me. There are no ultrabright light bulbs not one . . . . Always I hear a river. . . . I could if I chose renew my lease indefinitely in this glasshouse, quite forget write off my past take my chances on new territory. I shall not. Because I'm a helpless captive of place and to come to terms with the tyranny of place is to have something to live for to save me from stagnation, anonymity.
>
> Time to take stock of the ego center wait and listen to the river washing its shores, to the echoes of the hounds across Limpopo and Zambesi. (Lindfors 1985, 33–34)

Given the "cultural wilderness" of political exile, the alienation of having no roots in the community, and the loss of the African humanist writer in his glass house in a Denver suburb, it is understandable why it became necessary for him to return to the wellspring of inspiration, to seek renewal in a place where one could meaningfully serve one's community—and to grow old in a society where elders and ancestors are respected and revered. Mphahlele feared dying in America, but in his free-associating poetic fragment there are already signs of spiritual death.

Mphahlele's timing with regard to his critical thought and literary thrust in the context of the new South Africa could not have been better. His philosophical and literary ideas about reclaiming African history and culture have recently gained currency. They are particularly relevant in what some critics and writers have called the "post-1990 moment." This is the moment when South Africa "continues its long march to modernity," and, in the process, undertakes to fill the vacuum left by apartheid and the obsolescence of some black resistance movements. As it does so, it seeks out "new directions in intellectual and cultural practice" (Minkley and Steyn 1996, 196). As South Africa is integrated into the global community, after years of cultural and political isolation, it may respond to the dialectic between local and global identities in any one of several ways. National identities, in response to the influence of the global village and marketplace, may erode, local identities may strengthen in resistance to global influences, or new hybrid identities may evolve (198).

Gary Minkley and Andrew Steyn quote George Marcus to support their point that within the postmodernist frame, the "most energetic thinking about culture, especially in cross-cultural and transcultural frameworks, had been coming from among literary scholars" (199). At the core of the new discourse culture, as defined by anthropology and literary studies, is supplanting history. What Minkley and Steyn refer to as a "new theory" displaying rigor and imagination is really, however, an old but highly relevant theory, dressed up in new postmodernist language for a new postmodernist South Africa.

Mphahlele has for decades been thinking energetically, imaginatively, and with intellectual rigor within these same frameworks in which culture is located "at the center of analysis," and which culture is also vitally linked to nation building and education. According to Minkley and Steyn, "*Current* debates within Africa and African studies have highlighted both the problematic basis to conceptions of its colonial past . . . but also drawn serious debate back to the attempt *to reclaim African history and culture*" (205).

To reclaim African history and culture has been Mphahlele's lifelong pursuit. There is little doubt that in the unfolding dialogue of two selves, Mphahlele will be remembered as an African writer with a distinctive way of life, transformed into a body of literature. He will be remembered for his landmark works of criticism, and as the primogenitor of the black South African short story and township autobiography. He will be remembered for his contribution to the cause of black education. Perhaps the time will also come when *Chirundu* is given the attention it deserves, *Voices in the Whirlwind* and *The African Image* appear on university syllabuses, and the 1974 edition of *The African Image* sees the light of day. It is time this Nobel prize nominee, internationally known scholar and writer who has been "at the very hub of a burgeoning literature," this pioneering figure and catalyst in South Africa's black literary renaissance becomes a role model and household word, even and especially among the black youths in South African townships (Thuynsma 1989, 93).

Finally, Mphahlele deserves recognition for his imaginative and liberating act of cultural retrieval in bringing to light and adapting a concept of African humanism particularly well suited to the needs of the time, one that, in turn, has served as an inspiration and stimulus for black nationalist thought. In literature as in life, African humanism serves to equalize painful forces of alienation.

Mphahlele says he admires "the white man's achievements, his mind that plans tall buildings, powerful machinery," but that his "forebears and I could teach him a thing or two if only he would listen" (1985, 218). Balance is achieved by resolving this dialectic into a synthesis—and black and white would profit each by learning from the other. Mphahlele cites one of his favorite poets, Rabindranath Tagore, to make his point. Tagore writes that balance is achieved by understanding man in his entirety. Says Tagore, "we must not reduce him to the requirements of any particular duty. To look on trees only as firewood, is not to know the tree in its entirety" (Mphahlele 1986, 24).

In literature, a dialogue of two selves embraces the need "to strike and hold the delicate balance between immediate social relevance and the act of language as a vehicle of truth" while, metaphysically, it involves a need for balance between "attachment to material life with its social demands and detachment from it in order to attain spiritual or intellectual freedom" (Mphahlele 1986, 24).

In the dialogue of two selves, African humanism serves not only as an effective and illuminating thematic counterpoint to themes of alienation, spilling over into style, narrative techniques, plot and characterization, but it also serves as an affirmation and bridging point, a meeting place between Africa and the West, where African communalism and Western individualism meet—a coming together of the Renaissance, the English language, and a humanism that is purely African.

Notes

Chapter 1

1. After conducting a thorough search over several months of South African used book stores and the UNISA library, I was informed that the UNISA library had a banned book section and that I might discover a copy of the unobtainable revised edition of *The African Image* in safe keeping there. The detective work paid off. At long last, I secured the much-desired and sought-after book. This was accomplished with the aid of a signed note to the effect that permission was granted the signee for *The African Image* be taken out of the "Banned Collection" for a period of 42 days. The date of issuance of the special permit is March 19, 1991. Further research revealed that the first edition of *The African Image* (1962) had been banned on January 14, 1977; and the ban lifted on April 4, 1987, as listed in the voluminous *Jacobsens Index of Objectionable Literature,* in which thousands of banned book titles were printed and updated monthly. The revised edition of the *The African Image* (1974) was banned on January 7, 1983, under Gazette no. 8506, notice no. 20, section 4, paragraphs c, d, and e of the 1973 Publications Act. Since it is difficult to imagine how a work of literary criticism might be either "harmful to the relations between any section of the inhabitants of the Republic" (d) or "prejudicial to the safety of the state" (e), the question arises as to what rationale the censorship board had in mind when it banned the book. The rationale, in this event, was quite likely based on paragraph "c" which prohibits literature that "brings any section of the inhabitants of the Republic into ridicule or contempt." In Chapter Two, I will explore this question further and cite what may well have been viewed by the censorship board as the offending passage.

Regardless of the legalities and rationales for the Publications Acts, all of Mphahlele's works were, in any case, automatically banned, along with those of countless other black writers who left the country, because black writers who left the country were declared "'prohibited immigrants' and listed as writers whose utterances and writings cannot be quoted or read in the country" (Mphahlele 1967, 213).

Equally puzzling is the question why it took nearly ten years for the revised edition of *The African Image* to be officially proscribed. According to Lawrence

Berman in the English Department, UNISA, the membership of the Censorship Board was secret, any member of the reading public could call attention to a book deemed questionable (perhaps, in this case, it took ten years for the right person to stumble across the offending passage) and what was desirable or undesirable was not clearly defined. A book, for example, might be deemed undesirable according to the Immorality Act simply because it described interacial intercourse, "but there was no way you could arrest characters in a book."

Furthermore, anyone could institute a banning at any time, even years after a book's publication. The author, however, was not informed of the banning, but notice was "merely published in the *Government Gazette*," so that a month might transpire before the author came to know of it. Moreover, the censorship committee had no literary or legal training and the "appellant had no right of audience" (Gordimer 1988, 62, 252).

A call to the Censorship Board in Cape Town elicited no further information about the current status of the revised *The African Image*. The person answering the call was unable to locate any listing of a work by that title.

2. Although copies of Don Mattera's *Memory Is the Weapon* are available in some bookstores in Washington, D.C., efforts to find copies of Mphahlele's *Down Second Avenue* either in public libraries or bookstores in Colorado, San Francisco, and Washington, D.C., proved fruitless. Mphahlele's novel *Chirundu* was reprinted by Ravan Press in 1994. As of this writing, *The African Image* (1962) is out-of-print. After a considerable search at used bookstores in Johannesburg and Cape Town, copies of both the novel and the criticism were eventually secured.

3. In an interview conducted by the author of this study with Gerald Chapman, head of the Department of English, at the University of Denver, on September 10, 1991, Chapman said about Mphahlele's popularity as a lecturer:

> At DU Zeke was a very popular lecturer. I recall a public lecture series where people came from all over the region to hear Mphahlele. I have never seen such a worshipful crowd. He was the spokesman for the writer in exile and I was really very moved by the expression I saw on their [the students'] faces. That was the kind of teaching that I remember most. He had a way of reaching students' hearts.
>
> For a short time when Zeke came back here we had a very strong graduate program in African studies at DU. Zeke brought out large numbers of very gifted black students. I don't know whether this had anything to do with his [Zeke's] African Humanism or not, but I think it surely must have had something to do with it.

4. The author is fortunate to have lived in some of the same countries and geographic locales as Es'kia Mphahlele—from Colorado to the East Coast of the USA, from Dar es Salaam in East Africa to South Africa, including three years in Pretoria. In 1990, she and other expatriates living in South Africa at the time bore witness to history in the making when Nelson Mandela was released after twenty-seven years held as a political prisoner. The author lived in Tanzania in the era of *Ujamaa* socialism under Julius Nyerere. Over a four-year-period, she studied Kiswahili and translated and retold some oral folk tales later published in *Short Story International*. She traveled extensively in rural East Africa in the early 1970s and in Southern Africa in the early 1990s, including Lesotho (formerly Basutoland) where Mphahlele in 1954 experienced his "first exile." In Colorado, she interviewed Gerald Chapman, chairman of the Department of English at Denver University, where Es'kia Mphahlele registered for his Ph.D. in 1965. Chapman, one of the foremost Elizabethan scholars in the USA, is a long-time colleague and close personal friend of Mphahlele's (Thuynsma 1989, 267).

It is hoped that firsthand knowledge of a Bantu-based African language, of African "orature" and village living, and of some of the key people and places that have influenced Mphahlele's writings will enable the author to bring to the close examination of the text special insights and a deeper understanding of context not readily available to the purely abstract theorist. In addition, the author has met Mphahlele, heard him speak, exchanged letters and telephone calls with him, and conducted a personal interview with him. This enriched, particularized experience complements and adds substance to those essential literary tools of critical theory, analysis, and academic discipline.

Chapter 2

1. *Man Must Live* is out of print. The copy I secured was through the courtesy of Peter Thuynsma at the University of the Witwatersrand. Two chronologies I have seen in books devoted to the life and works of Mphahlele incorrectly list the date of publication as 1947. On the title page of *Man Must Live*, the date of publication of this first collection of short stories to be published by a black South African writer is given as 1946—that is, "designed and published in 1946 by the African Bookman . . . Cape Town."

Chapter 3

1. Mphahlele dedicated his thesis to his promoter who was then head of the

Department of English (UNISA), Edward Davis. Mphahlele tells his autobiographer Chabani Manganyi that he recalls Davis as being "a short little man, unorthodox in many ways, and [as someone who] had decidedly independent views about literature. He had studied in South Africa and at Oxford. . . . I remember him as a very astute scholar—a stimulating person and the most outstanding professor I ever had the pleasure to study under. . . . I profited from his incisive criticism" (Manganyi 1983, 146). Mphahlele describes the commencement exercise, a segregated event with separate tea services and separate seating, in *Down Second Avenue* (Mphahlele 1959, 198).

Chapter 6

1. Chimane's parents were clearly victims of the Land Act which, as historian T. R. H. Davenport writes, "imposed a policy of territorial segregation with a very heavy hand. It aimed specifically to get rid of those features of African land ownership and share-cropping which white farmers found undesirable" (Davenport 1989, 259).

Chapter 7

1. In a September 10, 1991, interview I asked Gerald Chapman whether Mphahlele might have entertained the idea of staying permanently in America. He replied that, while one could not always be certain whether Mphahlele (who had an immigrant visa) might or might not have considered U.S. citizenship, he believed that Mphahlele always had in mind a "larger purpose"—the commitment to the community at home.

References

Abbagnano, Nicolo. 1967. "Humanism." *The Encyclopedia of Philosophy.* New York: Macmillan. 3:69–72.

"Abortion on Demand Legalized in South Africa." 1997. *Colorado Springs Gazette* February 2:A17.

Abraham, W. E. 1962. *The Mind of Africa.* London: Weidenfeld and Nicolson.

Abrahams, Peter. 1946. *Mine Boy.* Oxford: Heinemann International.

———. 1988. *Tell Freedom.* London: Faber and Faber.

Achebe, Chinua. 1991. *Things Fall Apart.* Oxford: Heinemann.

Allen, N. R., Jr. 1991. *African-American Humanism: An Anthology.* Buffalo: Prometheus Books.

Amuta, C. 1989. *The Theory of African Literature: Implications for Practical Criticism.* London: Zed Books.

Ashcroft, Bill et al. 1991. *The Empire Writes Back: Theory and Practice in Post-Colonial Literatures.* New York: Routledge.

"Autobiographies Tell a Rich Story." 1989. *New Nation: People's History!* 1:123–24.

Ba, Mariama. 1989. *So Long a Letter.* Portsmouth: Heinemann.

Bakhtin, Mikhail M. 1981. *The Dialogic Imagination.* Edited by M. Holquist. Austin: University of Texas Press.

Barboure, Dorian. 1984. "Mongane Serote: Humanist and Revolutionary." *Momentum: On Recent South African Writing.* M. J. Daymond, et al. (eds.). Pietermaritzburg: Natal University Press. 171–182.

Barnett, Ursula A. 1976. *Ezekiel Mphahlele.* Boston: Twayne.

———. 1983. *A Vision of Order: A Study of Black South African Literature in English (1914–1980).* Cape Town: Maskew Miller Longman.

———. 1984. "Africa or the West?—Cultural Synthesis in the Work of Es'kia Mphahlele." *Africa Insight* 14:59–63.

Bates, Mudimbe, and Jean O'Barr. 1993. *Africa and the Disciplines.* Chicago: University of Chicago Press.

Beier, U., ed. 1979. *Introduction to African Literature: An Anthology of Critical Writing.* Harlow: Longman.

Beckson, K. and A. Ganz. 1990. *Literary Terms: A Dictionary.* New York: Noonday Press.

Bernstein, Richard. 1997. "Apartheid from Under: One Man's Long Life." *New York Times* 24 April:B4.

Biko, Steven. 1979. *Black Consciousness in South Africa: Steve Biko.* Edited by Millard Arnold. New York: Vintage Books.

———. 1978. *I Write What I Like: A Selection of His Writings.* San Francisco: Harper.

Boyne, Roy and Ali Rattansi. 1990. *Postmodernism and Society.* New York: St. Martin's Press.

Bravo, Nelda Emery. 1991. "The Agrarian Manifesto and the Plan *Espiritual de Aztlan:* Cultural Nationalism and American Literary Tradition." Ph.D. diss. Texas A & M.

Brink, André. 1979. *A Dry White Season.* London: Collins.

———. 1983. *Writing in a State of Siege.* New York: Summit Books.

———. 1988. *States of Emergency.* London: Collins.

———. 1991. "A Culture of Reading." *The Weekly Mail* 12:1.

Brown, Linda. 1996. Unpublished letter to Ruth Obee, December 9.

Brutus, Dennis. 1973. *A Simple Lust.* Portsmouth: Heinemann.

Butler, Guy. 1984. "A Search for Synthesis." In *Momentum: On South African Writing.* Edited by M. J. Daymond et al. Pietermaritzburg: Natal University Press.

Butler, Jeffrey, Richard Elphick, and David Walsh. 1987. *Democratic Liberalism in South Africa: Its History and Prospect.* Middletown: Wesleyan University Press.

Byrne, Deirdre. 1994. "A Different Kind of Resistance: An Overview of South African Black Women's Writing." *UNISA English Studies* 32.2 (September): 23-24.

Chapman, M., ed. 1989. *The Drum Decade: Stories from the 1950s.* Pietermaritzburg: Natal University Press.

Chapman, M., Colin Gardner, and Es'kia Mphahlele, eds. 1992. *Perspectives on South African English Literature.* Johannesburg: AD. Donker.

Chinweizu, Onwuchekwa Jemie, and Ihechukwu Madubuike. 1983. *Toward the Decolonization of African Literature.* Washington, D.C.: Howard University Press.

Coetzee, J. M. 1980. *Waiting for the Barbarians.* London: Penguin Books.

———. 1985. *Life and Times of Michael K.* London: Penguin Books.

———. 1988. *White Writing: On the Culture of Letters in South Africa.* New Haven: Yale University Press.

Cole, S. and J. Lindemann. 1990. *Reading and Responding to Literature.* San Diego: Harcourt Brace Jovanovich.

Cooper, Brenda and Andrew Steyn, eds. 1996. *Transgressing Boundaries: New Directions in the Study of Culture in Africa.* Athens: Ohio University Press.

Courlander, Harold. 1975. *A Treasury of South African Folklore.* New York: Crown.

Couzens, T. J. 1971. "The Dark Side of the World: Sol Plaatje's 'Mhudi.'" *English Studies in Africa* 14:187–203.

———. 1973. "Sol Plaatje's 'Mhudi.'" *The Journal of Commonwealth Literature* 8:1–18.

———. 1974. "The Continuity of Black Literature in South Africa before 1950." *English in Africa* 1:11–23.

———. 1978. "Printers' and other Devils: The Texts of Sol T. Plaatje's 'Mhudi.'" *Research in African Literature* 9:198–215.

———. 1987. "Sol T. Plaatje and the First South African Epic." *English in Africa* 14:41–63.

Couzens, T. J., et al. 1987. "Looking In: Interviews with Es'kia Mphahlele." *The Council of the English Academy* 4:114–41.

Crews, F., ed. 1970. *Psychoanalysis and Literary Process.* Cambridge, Mass.: Winthrop.

Daley, Suzanne. 1997. "Blacks in South Africa Find New Wealth but Old Biases." *New York Times* October 2:1.

Damian, R. 1986. "Through the Keyhole: Masters and Servants in the Work of Es'kia Mphahlele." *English in Africa* 13:64–88.

Danow, David K. 1991. *The Thought of Mikhail Bakhtin: From Word to Culture.* New York: St. Martin's Press.

Dathorn, O. R. 1974. *African Literature in the Twentieth Century.* Minneapolis: Heinemann Educational Books.

Davenport, T. R. H. 1989. *South Africa: A Modern History.* Bergvlei: Southern Book Publishers.

Davidson, Basil. 1991. *Africa in History.* New York: Macmillan.

De Kock, L. 1987. "Literature, Politics and Universalism: A Debate between Es'kia Mphahlele and J. M. Coetzee." *Journal of Literary Studies* 3:35–48.

De Vries, Abraham H. 1989. "An Interview with Richard Rive." *Current Writing* 1:45–56.

Dunn, A. 1991. "PW Still Fears Hellish Reds." *The Pretoria News* 16 November 16:1.

Du Plessis, M. 1983. *A State of Fear.* Cape Town: David Philip.

Eagleton, T. 1986. "Marxism and Literary Criticism." In C. Kaplan, ed. *Criticism: The Major Statements.* New York: St. Martin's Press. 532–54.

Eakin, John Paul. 1984. *Fictions in Autobiography: Studies in the Art of Self-Invention.* Princeton, N.J.: Princeton University Press.

Ebersohn, W. 1986. *Momentum: On Recent South African Writing.* M. J. Daymond et al. (eds.). Pietermaritzburg: Natal University Press. 16–19.

Fanon, Frantz. 1963. *The Wretched of the Earth.* New York: Grove Press.

Foucault, Michel. 1979 (1975). *Discipline and Punish: The Birth of the Prison.* New York: Vintage Books.

Fromm, Erich. 1965. *Socialist Humanism.* New York: Doubleday.

Fry, Northrop. 1957. *Anatomy of Criticism: Four Essays.* Princeton: Princeton University Press.

Gardiner, Michael. 1991. *The Dialogics of Critique: M. M. Bakhtin and the Theory of Ideology.* London: Routledge.

Gerhart, Gail M. 1979. *Black Power in South Africa: The Evolution of an Ideology.* Berkeley: University of California Press.

Goldmann, Lucien. 1964. *The Hidden God.* Translated by Philip Thody. New York: Humanities Press.

Gordimer, Nadine. 1982. *Six Feet of the Country.* London: Penguin Books.

———. 1988. *The Essential Gesture: Writing, Politics and Places.* New York: Alfred A. Knopf.

———. 1990. *My Son's Story.* Cape Town: David Philip.

———. 1995. *None to Accompany Me.* New York: Penguin.

Gravitz, Herbert L., and Julie D. Bowden. 1985. *A Guide for Adult Children of Alcoholics.* New York: Simon and Schuster.

Gray, S. 1990. "The Long Eye of History: Four Autobiographical Texts by Peter Abrahams." *Pretexts* 2:99–115.

———. 1991. "Basking in Gordimer's Reflected Nobel Glory." *Weekly Mail* October 6:1.

Gray, S., ed. 1984. *Modern South African Poetry.* Craighall: AD. Donker.

Gwala, M. 1989. "Es'kia Mphahlele: A Divided Self?" *Third World Quarterly* 11:198–202.

Haggard, H. R. 1962. *King Soloman's Mines.* New York: Collier.

Hansen, Karen Tranberg. 1989. *Distant Companions: Servants and Employers in Zambia, 1900–1985.* Ithaca, N.Y.: Cornell University Press.

Harvey, David. 1989. *The Condition of PostModernity: An Enquiry into the Origins of Cultural Change.* Oxford: Blackwell.

Head, Bessie. 1990. *A Woman Alone.* Portsmouth: Heinemann.

———. 1995. *Maru.* Portsmouth: Heinemann.

———. 1981. *Serowe: Village of the Rain Wind.* Portsmouth: Heinemann.

———. 1987. *When Rain Clouds Gather.* Oxford: Heinemann.

Heard, Tony. 1990. *The Cape of Storms.* Johannesburg: Ravan.

Herde, Peter. 1973. "Humanism in Italy." *Dictionary of the History of Ideas.* Edited by Philip P. Wiener. New York: Charles Scribner's Sons. 2:515–24.

Hodge, Norman. 1981. "Dogs, Africans and Liberals: The World of Mphahlele's 'Mrs Plum.'" *English in Africa* 8:33–45.

———. 1986. "The Way I Looked at Life Then: Es'kia Mphahlele's *Man Must Live and Other Stories.*" *English in Africa* 13:47–65.

Horney, Karen. 1937. *The Neurotic Personality of Our Time.* New York: W. W. Norton.

"Humanism." 1967. *Encyclopaedia Britannica.* Chicago: William Benton. 9: 825–26.

Ibrahim, Huma. 1996. *Bessie Head: Subversive Identities in Exile.* Charlottesville: University of Virginia Press.

Irele, Abiola. 1990. *The African Experience in Literature and Ideology.* Bloomington: Indiana University Press.

Iser, Wolfgang. 1975. *The Implied Reader: Patterns of Communication in Prose Fiction from Bunyan to Beckett.* Baltimore: Johns Hopkins University Press.

Jabavu, Noni. 1982. *The Ochre People.* Cape Town: Ravan Press.

James, William. 1990. *The Varieties of Religious Experience.* New York: Vintage.

JanMohamed, Abdul R. 1988. *Manichean Aesthetics: The Politics of Literature in Colonial Africa.* Amherst: University of Massachusetts Press.

Johnson, Joyce. 1984. "Culturally Derived Motifs and Symbols as Structural Features in Es'kia Mphahlele's *Chirundu.*" *Kunapipi* 6:109–19.

Joubert, E. 1985. *Poppie.* Johannesburg: Southern Book.

Kane-Berman, John. 1981. *Soweto: Black Revolt White Reaction.* Johannesburg: Ravan Press.

Kaplan, C., ed. 1986. *Criticism: The Major Statements.* New York: St. Martin's Press.

Kesteloot, Lilyan. 1963. *Black Writers in French: A Literary History of Negritude.* Translated by Ellen Conroy Kennedy. Washington, D.C.: Howard University Press, 1991.

Khapoya, Vincent B. 1994. *The African Experience: An Introduction.* Englewood Cliffs, N.J.: Prentice Hall.

King, R. H. 1992. *Telling Facts: History and Narration in Psychoanalysis.* In Smith, M.D. (ed.). Baltimore: Johns Hopkins University Press.

Klein, Leonard S. 1986. *African Literature in the 20th Century: A Guide.* New York: Unger Publishing Co.

Klima, V., K. F. Ruzicka, and P. Zima. 1976. *Black Africa: Literature and Language.* Dordrecht: D. Reidel Publishing.

Kuzwayo, E. 1985. *Call Me Woman.* Johannesburg: Ravan Press.

Larson, C. 1978. *The Emergence of African Fiction.* London: Macmillan.

Lelyveld, J. 1980. "Black South African Goes Home Again." *New York Times* November 16:3.

———. 1986. *Move Your Shadow.* London: Macdonald and Co.

Lessing, D. 1950. *The Grass Is Singing.* London: Heinemann.

"Liberalism." 1973. *Dictionary of the History of Ideas.* Edited by Philip P. Weiner. New York: Charles Scribner's Sons.

Lindfors, Bernth. 1985. Symposium on Contemporary South African Literature. University of Texas at Austin, March 20–22, 1975.

———. 1994. "Many Happy Returns? Repatriation and Resistance Literature in a New South Africa." *Cross/Cultures* 14:63–72.

Lodge, Tom. 1990. *Black Politics in South Africa Since 1945.* Johannesburg: Ravan Press.

"Major Easing of Some Security Laws Planned." 1991.*The Star* May 3:6.

Makgabutlane, Sol. 1990. "Mightier than the Sword." *Tribute* May:32–38.

Malan, C., ed. 1987. *Race and Literature.* Pinetown: Owen Burgess Publishers.

Malan, Rian. 1990. *My Traitor's Heart.* London: The Bodley Head.

Manganyi, N.C. 1983. *Exiles and Homecomings: A Biography of Es'kia Mphahlele.* Johannesburg: Ravan Press.

———, ed. 1984. *Bury Me at the Marketplace: Selected Letters of Es'kia Mphahlele 1943–1980.* Johannesburg: Skotaville Publishers.

Maritain, J. 1950. *True Humanism.* Trans. M. R. Adamson. London: Geoffrey Bles.

Mathabane, M. 1986. *Kaffir Boy.* New York: Plume, New American Library.

Mathiane, N. 1990. *Beyond the Headlines: Truths of Soweto Life.* Johannesburg: Southern Book Publishers.

Matshikiza, T. 1961. *Chocolates for My Wife.* Cape Town: David Philip.

Mattera, D. 1987. *Memory Is the Weapon.* Johannesburg: Ravan Press.

Mbiti, John. 1985. *Prayers in African Religion.* New York: Orbis Books.

Meebelo, Henry S. 1973. *Main Currents of Zambian Humanist Thought.* Lusaka: Oxford University Press.

Modisane, B. 1990. *Blame Me on History.* Parklands: AD. Donker.

Moody, C. 1991. "Authors Mindlessly Denigrated." *The Star* October 23:13.

Moore, G. 1962. *Seven African Writers.* London: Oxford University Press.

———. 1969. *The Chosen Tongue: English Writing in the Tropical World.* London: Longmans, Green and Co.

Mphahlele, Es'kia. 1946. *Man Must Live and Other Stories.* Cape Town: African Bookman.

———. 1955. "The Non-European Character in South African English Fiction." MA thesis. Pretoria: University of South Africa.

———. 1956–57. Lesane short stories. *Drum.*

———. 1959. *Down Second Avenue.* London: Faber and Faber.

———. 1960. "Black and White." *New Statesman.* 342–43, 346.

———. 1962. *The African Image.* London: Faber and Faber.

———. 1964. *Modern African Stories.* London: Faber and Faber.

———. 1966. *A Guide to Creative Writing: A Short Guide to Short Story and Novel Writing.* Dar-es-Salaam: East African Literature Bureau.

———. 1967. *In Corner B and Other Stories.* Nairobi: East African Publishing House.

———. 1971. *The Wanderers.* New York: Macmillan.

———. 1972. *Voices in the Whirlwind and Other Essays.* New York: Hill and Wang.

———. 1973. "Why I Teach My Discipline." *The University of Denver Quarterly* 18:32–43.

———. 1974. *The African Image.* New and rev. ed. London: Faber; New York: Praeger.

———. 1979. "Exile, the Tyranny of Place and the Literary Compromise." *UNISA English Studies: Journal of the Department of English* 17:37–44 (Pretoria).

———. 1980. *Chirundu.* Johannesburg: Ravan Press; New York: Thomas Nelson.

———. 1981a. Introduction to *Conversations with African Writers* by Lee Nichols and taped interview with Lee Nichols. Washington, D.C.: Voice of America.

———. 1981b. *Let's Write a Novel: A Guide.* Cape Town: Maskew Miller.

———. 1981c. *The Unbroken Song: Selected Writings of Es'kia Mphahlele.* Johannesburg: Ravan Press.

———. 1984a. *Father Come Home.* Johannesburg: Ravan Press.

———. 1984b. *Poetry and Humanism: Oral Beginnings.* Johannesburg: Institute for the Study of Man in Africa, University of the Witwatersrand.

———. 1985. *Let's Talk Writing: Prose.* Johannesburg: Skotaville Publishers.

———. 1986. "Remarks on Chirundu." *English in Africa* 13.2 (October): 21–37.

———. 1990a. "The Art of the Writer and His Function." *UNISA African Studies Forum* 33:2–19.

———. 1990b. "Publisher at Your Doorstep." *Tribute* April:128

———. 1991a. "Back from the Wilderness." *Tribute* May:144

———. 1991b. "Decolonising the Mind." *New Nation* November 1–7:8.

———. 1993a. "Educating the Imagination." *College English* 55:179–86.

———. 1993b. Unpublished letter to Ruth Obee, March 31.

———. 1994a. "Silences." Unpublished poem (from August 1992–93) sent to Ruth Obee, March 15.

———. 1994b. Unpublished letter to Ruth Obee, April 30.

———. ed. 1967. Introduction. *African Writing Today.* Harmondsworth: Penguin.

————, ed. 1970. *Thought, Ideology and African Literature*. Denver: University of Denver.

————, with Michael Chapman and Colin Gardner, eds. 1992. *Perspectives on South African Literature*. Parklands: AD. Donker.

Mulaudzi, Amy Bell. 1994. Unpublished letter to Ruth Obee, August 14.

Ndebele, N. S. 1983. *Fools and Other Stories*. Johannesburg: Ravan Press.

————. 1988. "Turkish Tales and Some Thoughts on South African Fiction." In *Ten Years of Staffrider (1978–1988)*, 318–40.

————. 1991. *Rediscovery of the Ordinary*. Johannesburg: COSAW.

Ngara, E. A. 1987. *Art and Ideology in the African Novel: A Study of the Influences of Marxism on African Writing*. London: Heinemann.

Ngugi, wa Thiong'o. 1992. *Decolonising the Mind: The Politics of Language in African Literature*. London: Heinemann.

————. 1938. *Moving the Centre: The Struggle for Cultural Freedoms*. London; Portsmouth: Heinemann, 1993.

Ngwenya, Thengani H. 1989. "The Ontological Status of Self in Autobiography: The Case of Bloke Modisane's *Blame Me on History*." *Current Writing* 1:67–77.

Nkosi, L. 1981. *Tasks and Masks: Themes and Styles of African Literature*. Essex: Longman.

————. 1983. *Home and Exile and Other Selections*. Essex: Longman.

"Nobel Prizes." 1967. *Encyclopaedia Britannica*. 26:548–52.

Nussbaum, Felicity A. 1991. "Autobiographical Spaces and the Postcolonial Predicament." *Current Writing* 3:24–31.

Obee, Ruth. 1991a. Interview with Es'kia Mphahlele, Professor Emeritus of African Literature, University of the Witwatersrand, Soweto.

————. 1991b. Inteview with Gerald Chapman, Professor of English, University of Denver, Colorado.

O'Brien, Anthony. 1992. "Literature in Another South Africa: Njabulo Ndebele's Theory of Emergent Culture." *Diacritics* 22:67–85.

Obiechina, Emmanuel N. 1990. *Language and Theme: Essays on African Literature*. Washington, D.C.: Howard University Press.

Ogungbesan, Kolawole. 1992. "A Long Way from Vrededorp: The Reception of Peter Abrahams' Ideas." In *Perspectives on South African English Literature*. Edited by Michael Chapman, et al. Johannesburg: AD. Donker.

Oliphant, A. W. and I. Vladislavic, eds. 1988. *Ten Years of Staffrider (1978–1988)*. Johannesburg: Ravan Press.

Olney, J. 1973. *Tell Me Africa*. Princeton, N.J.: Princeton University Press.

————. 1988. *Studies in Autobiography*. Oxford: Oxford University Press.

Omo Asein, S. 1980. "The Humanism of Ezekiel Mphahlele." *Journal of Commonwealth Literature* 15.1 (August): 39–49.

Parker, Kenneth, ed. 1978. *The South African Novel in English: Essays in Criticism and Society.* New York: Holmes & Meier.

Patel, Essop. 1986. "Towards Revolutionary Poetry." In *Momentum: On Recent South African Writing.* Edited by M. J. Daymond, et al. Pietermaritzburg: Natal University Press.

Paton, Alan. 1953. *Too Late the Phalarope.* New York: Charles Scribner's Sons.

———. 1961. *Debbie Go Home.* London: Penguin Books.

———. 1988. *Cry, The Beloved Country.* London: Penguin Books.

Pawlowski, Robert. 1991. Letter to Ruth Obee, November 21.

Pereira, E. et al., ed. 1987. *South African English Literature: 1900–1950s.* Pretoria: University of South Africa.

———. 1987b. *South African English Literature: 1950s–1980s.* Pretoria: University of South Africa.

Plaatje, Sol T. 1989. *Mhudi.* Parklands: AD. Donker.

Plomer, W. 1925. *Turbott Wolfe.* Oxford: Oxford University Press, 1985.

Popken, Michael, ed. 1978. *Modern Black Writers.* New York: Frederick Ungar Publishing.

Rhodes, Richard. 1995. *How to Write: Advice and Reflections.* New York: William Morrow.

Rieff, Philip. 1959. *Freud: The Mind of the Moralist.* New York: Viking Press.

Rive, R. 1986. *'Buckingham Palace,' District Six.* Cape Town: David Philips.

Ruth, Damian. 1986. "Through the Keyhole: Masters and Servants in the Work of Es'kia Mphahlele." *English in Africa* 13.2 (October): 65–87.

Saunders, C. et al., eds. 1988. *Reader's Digest Illustrated History of South Africa: The Real Story.* Cape Town: The Reader's Digest Association.

Schreiner, O. 1978 (first publ. 1883). *Story of an African Farm.* New York: Schocken.

Serote, W. M. 1981. *To Every Birth Its Blood.* London: Heinemann.

———. 1982. *Selected Poems.* Johannesburg: AD. Donker.

———. 1990. *On the Horizon.* Fordsburg: Congress of South African Writers.

Shava, P. V. 1989. *A People's Voice: Black South African Writing in the Twentieth Century.* London: Zed Books.

Shear, Keith. 1989. "Depictions of Childhood in South African Autobiography, with Particular Reference to the 1920s." *English in Africa* 16:39–69.

Smith, David G. "Liberalism." *Dictionary of the History of Ideas.* Philip P. Wiener (ed.). New York: Charles Scribner's Sons. 3: 276–282.

Smith, P. 1925. *The Little Karoo.* Cape Town: David Philip.

Sono, Themba. 1993. *Reflections on the Origins of Black Consciousness in South Africa.* Pretoria: HSRC Publishers.

South African Wimmin. 1996. *The Economist* October 5:79–80.

Soyinka, Wole. 1967. "The Writer and the Modern African State." *Transition* 31:13.

———. 1992. *Myth, Literature and the African World.* Cambridge: Cambridge University Press.

Sparks, Allister. 1990. *The Mind of South Africa.* New York: Alfred A. Knopf.

Staples, Brent. 1994. "The Good Son." *Washington Post* March 17:D2.

Taylor, Paul. 1994. "A Fearful Leap Into the Unknown." *Washington Post* March 9:A1.

Thompson, L. 1990. *A History of South Africa.* New Haven: Yale University Press.

Thuynsma, Peter N., ed. 1989. *Footprints along the Way: A Tribute to Es'kia Mphahlele.* Braamfontein: Skotaville Publishers.

———. 1990. Class lectures on Mphahlele's *Down Second Avenue,* University of the Witwatersrand, Johannesburg.

Trosman, H. 1967. "Neuroses." *Encyclopaedia Britannica* 16: 295–301.

Tsedu, Mathana. 1991. "Sarah—the Widow the World Forgot." *Sowetan* April 11:6.

Van der Spuy, H. I. J. 1974. "The Psychology of South Africa." *New Society* 27 (January–March): 197.

———. 1978. *The Psychology of Apartheid: a Psychosocial Perspective on South Africa.* Washington: The University Press of America.

———. 1997. Unpublished letter to Ruth Obee, January 7.

Visser, N. W. 1976. "South Africa: The Renaissance That Failed." *Journal of Commonwealth Literature* 2:118–133.

Waldmeir, Patti. 1997. *Anatomy of a Miracle.* New York: W. W. Norton.

Walker, S., ed. 1989. *Stories from the Rest of the World.* St. Paul: Graywolf Press.

Wallerstein, Immanuel. 1961. *Africa: The Politics of Independence.* New York: Random House.

Watson, Stephen. 1982. "'Cry the Beloved Country' and the Failure of Liberal Vision." *English in Africa* 9:232–48.

Watts, J. 1989. *Black Writers from South Africa.* London: Macmillan.

Wauthier, Claude. 1979. *The Literature and Thought of Modern Africa.* Washington, D.C.: Three Continents Press.

Woeber, C. and J. Read. 1989. *Es'kia Mphahlele: A Bibliography.* Grahamstown: National English Literary Museum.

Zell, M. Hans and Silver, H. (comp. and ed.). 1972. "Ezekiel Mphahlele." *A Reader's Guide to African Literature.* London: Heinemann. 154–56.

Index